The OXFORD BOOK *of* CAROLS

The Oxford Book of Carols is published in two editions:

Music Edition, complete

Words Edition, without notes.

There are over 200 carols in the book, including unison and four-part arrangements. Many of the carols can be obtained separately with music for the use of choirs.

The OXFORD BOOK *of* CAROLS

By

PERCY DEARMER

R. VAUGHAN WILLIAMS

MARTIN SHAW

GEOFFREY CUMBERLEGE

OXFORD UNIVERSITY PRESS

LONDON

Oxford University Press, Amen House, London E.C. 4
GLASGOW NEW YORK TORONTO MELBOURNE WELLINGTON
BOMBAY CALCUTTA MADRAS CAPE TOWN
Geoffrey Cumberlege, Publisher to the University

FIRST PUBLISHED 1928
TWENTY-THIRD IMPRESSION 1956

PRINTED IN THE NETHERLANDS

PREFACE

CAROLS are songs with a religious impulse that are simple, hilarious, popular, and modern. They are generally spontaneous and direct in expression, and their simplicity of form causes them sometimes to ramble on like a ballad. Carol literature and music are rich in true folk-poetry and remain fresh and buoyant even when the subject is a grave one. But they vary a good deal: some are narrative, some dramatic, some personal, a few are secular; and there are some which do not possess all the typical characteristics. Simplicity, for instance, was often lost in the conceits of Jacobean poets, who yet wrote some charming carols.

Hilarity also has been sometimes forgotten, or obscured in the texts. The word 'Carol' has a dancing origin, and once meant to dance in a ring: it may go back, through the Old French '*caroler*' and the Latin 'CHORAULA', to the Greek 'CHORAULES', a flute-player for chorus dancing, and ultimately to the 'CHOROS' which was originally a circling dance and the origin of the Attic drama. The carol, in fact, by forsaking the timeless contemplative melodies of the Church, began the era of modern music, which has throughout been based upon the dance. But, none the less, joyfulness in the words has been sometimes discarded by those who were professionally afraid of gaiety. Some French carols were rewritten by well-meaning clergymen into frigid expositions of edifying theology; some of the English tunes were used by excellent Methodists of the eighteenth century to preach their favourite doctrines. Before their time the British tendency to lugubriousness had occasionally shown itself in the folk-carol: but even in such cases the dancing tunes remained, happily to belie the words; and in France behind the ecclesiastical propriety of modern noëls there lurk many carols like 'Guillô, pran ton tamborin' (No. 82) to bear witness to the spirit of a more spontaneous and undoubting faith.

The typical carol gives voice to the common emotions of healthy people in language that can be understood and music that can be shared by all. Because it is popular it is therefore genial as well as simple; it dances because it is so Christian, echoing St. Paul's conception of the fruits of the Spirit in its challenge to be merry—

'Love and joy come to you'. Indeed, to take life with real seriousness is to take it joyfully, for seriousness is only sad when it is superficial: the carol is thus all the nearer to the ultimate truth because it is jolly. So, on the one hand, the genius of the carol is an antidote to the levity of much present-day literature, music, and drama, made by men who are afraid to touch the deeper issues of life because seriousness is associated in their minds with gloom; for its jubilant melodies can encircle the most solemn of themes: on the other hand, it is an antidote to pharisaism, the formalism which is always morose, as Paul Sabatier says in his life of Francis of Assisi—that most Christian of saints, who as scenic artist at the Greccio crib, and as the sweet-voiced troubadour of the Holy Spirit, the 'joculator Dei', was the precursor if not the parent of the carol: 'Le formalisme religieux, dans quelque culte que ce soit, prend toujours des allures guindées et moroses. Les pharisiens de tous les temps se défigurent le visage, pour que nul ne puisse ignorer leurs dévotions: François non seulement ne pouvait souffrir ces simagrées de la fausse piété, mais il mettait la gaieté et la joie au nombre des devoirs religieux . . . le maître alla jusqu'à en faire un des préceptes de la Règle. Il était trop bon général pour ne pas savoir qu'une armée joyeuse est toujours une armée victorieuse. Il y a dans l'histoire des premières missions franciscaines des éclats de rire qui sonnent haut et clair.'

Carols, moreover, were always modern, expressing the manner in which the ordinary man at his best understood the ideas of his age, and bringing traditional conservative religion up to date: the carol did this for the fifteenth century after the collapse of the old feudal order, and should do the same for the twentieth. The charm of an old carol lies precisely in its having been true to the period in which it was written, and those which are alive to-day retain their vitality because of this sincerity; for imitations are always sickly and short-lived. A genuine carol may have faults of grammar, logic, and prosody; but one fault it never has—that of sham antiquity.

§ 1. *History of the Carol.*

Because the carol was based upon dance music, it did not appear until the close of the long puritan era which lasted through the Dark Ages and far into the Medieval period. The word meant something Terpsichorean and evil in the seventh century, as we can see in St. Ouen's *Life* of the contemporary St. Eligius (ii. 15): 'Nullus in festivitate S. Joannis, vel quibuslibet sanctorum solemnitatibus, solstitia aut ballationes vel saltationes aut *caraulas* aut cantica diabolica exerceat': the people evidently wanted to dance on saints' days, especially on Midsummer Day, and the 'caraula' was condemned with the 'ballatio': from this latter example of Late Latin our 'ballad' is derived, and 'ball' (and ultimately 'ballet'). St. Augustine uses the verb 'ballare' of David dancing before the ark; but David's example was ignored, and the dance reprobated under all three names—ballatio, saltatio, and caraula. By the fourteenth century, however, the word carol had changed its meaning, and, though it retained its dancing associations, had become respectable. Dante, in the 24th canto of the *Paradiso*, could use it of the dancing band of saints in glory: 'Così quelle carole differentemente danzando': here 'carola' means a choir, but it is a choir that dances.

Therefore the carol made its appearance late in Christian history—not, indeed, until the modern spirit of humanism had dawned upon the Middle Ages. It was a creation of the fifteenth century. Popular singers and reciters had of course always existed; and the curious early thirteenth-century Anglo-Norman wassail song, 'Seignors ore entendez a nus', shows, as we should expect, that minstrels did not avoid the baronial hall at Christmas time; but it was not till the fourteenth century that English poetry developed from the homiletic verse, the metrical chronicle, and the melancholy elegiac poetry of the preceding two hundred years into the metrical romance, and Chaucer arrived with his Italian humanism and his new demonstration of the possibilities of verse. There was a marked growth of the democratic spirit in the fourteenth century; and religious literature in the vernacular, including hymns, spread as a result of this and of the activity of the preaching friars. Only in the lifetime of Chaucer are there signs of the carol beginning to emerge as something different from a poem, or from a sequence like 'Angelus ad virginem' (52) which can be treated as a carol only because of its enchanting melody. It is difficult, if not impossible, to find any example of an authentic carol which can with certainty be dated earlier than 1400 (Chaucer's roundel of *c.* 1382, No. 128, has to be arranged in order to be sung as a carol). Professor Saintsbury, indeed, says definitely that the oldest of our carols date from the fifteenth century.

The carol was in fact a sign, like the mystery play, of the emancipation of the people from the old puritanism which had for so many centuries suppressed the dance and the drama, denounced communal singing, and warred against the tendency of the people to disport themselves in church on the festivals. Instances abound of the struggle, as for instance when John of Salisbury in the twelfth century denounced the 'mimi', 'balatroni', 'praestigiatores', and others of an age which he declares 'non modo aures et cor prostituit vanitate sed oculorum et aurium voluptate suam mulcet desidiam', and no doubt in the Middle Ages, as under the Roundheads, such objections often found justification in the excesses of popular merriment. But even in the twelfth century and even in church the instinct for dramatic expression was in revolt, and we find Abbot Aelred of Rievaulx complaining of chanters who gesticulated and grimaced while singing the sacred offices, and imitated the sound of thunder, of women's voices, and of the neighing of horses. In other and more seemly ways anthems, sequences, and tropes were sung with increasing dramatic emphasis, till from them the mystery play developed. The struggle went on, and the Muses gradually won: about the time when the English barons rose against King John, Pope Innocent III forbad 'ludi theatrales' in church, and his order was repeated by Gregory IX. St. Francis, their contemporary, by his jovial singing as well as by his invention of the Christmas crib, gave, as we have said, a great impetus to the new conception of music and drama in the thirteenth century. We get a glimpse of the transition in such descriptions as that printed by Petit de Julleville in his *Histoire de Théâtre en France* of the crib ceremonies at Rouen in the fourteenth century: the crib was behind the altar, the shepherds came in by the great gates of the choir, a child on a platform represented the angel, and 'two priests of the first rank wearing dalmatics will represent the midwives and stand by the crib'. But by this time the mystery play had become in many places a real form of drama, performed outside the church. France, which was ahead of England with the play (as Germany seems to have been more than a generation ahead with the carol), had a secular drama in the thirteenth century, four examples of which, by Adam the Hunchback (†1288) and others, survive. English drama in the literary sense dates from about the year 1300; the Guilds took up the mystery play and brought it to full flower, gradually increasing the secular element at the same time: the York and Towneley Plays date from 1340 to 1350, the Chester Plays are *c.* 1400, and the Coventry Plays ran from 1400 to 1450; the old drama thus reached the top of its vigour in the fifteenth century. Such developments led naturally to the writing of religious songs in the vernacular, as in the Coventry Carol (22), and also to the gradual substitution of folk-song and dance tunes for the winding cadences of liturgical music. The time was ripe for the carol.

People were now accustomed to think vividly of many of the Bible stories: the influence of the constant dramatic visualization of such scenes as the Annunciation, the visit of the Shepherds ('And farewell, Joseph, with thy round cap') and of the legendary Three Kings, or the misdeeds of Herod, 'that moody king'—who was often out-Heroded long before *Hamlet* was written—is evident in many old carols, as well as in sculpture and painting; and some carols, like the two of which the tunes are preserved, the Coventry Carol (22) and the German 'Joseph lieber' (77), were definitely written for the mystery play or crib. Plainsong antiphons were not very suitable for the drama, and they gradually disappeared; for the fifteenth century was a great era also of musical development both in prick-song and counterpoint, and in the latter England for a while led the way for the Netherlands under the influence of composers like John Dunstable, who had a European reputation twenty years before he died in 1453: 'What tidings bringest thou, Messenger' (40) is from his school, if not by him. The fifteenth century was also the special time of ballad production in England—there was little, if any, before—and the ballad is another example of popular tradition: a narrative poem of communal origin, the ballad began in the dramatic singing of a throng of people under a leader, and in its earlier form was sung with a refrain: 'ballad', as we have seen, means a dancing song, just as 'carol' does.

There was thus a drawing together, with a new music, in what was still almost a new language, of minstrel, literary, and folk poetry in the fifteenth century. Chaucer was dead; and it was not a great age of English verse, except for the ballads and songs, and for the carols—those 'masterpieces of tantalizing simplicity', as Professor Manly calls them. The ballad was one of the forms in which many of our traditional carols have been cast, as for instance, 'The Carnal and the Crane' (53–5) and 'The Cherry

Tree Carol' 36). The lyric also sometimes takes on a new religious grace, a 'harp of Ariel' quality in such a poem as 'I sing of a maiden' (183), and thus becomes so much a carol that Professor Saintsbury quotes it in his *Short History of English Literature* as the typical carol of the age, though this is perhaps to go a little too far, since we do not know how or even whether it was sung. There also emerges a new form of verse with a lilting rhythm, evidently devised for singing (like 'Adam lay ybounden', 180). This form, with a refrain for the chorus to sing, is the carol *par excellence*, and the following are instances of it, all from between the years 1430 and 1460: 'When Christ was born of Mary free' (178), 'This endris night' (39), 'Welcome Yule' (174). One version of the last named occurs in the collection of John Awdlay (*c.* 1430), the blind chaplain of Haughmond Abbey in Shropshire, who 'at the end of a tedious versifying of the whole duty of man', as Sir Edmund Chambers says, suddenly changes his key: 'the gladdened scribe marks it with red letters':

I pray you, Sirs, both more and less
Sing these carols in Christèmas.

Here a priest is helping on the new movement. Another form of carol is the macaronic, in which lines of Latin, generally from the well-known office hymns, are interspersed with vigorous phrases in the vernacular, as in 'Make we joy' (23) and the famous 'In dulci jubilo' (86), both of which have retained their melodies. This last class has suggested to some writers the activity of innovating parsons; but the Latin often consists of tags like *A solis ortus cardine* (the first line of the hymn for Evensong on Christmas Day as well as for Lauds), which were familiar to any one who paid the least attention in church; and Latin was used by most people who were acquainted with letters in any form. Parsons doubtless wrote some of these carols and some of other kinds; but there were other classes in which poets and composers were found, not least the *scholares vagantes*, light-hearted products of all the universities of Europe, 'equally at home in ale-house, in hall, in market-place, or in cloister', who were busy making songs both secular and religious, and singing them (often improperly, as in the case of No. 36) to tunes both religious and secular. The truth is that carols are a national creation: if they represent the layman's contribution to religion, the clergy also have contributed much, though less from the musical side: like Gothic architecture they are unclerical in the sense that they are the work of all the people combined—including many parsons, who in this as in all succeeding ages of carol-making had their share with musicians, poets, and peasant folk.

The carol arose with the ballad in the fifteenth century, because people wanted something less severe than the old Latin office hymns, something more vivacious than the plainsong melodies. This century rang up the modern era: it was the age of the all-pervading Chaucerian influence and of the spread of humanism in England, where it culminates in the New Learning under Grocyn, Warham, Linacre, and Colet: in Italy the fifteenth century began with the full flood of the Renaissance, and Leonardo was in his prime when it ended: before its close, printed books were familiar objects, and the New World had been discovered. Our earliest carols are taken from manuscripts of this century and from the collection which Richard Hill, the grocer's apprentice (36, *note*), made at the beginning of the sixteenth. The earliest printed collection which has survived (and that only in one of its leaves containing one of the Boar's Head Carols, No. 19, and 'a caroll of huntynge') was issued in 1521 by Wynkyn de Worde, Caxton's apprentice and successor. A later extant collection was printed by Richard Kele, *c.* 1550. The metre of these earlier carols is most commonly a one-rime iambic tercet, eight syllables to each line, with a refrain (as in 'Tyrley, Tyrlow', 169), which is near to the familiar Long Measure of the vast majority of the ancient Latin hymns, and when the refrain is also in eight syllables (as in 'In Bethlehem that fair city', 120, and 'Out of your sleep', 177) is, but for the rime of the refrain, exactly in Long Measure. This metre continued in use—it is that, for instance, of the seventeenth-century 'The first Nowell' (27), with the addition of a refrain and some tripping extra syllables here and there. But the later traditional carols tend to employ the ordinary ballad metre or Common Measure, in which the second and fourth lines have six syllables only (as in 'The Holy Well', 56, and 'The moon shines bright', 46), and sometimes the D.C.M. (as 'The first good joy', 70) and other metres. The prevalent iambic metre of the old carols, and the rarity of feminine endings to lines, are the reason why English words which have lost their tunes can only occasionally be fitted to foreign substitutes; and for this reason new words have generally to be found for foreign tunes.

The carol continued to flourish through the sixteenth century, and until the recrudescence of puritanism in a new form suppressed it in the seventeenth. In the year 1644 the unfortunate people of England had to keep Christmas Day as a fast, because it happened to fall on the last Wednesday in the month—the day which the Long Parliament had ordered to be kept as a monthly fast. In 1647 the Puritan Parliament abolished Christmas and other festivals altogether. The new Puritan point of view is neatly expressed by Hezekiah Woodward, who in a tract of 1656 calls Christmas Day 'The old Heathen's Feasting Day, in honour to Saturn their Idol-God, the Papist's Massing Day, the Profane Man's Ranting Day, the Superstitious Man's Idol Day, the Multitude's Idle Day, Satan's—that Adversary's—Working Day, the True Christian Man's Fasting Day. . . . We are persuaded, no one thing more hindereth the Gospel work all the year long, than doth the observation of that Idol Day once in a year, having so many days of cursed observation with it.'

Thus, most of our old carols were made during the two centuries and a half between the death of Chaucer in 1400 and the ejection of the Reverend Robert Herrick from his parish by Oliver Cromwell's men in 1647.

The old masques and carols did not recover after the Restoration. New carols so-called continued indeed to be printed, throughout the eighteenth century, in such publications as *Poor Robin's Almanack* (1663–1776); but they were mere eating-songs about pork and pudding. Indeed, almost the only contribution of this static era was to print Nahum Tate's 'While shepherds watched' in the *Supplement* of *c.* 1698 to the *New Version*, as is mentioned in our foot-note to carol 33, and 'Hark! the herald angels' (altered from Charles Wesley's finer original of 1739) in the *Supplement* of 1782.

Meanwhile the old carols travelled underground and were preserved in folk-song, the people's memory of the texts being kept alive by humble broadsheets of indifferent exactitude which appeared annually in various parts of the country. The carol was ignored by the formal and prosaic world of the eighteenth century, and was slowly losing ground among the poor, though there is evidence of its continuance in many parts of England. Goldsmith in 1766 says that the parishioners of *The Vicar of Wakefield* 'kept up the Christmas carol'. A writer in the *Gentleman's Magazine* for May 1811 states that in the North Riding of Yorkshire he was awakened about six o'clock on Christmas Day 'by a sweet singing under my window', and looking out he saw six young women and four men singing. The American visitor, Washington Irving, in 1820 was surprised one Christmas night, also in Yorkshire, to hear beautiful music from rustics: 'I had scarcely got into bed', he writes in his *Sketch Book*, 'when a strain of music seemed to break forth in the air just below the window. I listened, and found it proceeded from a band, which I concluded to be the waits from some neighbouring village. They went round the house playing under the windows'; he listened with 'hushed delight', and notes half apologetically that 'even the sound of the waits, rude as may be their minstrelsy, breaks upon the mid-watches of a winter night with the effect of perfect harmony'.

The forgotten wealth of beauty was not restored by the pioneers of the Romantic Revival, nor even by that great rediscoverer of Christmas (and author of *A Christmas Carol*, which was magnificent but not a carol), Charles Dickens. Indeed, when Dickens was a boy the carol seemed to be on the verge of extinction, and William Hone, the author of *The Every Day Book*, anticipated that carol-singing would entirely disappear in a few years. At the same time, in 1822, Davies Gilbert published the first modern collection of traditional carols: he was a many-sided man—M.P. for Bodmin, he had given early help to Sir Humphry Davy, he chose Brunel's design for Clifton Suspension Bridge, and became President of the Royal Society. A second edition of his *Collection of Christmas Carols* was called for in 1823. But he also spoke of the carol as a thing of the past: these Cornish examples of his were sung, he said, 'in Churches on Christmas Day, and in private houses on Christmas Eve, throughout the West of England up to the latter part of the late century'. The next collector, William Sandys, the solicitor antiquary, in his *Christmas Carols Ancient and Modern*, 1833, did not take a much more hopeful view: carol singing, he wrote, still existed 'in the Northern counties and some of the Midland'; but, he added that the practice appeared 'to get more neglected every year'.

Indeed, the very meaning of the word 'carol' came to be forgotten. In 1831 a book called *Christmas Carols* was published by J. W. Parker for the S.P.C.K., and reprinted until 1857: it consisted entirely of new Christmas hymns, very poor in quality (and now forgotten), while the music included only one carol tune. We have before us another book, dated 1848, which, although it is called *Christmas Carols A Sacred Gift*, is really an anthology of poems on the Nativity without any musical suggestions whatever. 'Carol' had come to mean printed matter suitable for Christmas.

The broadsheets, however, continued to preserve the tradition among the common people, though they were deteriorating. W. H. Husk, in his *Songs of the Nativity*, 1868, reported that carols were still sung, but that the broadsheets showed that their printers, especially in London, 'find the taste of their customers rather incline towards hymns, mostly those in use amongst dissenting congregations, than to the genuine Christmas carol'. This was true also of the collection *The Christmas Box*, published as early as 1825 by the Religious Tract Society (mentioned in our note to No. 119), which contains several 'new carols' of a hymn-like description, including 'another new carol' for Spring, and a recast of 'God rest you merry', with 'merry' left out, but still appointed to be sung 'To the old tune,—*God rest you merry, Gentlemen*'; but beyond this and a second recast of the same, there is little that is not of a solemn and didactic character, addressed to 'Ye young and ye gay, ye lovers of sin, Who sportive with play, each new year begin': there are no real traditional carols, and the little book was evidently intended to supplant them.

In spite of such efforts of superior people, the neglected folk-carol continued to exist. Two examples may serve to give an idea of the position between about 1830 and 1870. We have before us a small paper book, *A New Carol Book*, published at Birmingham by J. Guest: it is undated, but does not look much later than 1830. It consists of forty-eight pages and contains, among several long compositions of no merit, 'Hark! the herald angels', 'On Christmas night all Christians sing' (our No. 24), 'Dives and Lazarus' (57), 'The moon shines bright' (46), 'God rest you merry' (11), and 'The holly and the ivy' (38). Our second example is from an article in the *Leisure Hour* for December 1869, which dwells on the enormous circulation of broadsheets at that time, but consoles its readers with unconscious irony, 'Village schools and village choirs have enlarged the rustic knowledge and improved the rustic ear'. The article reprints in full a typical broadsheet of the year, called *The Evergreen : Carols for Christmas Holidays* : its contents are 'God rest you merry', 'In friendly love and unity', 'The moon shines bright', 'Now cruel Herod', 'The first good joy' (our No. 70), and 'As I sat upon a sunny bank' (3). It is important to note that the people with their 'rustic' ears could always be depended on for the tunes.

But from another side a succession of scholars had been preparing the way for revival since the middle of George III's reign, as is shown by the names of Bishop Percy (whose *Reliques of Ancient English Poetry* had been published as far back as 1765), Joseph Ritson (his *Ancient Songs* were dated 1790), the Rev. John Brand († 1806), Sir Walter Scott († 1832), and William Hone († 1842). The work went on: in 1836 Thomas Wright began printing fifteenth-century *Songs and Carols* (from the Sloane MS. 2593), published more in 1847, and was still publishing ancient carols in 1856. Other scholars followed; and the valuable work of societies like the Percy Society and the Early English Text Society has assisted them down to our own day. Musicians began at last to be interested: in 1855–9 William Chappell published his two volumes of old music, but he ignored the living folk-song, alas, when it was still abundant. E. F. Rimbault, who did some useful but not always trustworthy work for music, had begun with a *Little Book of Carols* in 1846, though his more important small collections did not appear till 1863 and 1865.

Such was the position in the middle of the last century. In 1847 a genuine collector of folk-carols had published anonymously the valuable little book, *A Good Christmas Box*, at Dudley, unfortunately without tunes; and in 1852 Sandys added some new material in *Christmas Tide* to his first admirable collection. Thus, seventy years ago, when the folk-carol was slowly dying (in spite of the continuance of the broadsheets), at the other end of the scale the carol was being recovered: scholarly foundations had already been laid, and enough music had been published by Gilbert and Sandys to make carol-singing possible among the few educated people who were interested in it. The only men who were in touch with both sides and might therefore be able to effect a national revival were the clergy; and, as it happened, the new movement in the Church was causing some of the young high-church parsons to think wistfully about carols. But the first great impulse in the Church arose from an unexpected quarter.

A very rare Swedish book had come into the possession of the editors of the *Hymnal Noted* of 1852, the Rev. J. M. Neale and the Rev. T. Helmore: it was called *Piae Cantiones*, and was full of exquisite sixteenth-century tunes (see 141 *n.*). Neale translated some of the carols or hymns therein, and in 1853 he and Helmore published *Carols for Christmas-tide*, twelve carols, with music from the old book. This they followed up next year with twelve *Carols for Easter-tide*—the first recognition since old times of the carol apart from Christmas. Thus some of our finest carols both in words and music were given to the Church: the misfortune was that the traditional carols of this country were ignored, and their recovery was retarded. The Rev. J. E. Vaux indeed wrote in *Church Folk Lore*, 1894 (apparently without disapproval), that Neale and Helmore 'have done much to lead to the disuse of certain old favourites, which probably in a few years will be forgotten'; and he mentions that 'A Virgin unspotted' had been dropped at Grasmere about 1860, though recently it had been revived again 'to the great joy of the people'. But glamour at that time was sought among things ancient and foreign, and it is probable that Neale and Helmore hit upon the only way to recover prestige for the carol. Also they published their collection in cheaper form for use in church, and thus began to rebuild the broken bridge between poets and people. Fired by their example, Edmund Sedding published in 1860 nine *Antient Christmas Carols*, to which he added seven more in 1863, including a few English with some good Dutch and other foreign examples (e.g. 153). But Neale died in 1866 when he was only forty-eight, and Sedding followed him two years later. It was doubtless these men and their supporters whom Husk had in mind when in 1868 he said that 'a certain section of the clergy' had made attempts to revive a taste for the use of Christmas carols amongst their parishioners. 'But their efforts have been too intermittent and spasmodic to produce any successful result.' Anyhow the first chapter in the revival was ended.

The second chapter of the revival in the nineteenth century opens in 1871 with the publication of forty-two *Christmas Carols New and Old* by the Rev. H. R. Bramley, Fellow of Magdalen College, Oxford, and Dr. John Stainer, then organist of the college. The influence of this book was enormous: it placed in the hands of the clergy (who were perhaps not so 'intermittent' in their efforts as Husk had thought) a really practicable tool, which came into general use, and is still in use after nearly sixty years. The great service done by this famous collection was that it brought thirteen traditional carols, with their proper music, into general use at once. There was another side, it is true. Twenty-four of the numbers were composed by contemporary Church musicians, and it was the heyday of *Hymns Ancient and Modern* ; of these, little perhaps, except the tune by Sir John Goss (30), deserves to survive ; the traditional melodies also lost some of their freshness and strength in the inappropriate harmonies which were made for them. Moreover, it must be confessed that the mantle of Neale had not fallen upon Bramley ; the new words were but sorry pietistic verse for the most part. It is nevertheless mainly to Bramley and Stainer that we owe the restoration of the carol ; and if they obscured as well as restored, the age must be blamed rather than the editors. With their fifteen or sixteen old carol tunes, and two more from Neale and Helmore (thus popularizing our no. 136, but unfortunately with inappropriate words) they repaired the breach : afterwards they made up their total to seventy, which increased the modern compositions to forty-three, and the traditional to twenty-seven.

Many other new carols and some collections were produced in the last quarter of the nineteenth century, for carol singing had now become popular ; but none of these attained to the standard of Bramley and Stainer. There is a carol-book, for instance, of 1875 which contains over sixty modern pieces—with poor tunes, and words pitifully jejune—to less than forty that can be called carols—and these often obscured almost out of recognition. Indeed, Bramley and Stainer's book supplied nearly all that there was, until in 1901 and 1902 Dr. G. R. Woodward in two editions of the *Cowley Carol Book* (First Series) reprinted twenty-one of Neale's carols, and thus reopened the precious little vein of foreign music which had been discovered fifty years before by Neale and Helmore.

The carol, in fact, was still in jeopardy fifty years ago, and even later. Our churches were flooded with music inspired by the sham Gothic of their renovated interiors : ' carol services ' are indeed not infrequently held even to-day at which not a single genuine carol is sung. On this bad music let us quote Sir Henry Hadow and have done with it. He writes, in his little book, *Church Music*

(1926): 'There has probably been no form of any art in the history of the world which has been so overrun by the unqualified amateur as English church music from about 1850 to about 1900. Many of our professional musicians at this time stood also at a low level of culture and intelligence and were quite content to flow with the stream. . . . Thirty years ago we were perhaps at our lowest ebb. This music was deplorably easy to write, it required little or no skill in performance, it passed by mere use and wont into the hearts of the congregation, it became a habit like any other, and it is only during comparatively recent years that any serious attempts have been made to eradicate it.'

Fortunately, however, some two dozen real carols had also become generally known, and these have won their way by their intrinsic merit. The position in 1875, when the flood of bad carols had but recently begun, was correctly described by a writer in the *Guardian* that year, who noted that some 'hearty' persons were bringing carols into 'the sacred precincts' and actually using them as an act of worship; he added that, 'During the last few years carol-singing has been extensively revived. It had never indeed quite died out in our rural districts, in which roughly printed broadsides, with grotesque woodcuts, were, and are to this day, annually purchasable at the village shop. These broadsides are issued from the neighbourhood of Seven Dials, in a type, or rather in a conglomeration of odd specimens of type, which would fairly shock the nerves of a good compositor; yet their circulation is enormous, and, if their printers cannot excite our admiration, they at least deserve our gratitude, for they have sustained the very existence of some of the most beautiful carols during the long period of neglect at the hands of musicians and men of letters.'

It was not, however, till the last decade of the nineteenth century that folk music began to be systematically collected. Indeed, the Folk-Song Society was not founded till 1898; and Cecil Sharp, in his *English Folk-Songs: Some Conclusions* (1907), says that 'Twenty years ago it was only by a very few people that folk-songs were known to exist in this country', and the very word 'folk-song' does not seem to have been coined (from 'Volkslied') till after 1880. England, almost alone among the countries of Europe, had not produced a book of national songs; for we were supposed to be an unmusical people, 'Das Land ohne

Musik'. At last it was realized that England, as well as Scotland and Germany, and the rest of the civilized world, had its songs; and that folk-music (from which art-music is derived as literature is derived from popular speech) had existed in England all along—tunes originally of individual invention having been gradually shaped to the communal feeling of the race, here not less than in other countries. Then began the search among the memories of old people in the country-side, only just in time; and to this we owe the recovery of one lost carol tune after another. So many have been discovered that there is now a fairly wide scope for the selection of those which are best and most distinctive.

It is a thrilling history, full of significance. Something transparently pure and truthful, clean and merry as the sunshine, has been recovered from under the crust of artificiality which had hidden it. The English-speaking peoples are now getting back what once belonged to them, both in poetry and in music, through the researches of a few scholars and through the conservatism of old village folk and the work of a few musicians who could recognize beauty when they saw it. The carol is established again, and not the carol only; for the work that men like Cecil Sharp did for traditional song and dance is being spread to many ends by the primary and secondary schools throughout the country; the deadly effects of imitation and affectation are passing away, and, by the recovery of our national music which the musicians had lost, an inspiration has come which has already restored English music to the position it held in Europe before the eighteenth century.

§ 2. *Selection and Arrangement.*

The selection of carols is not so easy a task as perhaps might be imagined. There are some genuine old tunes which no one would ever sing; others, like those of William Byrd in 1588–9 and 1611, which are really motets; there are also far more genuine old texts than could possibly be made use of; and, as we have said, there is a large body of recovered folk-carol tunes; there is, moreover, a debatable land between the hymn and the carol; and besides all this there are hundreds of foreign carols. Furthermore, new carols are produced every year, and there is a large accumulation of inferior material, especially imitative work of the self-conscious and artificial type and sentimental verses written for foreign tunes not of the first rank. Much of the labour in any comprehensive collection must therefore be directed to elimination; and this is ungrateful work which has to be done for conscience' sake, since it produces no visible result and may even give the impression that matter has been overlooked which in reality has been carefully considered. One carol, for instance, has recently obtained a certain vogue because it was ascribed to a famous historical personage (a man, by the way, who would have been surprised to find his work associated with so slight a tune): it was evident that the words as they stood were at best but an unskilled translation remote from the supposed original, but a long search had to be made before we could be sure that the historical personage was entirely innocent of the thing in any form whatever.

From the great body of foreign carols it has been our task to discover, so far as we could, the finest tunes, selecting only those which for beauty and distinction seemed to belong to all mankind, and translating or paraphrasing so far as possible the words. Although in a carol the tune generally has precedence, and not the text as in a hymn, this is no reason why perfunctory libretto or meaningless doggerel should be given to a fine melody; we have therefore sought the co-operation of poets in order that both the words and music of the foreign carols might be as good as we could manage. In some cases where no good text seemed to have survived, we have asked our collaborators to write entirely new words: there are therefore some twentieth-century poems in this book; and we hope they are as true to their age, as fresh and direct, as the fifteenth-century poems were. Some modern tunes are also included, most of them in order to carry a specially good fifteenth- or sixteenth-century carol whose tune has been lost. There is, indeed, no reason why the art of carol-making should die.

To avoid, however, a confusion between old and new weddings of tunes to words we have arranged the *Oxford Book of Carols* in a special way. In the First Part we have placed traditional carols which still have their proper tunes (excluding cases that are perhaps on the border-line, such as Nos. 114, 130, and 137, and those texts in Part III which are only based on foreign originals); in the Second Part, traditional carol tunes set to other traditional or old texts; in the Third, the words are not traditional;

in the Fourth, the tunes are by modern composers; and in the Fifth are a few entirely modern carols. We have not attempted a further chronological arrangement, since any such attempt would be misleading; but the carols are grouped according to their seasons, and in this Music Edition there is a complete table of carols arranged for use throughout the year.

§ 3. *The Texts.*

We have kept as close as possible to the original texts, and have endeavoured to avoid changing their character or modernizing them into dullness; but sometimes texts have to be slightly altered to make them singable. The problem is more confused than that of hymns; for every fifteenth-century carol that appears in more than one manuscript is in more than one form, and every traditional carol that has been recovered from the people is more or less changed or truncated, while the broadsides are by no means trustworthy. Again, the fifteenth-century carols lose their rhymes if all archaic words are changed, and their character if the sounded 'e' is always replaced by an epithet; but we have altered such things sometimes when the character of the line did not seem to suffer by the change, since this is not a collection of texts but a practical book for choir and people. Especially when a carol is well known, as 'A babe is born all of a may' (116), it would seem perverse to restore 'A merye song then sungyn he', when 'A merry song that night sang he' (or they) has been familiar for the last fifty years, and gives to a reader of-to-day more of the character of the original than would the original words themselves, which in fact were not at all archaic to the author. On the other hand, carols like 'Lullay my liking' (182) and 'Adam lay ybounden' (180) would lose their character if the sounded 'e' were eliminated; they are perfectly intelligible as they stand, and they are not popularly associated with any other version.

The best texts of traditional carols can only be arrived at by copying from the more trustworthy collections, which are few in number, and sometimes by collating various versions. Davies Gilbert in 1822 evidently wrote down the words almost as he heard them, and like William Sandys he sometimes preserved the tunes. Sandys's collection of 1833 is larger; he was a scholarly editor and preserves the character of the originals, though he must have smoothed them a little. The anonymous editor of *A Good Christmas*

Box, Dudley, 1847, did in a modest way for the Midlands what Gilbert had done for Cornwall, and seems to have taken down exactly what he heard. W. H. Husk (*Songs of the Nativity*, 1868) deserves much credit for having made use of the broadsides. Most other compilers of the nineteenth century copied from these and from one another; and though some of them recovered a few more old carols, they tried so much to improve on their originals that their texts have seldom much value. Indeed, few subjects have suffered more than the traditional carol from the want of careful research and accurate presentation. The Hanoverian and Victorian scholars and musicians, with a few exceptions, ignored it; and some collections were made by people not well fitted for the task: there was, indeed, only just enough good work—in this country as distinct from Germany—to carry what was left of the old tunes and texts precariously over the gulf. Not even to-day does there yet exist a standard book on the carol, nor anything like a complete and trustworthy collection. On this subject the *Encyclopaedia Britannica* fails, and even the *Cambridge History of English Literature* stumbles a little. One result of these misfortunes is that when people give lectures or addresses about carols, few of their statements are correct; another is that the task of workers in the field is heavy, and beset with pitfalls.

None the less, during the nineteenth century the learned societies were active in printing the old manuscripts, and towards the end of the century some work was done for the later carols which was more worthy of the beginning made by Gilbert and Sandys. A. H. Bullen produced his volume of *Carols and Poems* in 1885; and on another side the Folk Song Society has brought accurate and thorough methods into a department which had suffered long from the lack of them. Among editors of varying degrees of accuracy at the present day Edmund K. Chambers and Frank Sidgwick stand out for their scholarly methods (*Early English Lyrics*, 1921), and lead us to hope that such flawless work may be extended, and that one day there may appear a complete collection of English carols of all ages in trustworthy form. This is not such a collection, but a practical book of carols intended to be sung. We have, indeed, supplied foot-notes, but only so far as seemed necessary to make each number as intelligible and interesting as the space allowed.

§ 4. *Carol Music.*

The tunes in this book are real carol tunes, and we have endeavoured to secure that their harmonies shall be appropriate to their character, preserving the freshness and buoyancy of the true carol. We have made it a principle not to attempt to provide words for other traditional music. It would be possible to take thousands of folk-tunes like 'The Raggle-taggle Gipsies' or 'Mowing the Barley' and write interminable new instalments of *pastiche* verses for them; but the result would be counterfeits and not carols. When an old tune like 'Greensleeves' (28) or 'Nous voici dans la ville' (91) has been for ages associated both with a carol and a folk-song, it can rightly be claimed as a carol tune; but to go beyond this class is to incur the danger of that artificiality which is still the great enemy of the carol.

There is a point where carols overlap with hymns, especially on their musical side. We have included 'While shepherds watched' (33) because of the traditional carol tune which belongs to it; and, passing over hymns like 'Christians, awake', we have also included for the sake of their carol music 'O little town' (138), 'In the bleak mid-winter' (187), and 'How far is it' (142) from the *English Hymnal* and *Songs of Praise*. A few outstanding carol tunes (Nos. 39, 76, 77, 78, 79), which are set to other words in these two books, we have also included because we think that no carol-book would be complete without them.

Variety in the method of singing is even more important with carols than with hymns, and the verses should never be sung straight through all in the same way. The first and last verses, for instance, can be sung in unison, and other verses also in the case of long carols; a fine antiphonal effect can often be got by the alternate singing of choir and people. Sometimes a carol can be treated as a solo, the harmonies being sung *bouche fermée* by the choir; and sometimes the organ or orchestra can be brought in with fine effect after it has been silent during two or three verses. Suggestions for variations of this sort, as well as varied harmonies and fa-burdens, will be found in this Music Edition of the *Oxford Book of Carols*. Whatever is to be done should be thought out beforehand and announced before the carol is sung, so that the people can do their part with confidence. Choir and people alike will be greatly helped if the choirmaster stands in a place from which he can conduct them both. Since a few carols are very short and others even after abridgement are long, and since the music enjoys a certain precedence, a very short carol like 'A little child' (74) may well be sung twice over, and the first verse at least repeated in a carol like 'Patapan' (82) or 'Rocking' (87), while a long carol like 'A New Dial' (64) may be more summarily abbreviated than is advisable in the case of a hymn.

§ 5. *The Use of Carols.*

By no means all the old carols are about Christmas. If, for instance, we analyse Richard Hill's typical manuscript collection (described under No. 36), we find that his 62 sacred songs in the Early English Text Society edition—all true carols with refrains—can be classified thus: A. *Carols of a general character* suitable at any time of the year, 18 (there are no narrative ballad carols and no May carols in the collection). B. *Carols bearing on the Nativity*, specifically Christmas, 17; Christmastide saints, 4; Epiphany, 2 (making the total for the Christmas season 23); Nativity, 4, one of these being mainly on the Passion; to the Virgin, 2; on the Annunciation, 5 (making a total in Section B of 34). C. *Carols on other subjects*, Baptism of Christ, 1; the Passion, 6; the Eucharist, 3. In other parts of the book are the Corpus Christi Carol (61 *n.*), 'Nay, nay ivy', and several devotional poems unconnected with Christmas. The absence of Easter is remarkable; for carols represent those aspects of religion in which the fifteenth-century Englishman was most interested: there are many foreign Easter carols, but abroad as well as in England the great subjects commemorated in the festivals after Easter evoked little or no lyrical response. The iconography of painting, as a visit to any picture gallery will show, has much the same characteristics, and evinces the same absence of interest in the works and teaching of Christ. This last subject appears in English seventeenth-century carols, in which also Easter finds mention as the sequel to the Passion.

There seems to have been a constant tendency of the people to sing carols all the year, and of those in authority (at least as early as the sixteenth century) to restrict festivities to the Twelve Days. After the Epiphany, labourers and apprentices were required to settle down to work again for the rest of the year—reluctantly, poor things: the young men used to hinder the maids by setting fire to their flax on the 7th of January, 'St. Distaff's Day', as Herrick tells us:

> Partly work and partly play,
> You must on Saint Distaff's day
> From the plough soon free your team,
> Then come home and fodder them:
> If the maids a-spinning go
> Burn the flax and fire the tow.

After this stolen day they 'bid Christmas sport goodnight'; and, concludes Herrick, 'next morrow, every one To his own vocation'. It is easy to see how the carol came to be restricted at least in its more festive aspects to Christmas, and occasional holidays like May Day, so that before the nineteenth century the conveniently alliterative title 'Christmas Carol' held the field. Bramley and Stainer completed the temporary disappearance of other carols by the popularity of their *Christmas Carols*, and thenceforward authors seldom attempted carols on any theme outside the Twelve Days.

The old people in the villages, however, held on to the other carols, and thus many have been recovered in recent years. In earlier days the waits, as they tottered towards extinction, had apparently found that some excuse was needed for singing such carols, since we can hardly account otherwise for the tags about Christmas or New Year which occur sometimes at the end of Passion and General Carols. Poor rustics! ever since the Methodist Revival people had been teaching them to drop carols altogether. The fact that so much has survived in the little private repertories of peasants and gipsies down to our own day is a tribute to the quality of the folk-carol. It should be easily possible to restore such spontaneous and imperishable things to general use, in the home as well as in church, and to have the waits at work again, not only out of doors but in halls and public rooms, all the year round.

Carols have been used in more than one way—out of doors, in church, at masques and concerts, in the home. As early as Chaucer, the Clerk of Oxenford could sing his carol-like sequence (52) 'So swetely that al the chambre rong'; and we hope that the lovely old tunes in this book will be more and more sung by people in their own homes. We hope also that they will be increasingly sung in halls, from the modest village institute to the fully equipped concert hall. The revival of village life and the desire to relieve the hideous secularity of our great towns may well lead to a demand for the use of carols in out-door processions and festivities in spring and summer as well as at Christmas. Clubs, guilds, women's institutes should find carols a constant source of happiness and inspiration. Those gatherings also of the 'Pleasant Sunday Afternoon' type, where young men and women often sing 'sacred' solos and duets of the most inconceivable depravity, might be made both religious and delightful if those young people were encouraged to sing carols every Sunday: on such occasions many of the Christmas numbers are not out of place even in the summer or autumn, while those we have classed as Nativity or General Carols are suitable all the year round. A new type of informal Sunday service is possible now that so many carols are readily accessible—a 'Carol Service' on every Sunday in the year: such a service (described in the notes to this Music Edition) is to be begun in at least one important centre as soon as this book is published.

We think also that carols might be continuously sung in ordinary parish churches and in chapels, where the choir often try to emulate the too difficult anthem of cathedral and collegiate churches. On p. 717 of the Music Edition of *Songs of Praise* we gave a list of hymns that are suitable to be sung instead of the anthem so often disastrous to the normal parish choir. What might not be done with carols? On every Sunday, in the place of the anthem, or after service, glorious carols can be sung by the choir, the people joining in the refrains, or singing the third and subsequent alternate verses. Perhaps nothing is just now of such importance as to increase the element of joy in religion; people crowd in our churches at the Christmas, Easter, and Harvest Festivals, largely because the hymns for those occasions are full of a sound hilarity; if carol-books were in continual use, that most Christian and most forgotten element would be vastly increased, in some of its loveliest forms, all through the year.

P. D.

ACKNOWLEDGEMENTS

BESIDES those whose contributions we gratefully acknowledge below, the translators, poets, and musicians who have taken so much trouble in helping us, we owe special thanks to Mr. Walter Gandy for his prolonged musical and literary researches; to the late Professor Röntgen for the Dutch and Flemish carols (73, 74); to Mr. J. B. Trend for Spanish carols (81, 113); to Canon R. E. Roberts for Welsh carols (9, 34, 50, 59); to the Rev. G. H. Doble and Mr. H. Jenner for Cornish carols (35, 41); to Miss Lucy Broadwood (45, 55); and especially to Miss Karpeles, the literary executrix to Cecil Sharp, for the English traditional carols acknowledged below. Also to Mr. J. H. Arnold, Miss E. Maconchy, and Dr. Geoffrey Shaw, for harmonizing melodies; to many who have helped and encouraged us, especially to Mr. Frank Sidgwick for his very kind help, and Mrs. Alexander Ferguson and Miss Violet Latford for their careful clerical assistance.

We acknowledge here the copyright texts under the initials A. F. D., A. G., B. M. G., E. B. G., G. D., L. M., N. S. T., O. B. C., S. P.; as well as those texts, melodies, and harmonies under the names of the Editors. Our thanks are due to Messrs. Stainer and Bell for allowing the reprinting of the following folk carols collected by Mrs. Leather and R. Vaughan Williams, 7, 43, 53, 57, 115, 131 (copyright, U.S.A. 1920, by Stainer & Bell, Ltd.); and by R. Vaughan Williams, 17, 24, 47, 51, 61, 68 (copyright, U.S.A. 1919, by Stainer & Bell, Ltd.); Messrs. Novello & Co., Ltd., for the following collected by Cecil Sharp, 8, 54, 60 (melody and words), and by Mr. W. P. Merrick and R. Vaughan Williams, 6 (1) in the Appendix of the Music Edition. Also to Messrs. Boosey for Miss Broadwood's Folk Carol, 45; Messrs. J. Curwen & Sons, Ltd., for tunes 78 (Curwen Edition, No. 71655, copyright, U.S.A. 1924, by Gustav Holst), 137 (Curwen Edition, No. 71656, copyright, U.S.A. 1924, by Gustav Holst), 172 (Curwen Edition, No. 2418, copyright, U.S.A. 1926, by Martin Shaw), 176 (Curwen Edition, No. 80663, copyright, U.S.A. 1928, by Armstrong Gibbs), also 182 and 189; also to Messrs. J. M. Dent & Sons, Ltd., for the late G. K. Chesterton's carol, 143; Miss Maud Karpeles for melody of 142; Messrs. Macmillan & Co., Ltd., for Christina Rossetti's carol, 187; Messrs. A. R. Mowbray & Co., Ltd., for tunes 22 (2), 29, 58, 178 (2), 184, 194, 195; Messrs. Novello & Co., Ltd., for tune 192; and the Caniedydd Committee, Welsh Congregational Union, for tunes 34 and 59.

Our heavy debt to the late Cecil Sharp is shown by our notes in many parts of the book, especially under Nos. 4, 8, 24, 32, 38, 44, 54, 60, 65, 70; our debt to the late Professor Julius Röntgen for help over Dutch tunes extends beyond the two numbers we have mentioned; and to Miss Jacubičková we owe the two Czech carols (87, 103) which she collected. Dr. Grattan Flood kindly gave us permission for Nos. 6 and 14 before he died; and to Trinity College, Dublin, we owe the permission to photograph the manuscript of No. 30. The Rev. J. R. Van Pelt kindly communicated the tune of No. 143; and Archdeacon Kewley gave permission for the melody of the Manx tune No. 167 collected by the late Dr. John Clague. Mr. H. J. L. J. Massé has helped us all by his publication of foreign carols, especially in *A Book of Old Carols*, which he edited in 1907 and 1910 with Mr. Charles Kennedy Scott.

We offer our best thanks to those who have made or translated carols for this book, or who have allowed their work to be included here: the Rev. H. N. Bate (191, 193); the Rev. Maurice F. Bell (75, 83); Mr. Laurence Binyon (161); Mr. Patrick R. Chalmers (101, 108, 110); the late G. K. Chesterton (143); Mrs. G. K. Chesterton (142); the Rev. J. M. C. Crum (149); Mr. Geoffrey Dearmer (111, 154, 155, 157); Mr. Walter de la Mare (163); Miss Eleanor Farjeon (88, 91, 97, 133, 158, 188); Miss Rose Fyleman (156); Mr. Robert Graves (80, 84); Mr. Selwyn Image (192, 194); Mr. Frank Kendon (140, 146); Professor George H. Leonard (145); Mr. A. A. Milne (106); Mrs. Roberts (9, 34, 50, 59); Mr. A. H. Fox-Strangways (95); Mr. R. C. Trevelyan (73, 74); Mr. H. D. Wade-Gery (179); and Mr. Steuart Wilson (98, 162, 164, 166, 167). Also to the following composers for permission to use their tunes: Mr. Rutland Boughton (168); Mr. E. Duncan Rubbra (175); Mr. Harry Farjeon (188); Mr. Armstrong Gibbs (176); the late G. Holst (187); Mr. John Ireland (170); Mr. R. O. Morris (190); Mr. S. H. Nicholson (174); and the late Peter Warlock (169, 180, 181); and to the following for their harmonizations: Mr. J. H. Arnold (67); the late Alan Gray and the Rev. the Abbot of Downside (52); Miss E. Maconchy (56, 69); Mr. C. Kennedy Scott (21); and Dr.

Geoffrey Shaw (2, 30, 48, 83, 92, 95, 98, 102, 105, 120, 135, 141, 148, 150, 151, 152, 158).

The arrangements of most of the tunes by (M. S.) and (R. V. W.), also No. 186, are the copyright of the Musical Editors. Also tunes Nos. 103, 123, 130, 177, and 183 are copyright, U.S.A. 1928, by Martin Shaw; and tunes Nos. 173, 185, and 196 are copyright, U.S.A. 1928, by R. Vaughan Williams. Tunes Nos. 169, 175, 180, 181, and 188 are copyright, U.S.A. 1925, and Nos. 21 and 67 are copyright, U.S.A. 1928, by the Oxford University Press. The following tunes are also the copyright of the Oxford University Press: Nos. 60 (2), 178 (1), App. 5.

We wish to take this opportunity of acknowledging our gratitude to the memory of J. M. Neale and the other pioneers in the revival of the carol: and also to all those old people in the villages of England who preserved and communicated so many traditional carols for our use to-day.

Explanatory Notes. Refrains are printed after the first verse, once for all, in italic. An asterisk suggests verses that may conveniently be omitted, but it is not intended to negative still further omissions. For the convenience of the reader a full-stop is printed after the number of the last verse of each carol. *Tr.* means 'translated by', and *Pr.* 'paraphrased by'. The sign † after an author's name means that a line has been altered from his original. The nature of the music is briefly stated at the head of each carol on the left side in all editions, and that of the words on the right side. Thus *Traditional* on the left means that the tune is taken from a traditional source, printed or oral. *Ibid.* means that the words are in the same book or other source or sources as the tune. In the Music Edition the composers of the harmonies, &c., are indicated by names or initials within brackets at the head of the music.

1 CHRISTMAS EVE FIRST TUNE.

(M. S.)

Traditional. *Ibid.*

THE Lord at first did Adam make
Out of the dust and clay,
And in his nostrils breathèd life,
E'en as the Scriptures say.
And then in Eden's Paradise
He placèd him to dwell,
That he within it should remain,
To dress and keep it well:
Now let good Christians all begin
An holy life to live,
And to rejoice and merry be,
For this is Christmas Eve.

2 Now mark the goodness of the Lord
Which he for mankind bore;
His mercy soon he did extend,
Lost man for to restore:
And then, for to redeem our souls
From death and hellish thrall,
He said his own dear Son should be
The Saviour of us all:

3 Now for the blessings we enjoy,
Which are from heaven above,
Let us renounce all wickedness,
And live in perfect love:
Then shall we do Christ's own command,
E'en his own written word;
And when we die, in heaven shall
Enjoy our living Lord:

4. And now the tide is nigh at hand,
In which our Saviour came;
Let us rejoice and merry be
In keeping of the same:
Let's feed the poor and hungry souls,
And such as do it crave;
Then when we die, in heaven we
Our sure reward shall have:

In Davies Gilbert's West-country collection, *Some Ancient Christmas Carols*, 1822, seven verses, with the first tune. The second tune is from Sandys, *Christmas Carols*, 1833.
Ibid. means that the words are in the original text with the tune.

1 CHRISTMAS EVE

SECOND TUNE.

(M. S.)

Chorus.

Traditional. *Ibid.*

THE Lord at first did Adam make
  Out of the dust and clay,
And in his nostrils breathèd life,
  E'en as the Scriptures say.
And then in Eden's Paradise
  He placèd him to dwell,
That he within it should remain,
  To dress and keep it well:

Now let good Christians all begin
  An holy life to live,
And to rejoice and merry be,
  For this is Christmas Eve.

2 Now mark the goodness of the Lord
  Which he for mankind bore;
His mercy soon he did extend,
  Lost man for to restore:
And then, for to redeem our souls
  From death and hellish thrall,
He said his own dear Son should be
  The Saviour of us all:

3 Now for the blessings we enjoy,
  Which are from heaven above,
Let us renounce all wickedness,
  And live in perfect love:
Then shall we do Christ's own command,
  E'en his own written word;
And when we die, in heaven shall
  Enjoy our living Lord:

4. And now the tide is nigh at hand,
  In which our Saviour came;
Let us rejoice and merry be
  In keeping of the same:
Let's feed the poor and hungry souls,
  And such as do it crave;
Then when we die, in heaven we
  Our sure reward shall have:

In Davies Gilbert's West-country collection, *Some Ancient Christmas Carols*, 1822, seven verses, with the tune. The second tune is from Sandys, *Christmas Carols*, 1833.

2 A CHILD THIS DAY

(CHRISTMAS)

The harmonies to verse 1 may be used throughout, if desired.
With vigour.
(G. S.)
f
1 A child this day is born, A child of high re-nown, Most wor-thy of a scep-tre, A scep-tre and a crown:
2 These tid-ings shep-herds heard, In field watching their fold, Were by an an-gel un-to them That night re-veal'd and told:
CHORUS.
Now-ell, Now-ell, Now-ell, Now-ell, sing all we may, Be-cause the King of all kings Was born this bless-ed day.
Be-
Fine.
Be-cause the King Was born . . . . this day.
-cause the King of all kings Was born this bless-ed day.

3 To whom the an - gel spoke, Say-ing, 'Be not a - fraid; Be
4 'For lo! I bring you tid - ings Of glad-ness and of mirth, Which

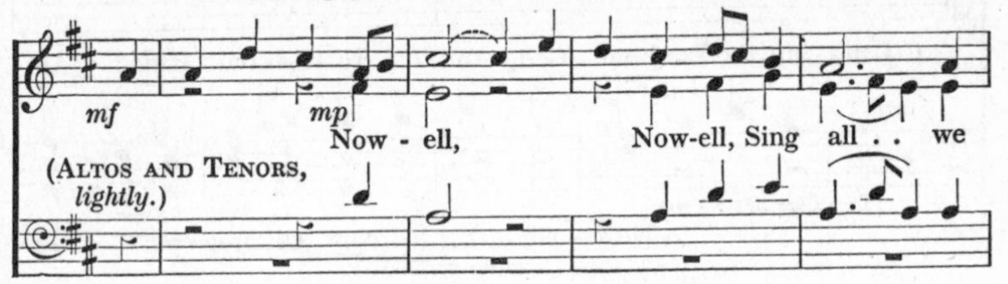

mf
mp
Now - ell, Now-ell, Sing all . . we
(ALTOS AND TENORS, lightly.)

Repeat CHORUS.

glad, poor sil - ly shep - herds—Why are you so dis - mayed?'
com - eth to all peo - ple by This ho - ly in - fant's birth':

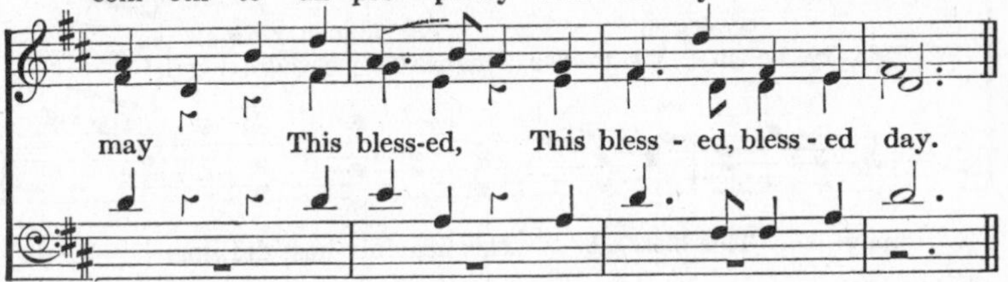

may This bless-ed, This bless - ed, bless - ed day.

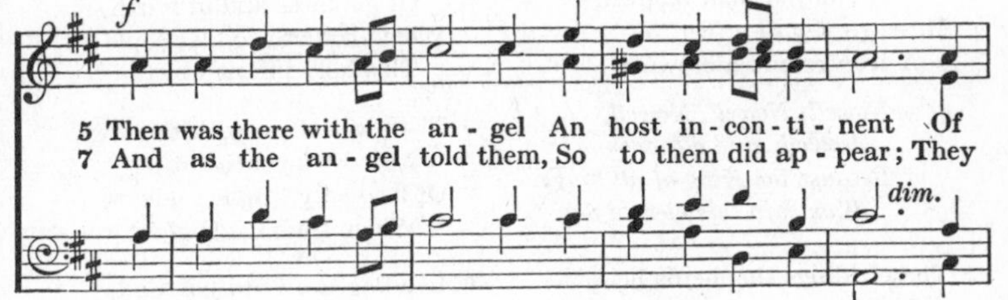

f
5 Then was there with the an - gel An host in - con - ti - nent Of
7 And as the an - gel told them, So to them did ap - pear; They
dim.

Repeat CHORUS.

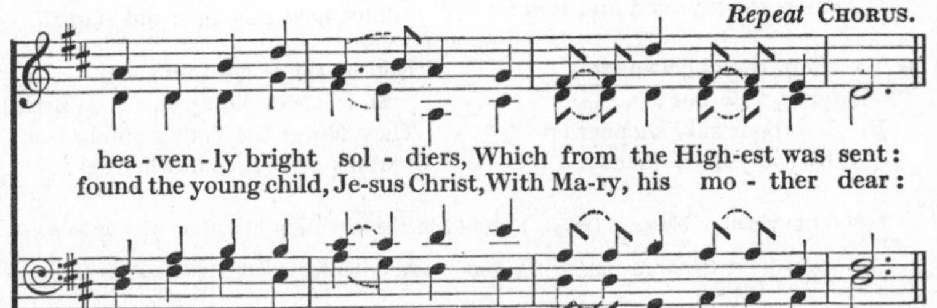

hea - ven - ly bright sol - diers, Which from the High - est was sent:
found the young child, Je - sus Christ, With Ma - ry, his mo - ther dear:

6 Laud-ing the Lord our God, And his ce-les-tial King; All
mf
(Two Bass parts.) mp
Now-ell, Now-ell, Sing all . . . we

CHORUS.
ff Now-
Now-ell, Now-ell, Now-ell,
glo-ry be in Pa-ra-dise, This heav'nly host did sing:
Now-
may This bless-ed, This heav'nly host did sing. Now-

Traditional. *Ibid.*

A CHILD this day is born,
A child of high renown,
Most worthy of a sceptre,
A sceptre and a crown:

Nowell, Nowell, Nowell,
Nowell, sing all we may,
Because the King of all kings
Was born this blessèd day.

2 These tidings shepherds heard,
In field watching their fold,
Were by an angel unto them
That night revealed and told:

3 To whom the angel spoke,
Saying, 'Be not afraid;
Be glad, poor silly shepherds—
Why are you so dismayed?

4 'For lo! I bring you tidings
Of gladness and of mirth,
Which cometh to all people by
This holy infant's birth':

5 Then was there with the angel
An host incontinent
Of heavenly bright soldiers,
Which from the Highest was sent:

6 Lauding the Lord our God,
And his celestial King;
All glory be in Paradise,
This heavenly host did sing:

7. And as the angel told them,
So to them did appear; [Christ,
They found the young child, Jesus
With Mary, his mother dear:

3. Silly] originally 'blessed' (*selig*), had still in the seventeenth century the meaning of 'simple'.

Ibid. means that the words are in the same book, or books, or other sources, as the tune to which they belong.

Words and tune from William Sandys, *Christmas Carols*, 1833 (West of England). The usual seven out of twenty-one verses are here given.

3 SUNNY BANK

(CHRISTMAS)

(M. S.)

Traditional. *Ibid.*

AS I sat on a sunny bank,
On Christmas Day in the morning,

2 I spied three ships come sailing by,
On Christmas Day in the morning.

3 And who should be with those three ships
But Joseph and his fair lady!

4 O he did whistle, and she did sing,
On Christmas Day in the morning.

5 And all the bells on earth did ring,
On Christmas Day in the morning.

6. For joy that our Saviour he was born
On Christmas Day in the morning.

Cf. No. 18. Melody, with some of the verses, taken by Mr. J. H. Blunt, in 1916, from Mr. Samuel Newman, at Downton, Wilts. 'A Sunny Bank' (either thus or as 'I saw three ships') is in most old broadsides and modern collections. It has been found in the North, and West, and Midlands; Cecil Sharp noted two versions, one in Worcestershire, and Bullen found it in Kent. There is an early version in Forbes's *Cantus* (Aberdeen), 1666. We print the usual broadside version of this form as given by Husk.

4 A VIRGIN MOST PURE FIRST TUNE.

(CHRISTMAS)

(M. S.)

3

CHORUS.

Aye and there - fore be mer - ry, re - joice and be you

mer - ry, Set sor - rows a - side; Christ

Je - sus our Sa - viour was born on this tide.

Traditional. *Ibid.*

A VIRGIN most pure, as the prophets do tell,
Hath brought forth a baby, as it hath befel,
To be our Redeemer from death, hell, and sin, [wrappèd us in :
Which Adam's transgression hath

Aye and therefore be merry, rejoice and be you merry,
Set sorrows aside ;
Christ Jesus our Saviour was born on this tide.

2 At Bethlem in Jewry a city there was, [did pass,
Where Joseph and Mary together
And there to be taxèd with many one mo', [should be so :
For Caesar commanded the same

3 But when they had entered the city so fair, [there,
A number of people so mighty was
That Joseph and Mary, whose substance was small,
Could find in the inn there no lodging at all :

4 Then were they constrained in a stable to lie, [for to tie ;
Where horses and asses they used
Their lodging so simple they took it no scorn : [Saviour was born :
But against the next morning our

5 The King of all kings to this world being brought, [him was sought ;
Small store of fine linen to wrap
And when she had swaddled her young son so sweet, [to sleep :
Within an ox-manger she laid him

6 Then God sent an angel from Heaven so high, [where they lie,
To certain poor shepherds in fields
And bade them no longer in sorrow to stay, [on this day :
Because that our Saviour was born

7. Then presently after the shepherds did spy [the sky ;
A number of angels that stood in
They joyfully talkèd, and sweetly did sing, [King :
To God be all glory, our heavenly

2. mo'] more.

Davies Gilbert, *Some Ancient Christmas Carols*, 1822. There is a printed version of 1734. Sandys (1833) prints a slightly different version with an eighth verse. Three versions are printed by W. H. Husk, *Songs of the Nativity*, 1868 (pp. 30, 56, 65). There are many tunes. The first we give from Gilbert ; the second from Cecil Sharp's *English Folk Carols*, noted by him from Mr. Henry Thomas at Chipping Sodbury (cf. Nos. 114 and 139).

4 A VIRGIN MOST PURE

SECOND TUNE.

(CHRISTMAS)

(M. S.)

CHORUS.
And there-fore be mer - ry, set sor - rows a - side; Christ

Je - sus our Sa - viour was born on this tide.

Traditional. *Ibid.*

A VIRGIN most pure, as the prophets do tell,
Hath brought forth a baby, as it hath befel,
To be our Redeemer from death, hell, and sin,
Which Adam's transgression hath wrappèd us in:

And therefore be merry, set sorrows aside;
Christ Jesus our Saviour was born on this tide.

2 At Bethlem in Jewry a city there was,
Where Joseph and Mary together did pass,
And there to be taxèd with many one mo',
For Caesar commanded the same should be so:

3 But when they had entered the city so fair,
A number of people so mighty was there,
That Joseph and Mary, whose substance was small,
Could find in the inn there no lodging at all:

4 Then were they constrained in a stable to lie,
Where horses and asses they used for to tie;
Their lodging so simple they took it no scorn:
But against the next morning our Saviour was born:

5 The King of all kings to this world being brought,
Small store of fine linen to wrap him was sought;
And when she had swaddled her young son so sweet,
Within an ox-manger she laid him to sleep:

6 Then God sent an angel from Heaven so high,
To certain poor shepherds in fields where they lie,
And bade them no longer in sorrow to stay,
Because that our Saviour was born on this day:

7. Then presently after the shepherds did spy
A number of angels that stood in the sky;
They joyfully talkèd, and sweetly did sing,
To God be all glory, our heavenly King:

2. mo'] more.

For note on this carol see p. 9.

5 THE PRAISE OF CHRISTMAS

(ADVENT : CHRISTMAS)

(M. S.)

Traditional. *T. Durfey and others.*

ALL hail to the days that merit more praise
  Than all the rest of the year,
And welcome the nights that double delights
  As well for the poor as the peer!
Good fortune attend each merry man's friend
  That doth but the best that he may,
Forgetting old wrongs with carols and songs,
  To drive the cold winter away.

2 'Tis ill for a mind to anger inclined
  To think of small injuries now;
If wrath be to seek, do not lend her thy cheek,
  Nor let her inhabit thy brow.
Cross out of thy books malevolent looks,
  Both beauty and youth's decay,
And wholly consort with mirth and with sport,
  To drive the cold winter away.

3 This time of the year is spent in good cheer,
  And neighbours together do meet,
To sit by the fire, with friendly desire,
  Each other in love to greet.
Old grudges forgot are put in the pot,
  All sorrows aside they lay;
The old and the young doth carol this song,
  To drive the cold winter away.

4. When Christmas's tide comes in like a bride,
  With holly and ivy clad,
Twelve days in the year much mirth and good cheer
  In every household is had.
The country guise is then to devise
  Some gambols of Christmas play,
Whereat the young men do best that they can
  To drive the cold winter away.

There is a black-letter copy of this wholesome song (of which twelve verses exist) in the Pepysian Collection. Rimbault preserved the tune. The first two verses are by Tom Durfey (1653–1723), the dramatist and friend of Charles II, in his *Pills to Purge Melancholy*, 1719.

6

IRISH CAROL

(CHRISTMAS)

(M. S.)

Ding dong, ding dong, etc.
(Tenor) Ding
dong, ding dong, ding dong, ding dong, ding dong, ding dong, ding

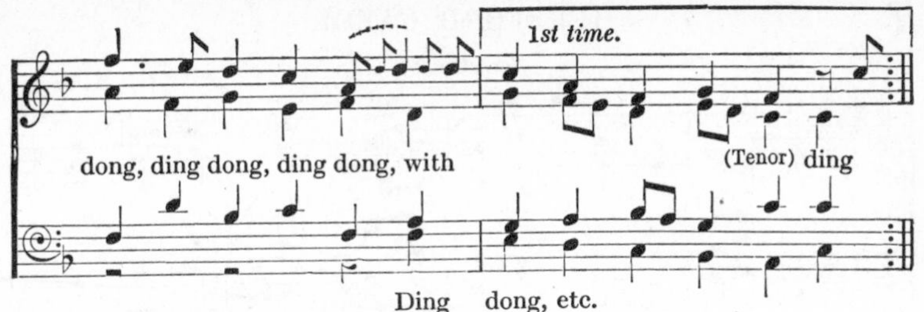
1st time.
dong, ding dong, ding dong, with
(Tenor) ding
Ding dong, etc.

2nd time.
with hum - ble faith ad - mires.
dong, etc.

Irish. *Ibid.*

CHRISTMAS Day is come; let's all prepare for mirth,
Which fills the heavens and earth at this amazing birth.
Through both the joyous angels in strife and hurry fly,
With glory and hosannas, 'All Holy' do they cry,
In Heaven the Church triumphant adores with all her choirs,
The militant on earth with humble faith admires.

2 But why should we rejoice? Should we not rather mourn
To see the Hope of Nations thus in a stable born?
Where are his crown and sceptre, where is his throne sublime,
Where is his train majestic that should the stars outshine?
Is there no sumptuous palace nor any inn at all
To lodge his heavenly mother but in a filthy stall?

3 Oh! cease, ye blessed angels, such clamorous joys to make!
Though midnight silence favours, the Shepherds are awake;
And you, O glorious star! that with new splendour brings
From the remotest parts three learned eastern Kings,
Turn somewhere else your lustre, your rays elsewhere display;
For Herod he may slay the babe, and Christ must straight away.

4. If we would then rejoice, let's cancel the old score,
And, purposing amendment, resolve to sin no more—
For mirth can ne'er content us, without a conscience clear;
And thus we'll find true pleasure in all the usual cheer,
In dancing, sporting, revelling, with masquerade and drum,
So let our Christmas merry be, as Christians doth become.

The words and tune kindly communicated by Dr. Grattan Flood. The words in their original form were probably written for the tune in the seventeenth century, when Bishop Luke Wadding (1588–1657) wrote many hymns and carols for folk-tunes which had become associated with 'coarse' words. Since then carols of this kind have been traditional in Kilmore, South Wexford. Cf. No. 14.

7 HEREFORD CAROL

(CHRISTMAS)

(R. V. W.)

Traditional.

Ibid.

COME all you faithful Christians
  That dwell here on earth,
Come celebrate the morning
  Of our dear Saviour's birth.
This is the happy morning,
  This is the blessèd morn:
To save our souls from ruin,
  The Son of God was born.

2 Behold the angel Gabriel,
  In Scripture it is said,
Did with his holy message
  Come to the virgin maid:
'Hail, blest among all women!'
  He thus did greet her then,
'Lo, thou shalt be the mother
  Of the Saviour of all men.'

3 Her time being accomplished,
  She came to Bethlehem,
And then was safe delivered
  Of the Saviour of all men.
No princely pomp attended him,
  His honours were but small;
A manger was his cradle,
  His bed an ox's stall.

4. Now to him that is ascended
  Let all our praises be;
May we his steps then follow,
  And he our pattern be;
So when our lives are ended,
  We all may hear him call—
'Come, souls, receive the kingdom,
  Preparèd for you all.'

Collated (with the omission of several verses) from three sources: (1) Mr. Hirons, Haven, Dilwyn; (2) Mr. Gallet, Leigh Linton, Worcestershire; (3) A ballad sheet published by R. Elliot, Hereford. Melody from Mr. Hirons. From *Twelve Traditional Carols from Herefordshire* (Leather and Vaughan Williams), Stainer & Bell.

8 SOMERSET CAROL

(CHRISTMAS)

(M. S.)

Traditional. *Ibid.*

COME all you worthy gentlemen
That may be standing by,
Christ our blessèd Saviour
Was born on Christmas Day.
The blessèd Virgin Mary
Unto the Lord did say,
O we wish you the comfort and
tidings of joy!

2 Christ our blessèd Saviour
Now in the manger lay—
He 's lying in the manger,
While the oxen feed on hay.
The blessèd Virgin Mary
Unto the Lord did say,
O we wish you the comfort and
tidings of joy!

3. God bless the ruler of this house,
And long on may he reign,
Many happy Christmases
He live to see again!
God bless our generation,
Who live both far and near,
And we wish them a happy, a happy New Year!

Cf. No. 11. Taken from Mr. Rapsey of Bridgwater, by Cecil Sharp, *Folk Songs from Somerset* (No. 126), and *English Folk Carols*, No. XI (*by permission of Novello & Co., Ltd.*). Mr Rapsey was taught the carol by his mother, and as a child used to sing it with other children in the streets of Bridgwater at Christmas time.

9 DARK THE NIGHT

(EPIPHANY: GENERAL)

Melody by CANON OWEN JONES.

SEREN BETHLEHEM. Harmonized by DR. CARADOG ROBERTS.

Welsh. *Tr. K. E. Roberts.*

DARK the night lay, wild and dreary
Moaned the wind by Melchior's tower, [weary
Sad the sage, while pondering
O'er the doom of Judah's power:
When behold, the clouds are parted—
Westward, lo, a light gleams far!
Now his heart's true quest has started,
For his eyes have seen the star.

2. Now, Lord Jesus hear our calling,
Deep the darkness where we stray;
How shall we, mid boulders falling,
Know for thine the rough-hewn way?
Lo, a light shines down to guide us
Where thy saints and angels are!
Now we know thy love beside us;
For our eyes have seen the star.

A free translation of a Welsh carol by the Rev. W. Lloyd. The tune and original Welsh words first appeared in *Carolan Nadolig* by Canon Owen Jones.

10

COME, LOVE WE GOD

(CHRISTMAS: EPIPHANY)

(v. 4 De - o . . Pa - tri)
O quan - ta, O quan-ta sunt haec op - e - ra.

Shann MS. *Ibid.*

COME, love we God! of might is most
The Father, the Son, the Holy Ghost,
Regnante jam in aethera;
The which made man, both more and less,
And create him to his likenéss,
O quanta sunt haec opera.

2 The herdmen came with their off'ring
For to presént that pretty thing
Cum summa reverentia.
They gave their gifts that child until;
They were received with full goodwill;
Quam grata sunt haec munera!

3 Three Kingès came from the east country,
Which knew they by astronomy,
Et Balam vaticinia;
They offered him gold, myrrh, incense;
He took them with great diligence:
Quam digna est infantia!

4. They turned again full merrily,
Each came unto his own country:
O Dei mirabilia,
They had heaven's bliss at their ending,
The which God grant us old and young.
Deo Patri sit gloria.

1. *Regnante*, &c.] Now reigning in the sky. *O quanta*, &c.] O how great are these works. 2. *Cum*, &c.] With utmost reverence. *Quam*, &c.] How welcome are these gifts. 3. *Et Balam*, &c.] And by the prophecy of Balaam. 3. *Quam*, &c.] How worthy is the infancy. 4. *O Dei*, &c.] O wonderful (works) of God. *Deo Patri*, &c.] Glory be to God the Father.

The tune and a selection from the partly illegible ten verses of the original are from 'Certaine pretie songes hereafter followinge drawn together by Richard Shanne, 1611', in the MS. of the Shann family of Methley, Yorks, now B.M., Add. 38599. Among various songs, some with music, is this: it is headed 'A Christmas Carroll maid by Sir Richard Shanne, priest', who may have been much earlier, since this has the characteristics of a fifteenth-century carol, and the tune is in a style contemporary with the words. We have altered the error 'These Kinges' in v. 3 to *Three* (the number of course is legendary); 'and sence' to *incense*. V. 4 has 'younge', but the original which Shann transcribed probably had 'ying'.

11 GOD REST YOU MERRY

(CHRISTMAS)

(M. S.)
O tid - ings, O tid - ings of com - fort and joy,
For
For Je - sus Christ our Sa - viour Was born on Christ - mas Day.
Je - sus Christ our Sa - viour Was born on Christ - mas Day.

Traditional. *Usual version.*

GOD rest you merry, Gentlemen,
Let nothing you dismay,
For Jesus Christ our Saviour
Was born upon this day,
To save us all from Satan's power
When we were gone astray:

O tidings of comfort and joy,
For Jesus Christ our Saviour
Was born on Christmas Day.

2 In Bethlehem in Jewry
This blessèd babe was born,
And laid within a manger,
Upon this blessèd morn;
The which his mother Mary
Nothing did take in scorn:

3 From God our heavenly Father
A blessèd angel came,
And unto certain shepherds
Brought tidings of the same,
How that in Bethlehem was born
The Son of God by name:

4 'Fear not,' then said the angel,
'Let nothing you affright,
This day is born a Saviour,
Of virtue, power, and might;
So frequently to vanquish all
The friends of Satan quite:'

5 The shepherds at those tidings
Rejoicèd much in mind,
And left their flocks a-feeding,
In tempest, storm and wind,
And went to Bethlehem straightway
This blessèd babe to find:

6 But when to Bethlehem they came,
Whereat this infant lay,
They found him in a manger,
Where oxen feed on hay;
His mother Mary kneeling,
Unto the Lord did pray:

7. Now to the Lord sing praises,
All you within this place,
And with true love and brotherhood
Each other now embrace;
This holy tide of Christmas
All others doth deface:

12 GOD REST YOU MERRY (LONDON)

(CHRISTMAS : NEW YEAR)

And it's
tid - ings of com - fort and joy, com-fort and joy : And it's
joy. . . . .
tid - ings of com - fort and joy, com-fort and joy.
joy. . . . .

Traditional, London.

GOD rest you merry gentlemen,
Let nothing you dismay,
Remember Christ our Saviour
Was born on Christmas Day,
To save poor souls from Satan's power
Which had long time gone astray,
And it 's tidings of comfort and joy,

2 From God that is our Father,
The blessèd Angels came,
Unto some certain Shepherds,
With tidings of the same ;
That there was born in Bethlehem,
The Son of God by name.
And it 's tidings of comfort and joy,

3 Go, fear not, said God's Angels,
Let nothing you affright,
For there is born in Bethlehem,
Of a pure Virgin bright,
One able to advance you,
And threw down Satan quite.
And it 's tidings of comfort and joy.

4 The Shepherds at those tidings,
Rejoiced much in mind,
And left their flocks a feeding
In tempest storms of wind,
And strait they came to Bethlehem,
The son of God to find.
And it 's tidings of comfort and joy.

Ibid., London.

5 Now when they came to Bethlehem,
Where our sweet Saviour lay,
They found him in a manger,
Where Oxen feed on hay,
The blessed Virgin kneeling down,
Unto the Lord did pray.
And it 's tidings of comfort and joy.

6 With sudden joy and gladness,
The Shepherds were beguil'd,
To see the Babe of Israel,
Before his mother mild,
On them with joy and chearfulness,
Rejoice each Mother's Child.
And it 's tidings of comfort and joy.

7 Now to the Lord sing praises,
All you within this place,
Like we true loving Brethren,
Each other to embrace,
For the merry time of Christmas,
Is drawing on a pace.
And it 's tidings of comfort and joy.

8. God bless the ruler of this House,
And send him long to reign,
And many a merry Christmas
May live to see again.
Among your friends and kindred,
That live both far and near,
And God send you a happy new Year.

'God rest you merry', which is, as Bullen says, 'the most popular of Christmas carols', has two magnificent tunes, and deserves to be given in two versions.

The first version, No. 11, gives the best-known text, as in Sandys, 1833, accepting Bullen's correction of 'Whereas' in v. 6. Sandys gives 'friends' in v. 4, though we fancy that the alternative 'fiends' was the word more generally sung. 'God rest you merry' means 'God keep you merry', but the comma after 'merry' is generally misplaced. There is a version in the *Roxburgh Ballads*, vol. iii, *c.* 1770.

The second version, No. 12 (with the tune 'as sung', said Rimbault, eighty years ago, 'in the London streets'), we have reprinted from a broadside printed by J. & C. Evans, Long-lane, London, some fifty years before Rimbault. In this case we have reproduced the spelling and punctuation exactly, only correcting the misprint 'comforts' in the first occurrence of the refrain ; otherwise the carol is exactly as in the broadside, except that we have numbered the verses.

Rimbault stated that the tune printed by Sandys of the first version is from Cornwall.

The words of No. 11 can be sung to the London tune (No. 12), by singing 'O tidings of comfort and joy' twice for the refrain.

13 GOD'S DEAR SON

(CHRISTMAS : EPIPHANY)

Traditional. *Ibid.*

GOD'S dear Son without beginning,
  Whom the wicked priests did scorn,
The only wise, without all sinning,
  On this blessèd day was born;
To save us all from sin and thrall,
  When we in Satan's chains were bound,
And shed his blood to do us good,
  With many a purple bleeding wound.

2 In Bethlehem, King David's city,
  Mary's babe had sweet creation;
God and man endued with pity,
  And a Saviour of each nation.
Yet Jewry land with cruel hand
  Both first and last his power denied;
Where he was born they did him scorn,
  And showed him malice when he died.

3 No kingly robes nor golden treasure
  Decked the birthday of God's Son;
No pompous train at all took pleasure
  To this King of kings to run.
No mantle brave could Jesus have
  Upon his cradle for to lie;
No music charms in nurse's arms,
  To sing the babe a lullaby.

4 Yet as Mary sat in solace,
  By our Saviour's first beginning,
Hosts of angels from God's palace
  Sounded sweet from Heaven singing;
Yea, Heaven and earth, at Jesus' birth,
  With sweet melodious tunes abound,
And everything for Jewry's King
  Upon the earth gave cheerful sound.

5 *Then with angel-love inspirèd,
  Three wise princes from the East,
To Bethlehem as they desirèd,
  Came where as our Lord did rest:
And there they laid before the maid,
  Unto her son, her God, her King,
Their offerings sweet, as was most meet,
  Unto so great a power to bring.

6. Now to him that hath redeemed us
  By his precious death and passion,
And us sinners so esteemed us,
  To buy dearly this salvation,
Yield lasting fame, that still the name
  Of Jesus may be honoured here;
And let us say that Christmas Day
  Is still the best day in the year.

In Gilbert (eight verses), with tune, 1822. A rougher version in nine verses is in *A Good Christmas Box*, Dudley, 1846. Here, as elsewhere, we have removed an accusation against the Jews.

14

WEXFORD CAROL

(CHRISTMAS)

(M. S.)

GOOD people all, this Christmas-time,
Consider well and bear in mind
What our good God for us has done,
In sending his belovèd Son.
With Mary holy we should pray
To God with love this Christmas Day;
In Bethlehem upon that morn
There was a blessèd Messiah born.

2 The night before that happy tide,
The noble Virgin and her guide
Were long time seeking up and down
To find a lodging in the town.
But mark how all things came to pass:
From every door repelled, alas!
As long foretold, their refuge all
Was but an humble ox's stall.

3 Near Bethlehem did shepherds keep
Their flocks of lambs and feeding sheep;
To whom God's angels did appear,
Which put the shepherds in great fear.
'Prepare and go', the angels said,
'To Bethlehem, be not afraid;
For there you'll find, this happy morn,
A princely babe, sweet Jesus born.'

4 With thankful heart and joyful mind,
The shepherds went the babe to find,
And as God's angel had foretold,
They did our Saviour Christ behold.
Within a manger he was laid,
And by his side the virgin maid,
Attending on the Lord of Life,
Who came on earth to end all strife.

5. There were three wise men from afar
Directed by a glorious star,
And on they wandered night and day
Until they came where Jesus lay.
And when they came unto that place
Where our beloved Messiah was
They humbly cast them at his feet,
With gifts of gold and incense sweet.

Kindly communicated, with No. 6, by Dr. Grattan Flood. The words (subsequently revised) and tune were taken down from a traditional singer in County Wexford. The words seem to have come from England: the first four and a half verses are in Shawcross's *Old Castleton Christmas Carols*, and the first verse was taken by R. Vaughan Williams from Mr. Hall, Castleton, Derbyshire (*Eight Traditional English Carols*, No. 7), with another tune. For another version see Sharp's *English Folk Carols*, viii.

15 WASSAIL SONG

FIRST TUNE.

(CHRISTMAS : NEW YEAR)

(M. S.)

Solo.
Chorus.
Love and joy come to you, And to you your was-sail too, And God bless you, and send you A hap - py new year, And God send you A hap - py new year.
Love and joy come to you, And to you your was-sail too, And God send you A hap - py new

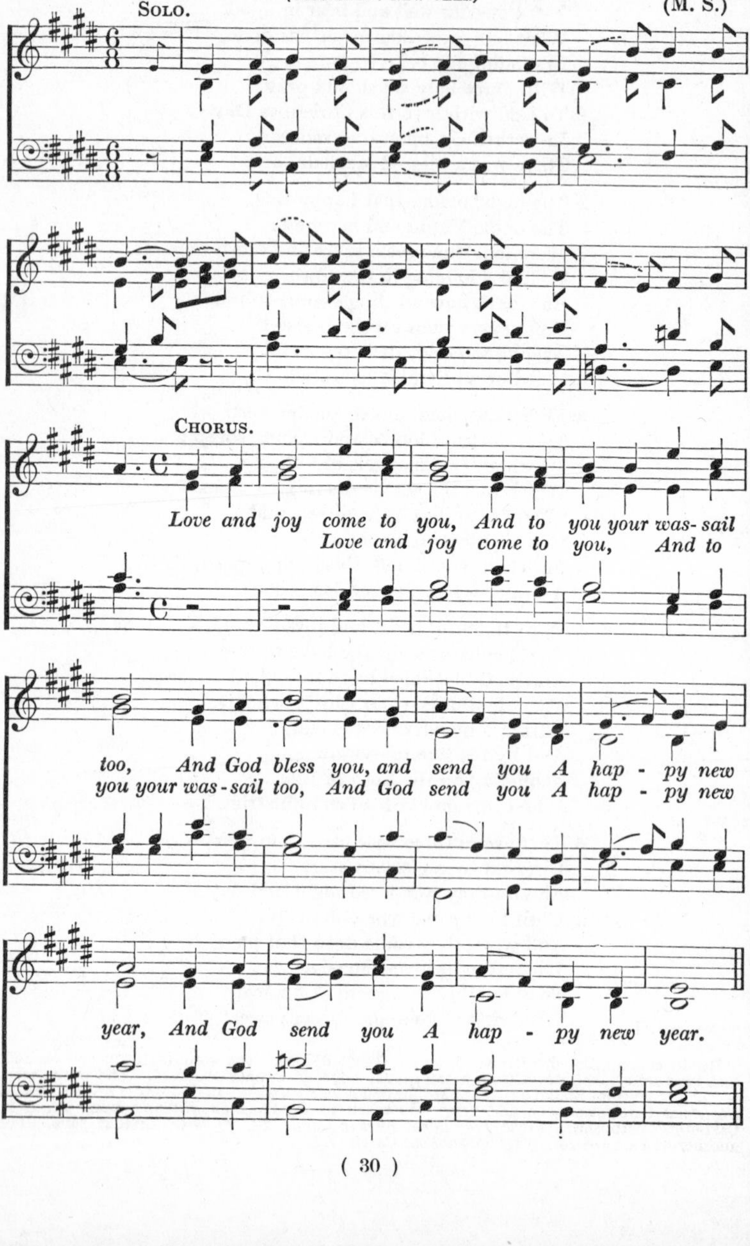

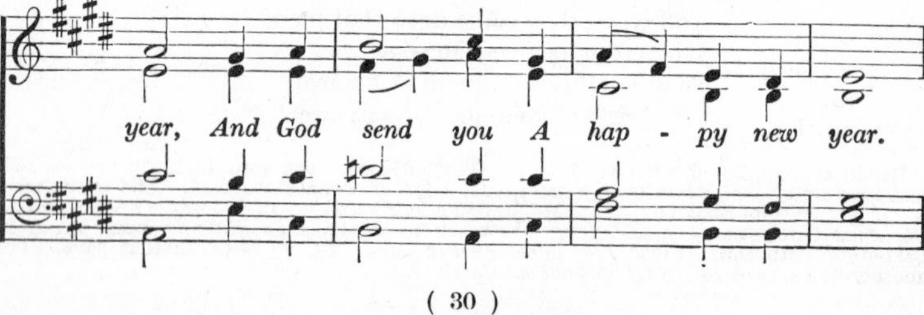

North of England. *Ibid.*

HERE we come a-wassailing
Among the leaves so green,
Here we come a-wandering,
So fair to be seen:

Love and joy come to you,
And to you your wassail too,
And God bless you, and send you
A happy new year.

2 *Our wassail cup is made
Of the rosemary tree;
And so is your beer
Of the best barley:

3 We are not daily beggars
That beg from door to door,
But we are neighbours' children
Whom you have seen before:

4 *Call up the butler of this house,
Put on his golden ring;
Let him bring us up a glass of beer,
And better we shall sing:

5 We have got a little purse
Of stretching leather skin;
We want a little of your money
To line it well within:

6 *Bring us out a table,
And spread it with a cloth;
Bring us out a mouldy cheese,
And some of your Christmas loaf:

7 God bless the master of this house,
Likewise the mistress too;
And all the little children
That round the table go:

8. Good Master and good Mistress,
While you're sitting by the fire,
Pray think of us poor children
Who are wandering in the mire:

The starred verses are not suitable when the carol is sung in church, but they give a vivid picture of the Waits of old times. Text from Husk's *Songs of the Nativity*, 1868, where he refers to a Yorkshire copy of the carol in a broadsheet printed at Bradford as late as *c.* 1850, and to a Lancashire copy in a Manchester chap-book. The first tune from Yorkshire has been familiarized by Stainer. The second tune was learnt by Martin Shaw when a boy from his father, James Shaw, who had often heard it in the streets of Leeds in the eighteen-fifties; the Rev. J. T. Horton of Bradford reported some fifteen years ago that it was still often sung by the Waits in the West Riding.

The charming seventh verse is also printed by Ritson in his *Ancient Songs and Ballads*, 1829, where he seems to have copied it from some source of the reign of James I or Charles I; he gives two verses only. Shakespeare may well have heard them sung outside his house on a Christmas night. We print them separately below, exactly as Ritson gave them, since they make a good conclusion to a carol-concert, and we have two tunes at our disposal:—

16 GOOD-BYE

17th century.

GOD bless the master of this house,
The mistress also,
And all the little children
That round the table go:

2. And all your kin and kinsfolk,
That dwell both far and near;
I wish you a Merry Christmas,
And a happy New Year.

15

WASSAIL SONG

SECOND TUNE.

Leeds.

(CHRISTMAS: NEW YEAR)

(M. S.)

TREBLE SOLO.

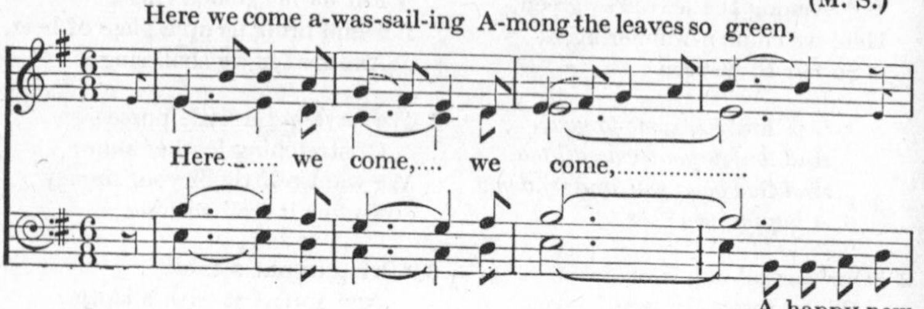
Here we come a-was-sail-ing A-mong the leaves so green,
Here...... we come,.... we come,..................
A happy new

Here we come a-wan-der-ing, So fair to be seen:
CHORUS.
Here........ we come,........ we come,.................. Love and
year........ we come,........ we come.........................

joy.... come to you, And to you your was-sail too, And God
Love and joy come to you,

bless you, and send you A hap - py new year.

In each verse the three under parts sing the same words during the Solo.

HERE we come a-wassailing
Among the leaves so green,
Here we come a-wandering,
So fair to be seen:

Love and joy come to you,
And to you your wassail too,
And God bless you, and send you
A happy new year.

2 *Our wassail cup is made
Of the rosemary tree,
And so is your beer
Of the best barley:

3 We are not daily beggars
That beg from door to door,
But we are neighbours' children
Whom you have seen before:

4 *Call up the butler of this house,
Put on his golden ring;
Let him bring us up a glass of beer,
And better we shall sing:

5 We have got a little purse
Of stretching leather skin;
We want a little of your money
To line it well within:

6 *Bring us out a table,
And spread it with a cloth;
Bring us out a mouldy cheese,
And some of your Christmas loaf:

7 God bless the master of this house,
Likewise the mistress too;
And all the little children
That round the table go:

8. Good Master and good Mistress,
While you're sitting by the fire,
Pray think of us poor children
Who are wandering in the mire:

For note on this carol, see p. 31.
No. 16 might be sung to the Second Tune when the First Tune is used for No. 15.

16 GOOD-BYE

17th century.

GOD bless the master of this house,
The mistress also,
And all the little children
That round the table go:

2. And all your kin and kinsfolk,
That dwell both far and near;
I wish you a Merry Christmas,
And a happy New Year.

17 ALL IN THE MORNING

(CHRISTMAS, &c.)

(R. V. W.)

[Copyright, 1919, by Stainer & Bell, Ltd.]

Traditional. *Ibid.*

IT was on Christmas Day,
And all in the morning,
Our Saviour was born,
And our heavenly King:
And was not this a joyful thing?
And sweet Jesus they called him by name.

2 *It was on New Year's Day,
And all in the morning,
They circumcised our Saviour
And our heavenly King:

3 It was on the Twelfth Day,
And all in the morning,
The Wise Men were led
To our heavenly King:

4 *It was on Twentieth Day,
And all in the morning,
The Wise Men returned
From our heavenly King:

5 *It was on Candlemas Day,
And all in the morning,
They visited the Temple
With our heavenly King:

Part 2

(LENT TO EASTER)

6 It was on Holy Wednesday,
And all in the morning,
That Judas betrayed
Our dear heavenly King:
And was not this a woeful thing?
And sweet Jesus we'll call him by name.

7 *It was on Sheer Thursday,
And all in the morning,
They plaited a crown of thorns
For our heavenly King:

8 It was on Good Friday,
And all in the morning,
They crucified our Saviour,
And our heavenly King:

9. It was on Easter Day,
And all in the morning,
Our Saviour arose,
Our own heavenly King;
The sun and the moon
They did both rise with him,
And sweet Jesus we'll call him by name.

The text has been completed from *Old Castleton Christmas Carols*, edited by the late Rev. W. H. Shawcross. Melody and first verse of text from Mr. Hall, Castleton, Derbyshire. From *Eight Traditional English Carols* (Vaughan Williams), Stainer & Bell.

18 I SAW THREE SHIPS

(CHRISTMAS)

(M. S.)

Traditional. *Ibid.*

I SAW three ships come sailing in,
On Christmas Day, on Christmas Day,
I saw three ships come sailing in,
On Christmas Day in the morning.

2 And what was in those ships all three ?

3 Our Saviour Christ and his lady.

4 Pray, whither sailed those ships all three ?

5 O, they sailed into Bethlehem.

6 And all the bells on earth shall ring,

7 And all the angels in Heaven shall sing,

8 And all the souls on earth shall sing.

9. Then let us all rejoice amain !

Cf. No. 3, 'As I sat on a sunny bank'. In one or other version this is in all the broadsides, sharing its popularity with 'God rest you merry' and 'The Seven Joys'. The version above (in Sandys, 1833) differs only in v. 3 from the Derbyshire version with our first tune in Bramley & Stainer, *Christmas Carols New and Old,* 1871. A unique version introducing the Passion ('As I sat by my old cottage door') was taken down by Cecil Sharp in Worcestershire. Our second tune is from Sharp's *English Folk Carols.* There is another tune in the *English Carol Book,* Second Series (P. Dearmer and M. Shaw), Mowbrays.

19 BOAR'S HEAD CAROL

(CHRISTMAS, SECULAR)

(M. S.)

SOLO VOICE.
1 The boar's head in hand bear I, Be-decked with bays and rose-ma-ry; And I
pray you, my mas-ters, be mer-ry, Quot es-tis in con-vi-vi-o:
CHORUS.
Ca-put a-pri de-fe-ro, Red-dens lau-des Do-mi-no.
End here.
SOLO VOICE.
2 The boar's head, as I un-der-stand, Is the rar-est dish in all this land, Which
Repeat CHORUS.
thus bedecked with a gay gar-land, Let us ser-vi-re can-ti-co:
3. Our stew-ard hath pro-vi-ded this, In hon-our of the King of bliss, Which
Repeat CHORUS.
on this day to be ser-ved is, In Re-gi-nen-si a-tri-o:

Traditional. *Queen's College, Oxford Version.*

THE boar's head in hand bear I,
  Bedecked with bays and rosemary;
And I pray you, my masters, be merry,
  Quot estis in convivio:

Caput apri defero,
Reddens laudes Domino.

2 The boar's head, as I understand,
  Is the rarest dish in all this land,
  Which thus bedecked with a gay garlànd,
    Let us *servire cantico:*

3. Our steward hath provided this,
  In honour of the King of bliss,
  Which on this day to be servèd is,
    In Reginensi atrio:

1. *Quot*, &c.] So many as are in the feast. *Caput*, &c.] The boar's head I bring, giving praises to God.
2. *Servire*, &c.] Let us serve with a song. 3. *In*, &c.] In the Queen's hall.

This version, as sung every Christmas at Queen's College, Oxford, is in Dibden's *Typog. Antiq.*, 1812, ii. 252, whence A. H. Bullen reprinted it in *Carols and Poems*, 1885 (p. 171), together with a version (p. 267) from Joseph Ritson's *Ancient Songs*, 1790 (from MS. Add. 5665 in the British Museum), the Wynkyn de Worde version correctly given with modern spelling (p. 170), and a quite different Boar's Head Carol (p. 172) sung at St. John's College, Oxford, in 1607. The carol in Hill's MS. (see No. 36) is a variant of the contemporary version of Wynken.

Jan van Wynken, of Worth, was Caxton's apprentice and successor: of his *Christmasse Carolles*, 1521, only the last leaf survives; it fortunately includes the colophon and is preserved in the Bodleian Library, Oxford: the text is reprinted with the original spelling in E. Flügel's *Neuenglisches Lesebuch*, 1895. Miss Rickert in *Ancient English Christmas Carols*, 1914, prints also three boar's head carols of the fifteenth century, but without references.

20 YEOMAN'S CAROL

(CHRISTMAS)

(M. S.)

Church-gallery book. *Ibid.*

LET Christians all with joyful mirth,
  Both young and old, both great and small,
Now think upon our Saviour's birth,
  Who brought salvation to us all:

  This day did Christ man's soul from death remove,
  With glorious saints to dwell in heaven above.

2 No palace, but an ox's stall,
  The place of his nativity;
This truly should instruct us all
  To learn of him humility:

3 Then Joseph and the Virgin came
  Unto the town of Bethlehem,
But sought in vain within the same
  For lodging to be granted them:

4 A stable harboured them, where they
  Continued till this blessèd morn.
Let us rejoice and keep the day,
  Wherein the Lord of life was born:

5. He that descended from above,
  Who for your sins has meekly died,
Make him the pattern of your love;
  So will your joys be sanctified:

The words and tune are from an old church-gallery tune-book, Dorset, and were discovered by the Rev. L. J. T. Darwall.

21 SIR CHRISTMAS

(CHRISTMAS, SECULAR)

In free rhythm. [Copyright, 1928, by Oxford University Press.]
ff SIR CHRISTMAS.
(Arr. by C. KENNEDY SCOTT.)
Now - ell, now - ell, now - ell, now - ell, now - ell,
mf
f
now - - ell, now - - - - - - - - - ell.
COMPANY.
(short.)
p
Who is there that singeth so, now-ell, now - ell, now - ell?
(SMALL CHOIR.) Ah . . . .
SIR CHRISTMAS.
COMPANY.
2. I am here, Sir Chris - tè - mas. Welcome, my lord Sir Chris - tè-mas.
SIR CHRISTMAS.
COMPANY.
Wel-come to ye all, both more and less, Come near, now - ell.

Sir Christmas.
3. Dieu vous gar - de, beaux sieurs, tid - ings I you bring:
A maid hath borne a child........... full............... young,
The which caus - eth you........ for........... to sing,
Company.
Sopranos.
Now - - ell, now - ell, now - - ell, now - ell.
(Small Choir.)
p
Ah ....
Ah ....
A Full Chorus.
ff
Now - ell, now - ell, now - ell, now - - ell, now - ell,
mf
ff
now - - - ell, now - - - - - - - - - - - - ell,

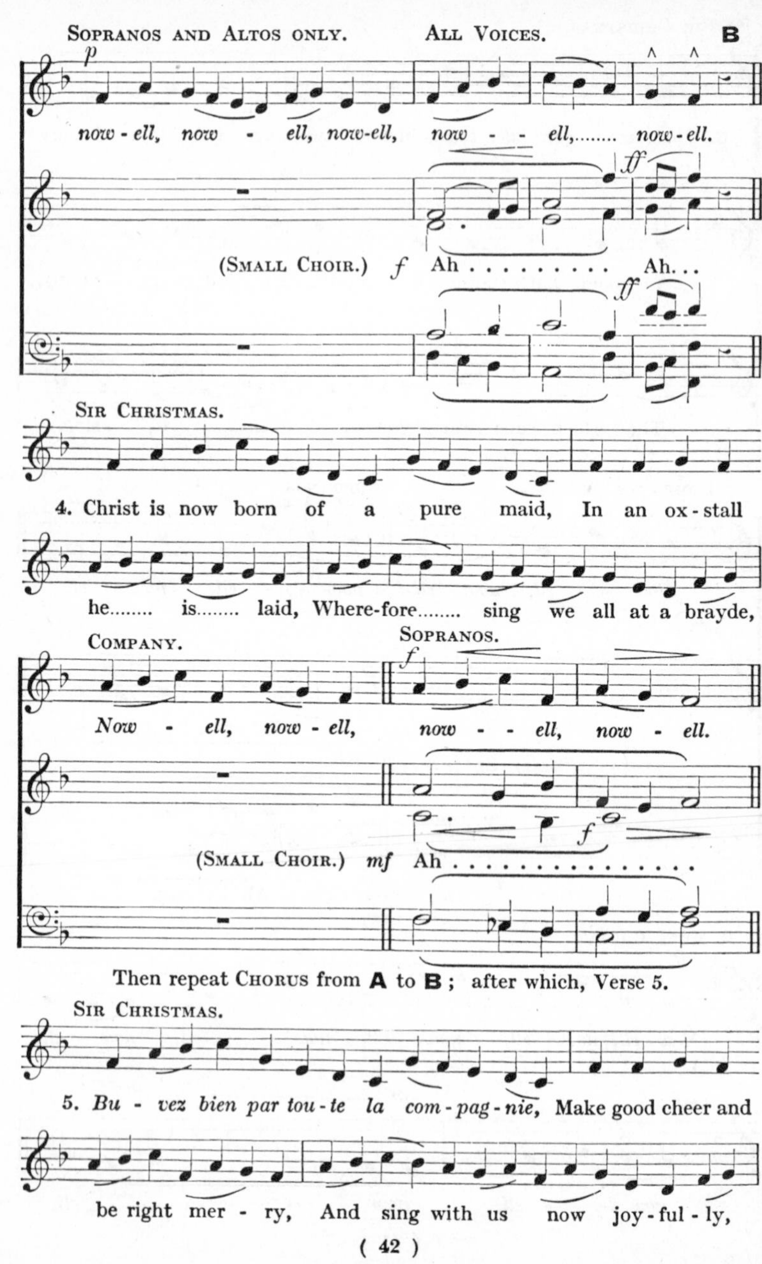
Sopranos and Altos only.
All Voices.
B
p
now - ell, now - ell, now-ell, now - - ell,........ now - ell.
(Small Choir.) f Ah . . . . Ah. . .
ff
ff
Sir Christmas.
4. Christ is now born of a pure maid, In an ox - stall
he........ is........ laid, Where-fore........ sing we all at a brayde,
Company.
Sopranos.
f
Now - ell, now - ell, now - - ell, now - ell.
(Small Choir.) mf Ah . . . .
f
Then repeat Chorus from A to B; after which, Verse 5.
Sir Christmas.
5. Bu - vez bien par tou - te la com - pag - nie, Make good cheer and
be right mer - ry, And sing with us now joy - ful - ly,

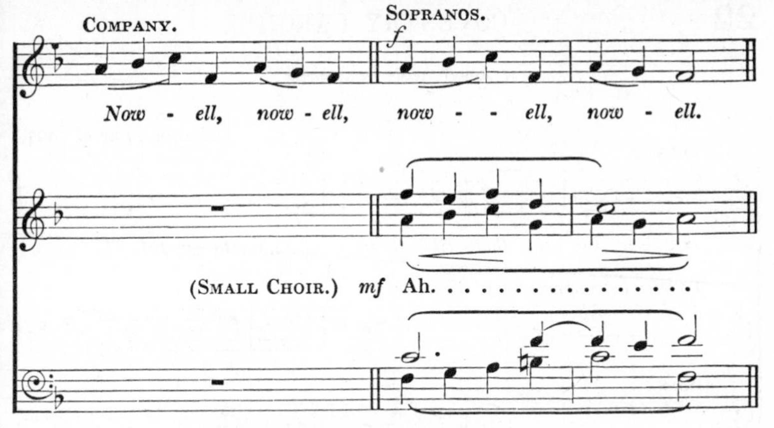
COMPANY.
SOPRANOS.
f
Now - ell, now - ell, now - - ell, now - ell.
(SMALL CHOIR.) mf Ah. . . . .

Then repeat from **A** to **B** and end.

c. 1500. (*Copyright, 1928, by Oxford University Press.*) *Ibid.*

Sir C.: NOWELL, *nowell, nowell, nowell.*
Comp.: Who is there that singeth so, *nowell, nowell, nowell?*

Sir C.: 2 I am here, Sir Christèmas.
Comp.: Welcome, my lord Sir Christèmas,
Sir C.: Welcome to ye all, both more and less,
Comp.: Come near, *nowell.*

Sir C.: 3 *Dieu vous garde, beaux sieurs,* tidings I you bring:
A maid hath borne a child full young,
The which causeth you for to sing,
Comp.: *Nowell.*

Sir C.: 4 Christ is now born of a pure maid,
In an ox-stall he is laid,
Wherefore sing we all at a brayde,
Comp.: *Nowell.*

Sir C.: 5. *Buvez bien par toute la compagnie,*
Make good cheer and be right merry,
And sing with us now joyfully,
Comp.: *Nowell.*

2. more and less] great and small. 3. *Dieu,* &c.] God keep you, fair gentlemen. 4. brayde] to start, here 'all at once'. 5. *Buvez,* &c.] Drink well, through all the company.

The parts are here marked so as to be sung by Sir Christmas and the Company. Words and tune from the MS. Add. 5665, which consists of English and Latin songs with music, dating probably from Edward IV to the early years of Henry VIII; the music seems to date the MS. itself c. 1520–30.

COVENTRY CAROL

(CHRISTMAS: INNOCENTS)

Original Tune of 1591.

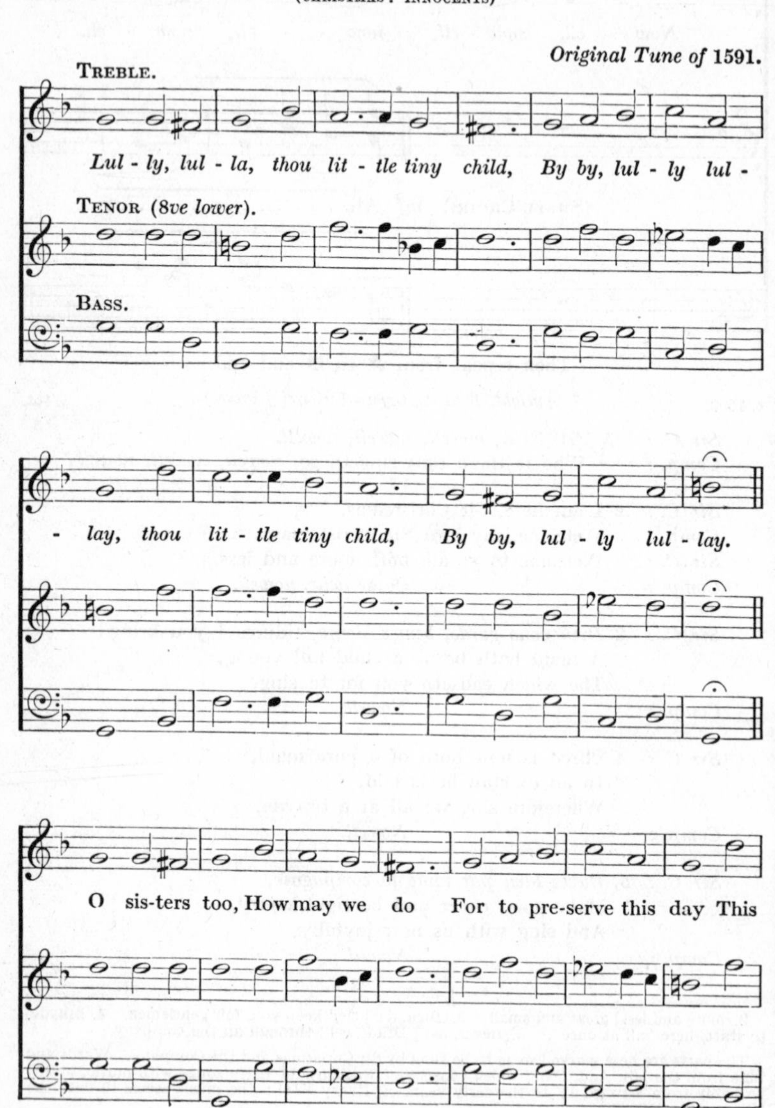
TREBLE.
Lul - ly, lul - la, thou lit - tle tiny child, By by, lul - ly lul -
TENOR (8ve lower).
BASS.
- lay, thou lit - tle tiny child, By by, lul - ly lul - lay.
O sis-ters too, How may we do For to pre-serve this day This

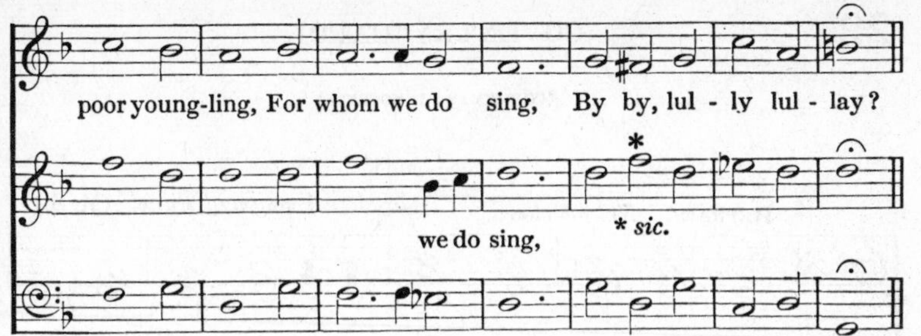
poor young-ling, For whom we do sing, By by, lul - ly lul - lay?
*
we do sing,
* sic.

The above Refrain and First Verse is scored from the original.

1591. *Pageant of the Shearmen and Tailors,* 15*th century.*

LULLY, lulla, thou little tiny child,
By by, lully lullay.
O sisters too,
How may we do
For to preserve this day
This poor youngling,
For whom we do sing,
By by, lully lullay ?

2 Herod, the king,
In his raging,
Chargèd he hath this day
His men of might,
In his own sight,
All young childrén to slay.

3. That woe is me,
Poor child for thee !
And ever morn and day,
For thy parting
Neither say nor sing
By by, lully lullay !

For the sake of the music the original spelling is retained in this version of the refrain.

This song is sung by the women of Bethlehem in the play, just before Herod's soldiers come in to slaughter their children.

The tune was discovered and printed by Thomas Sharp, *Dissertations*, 1825.

See the note on p. 47 for further particulars.

22 COVENTRY CAROL

(CHRISTMAS : INNOCENTS)

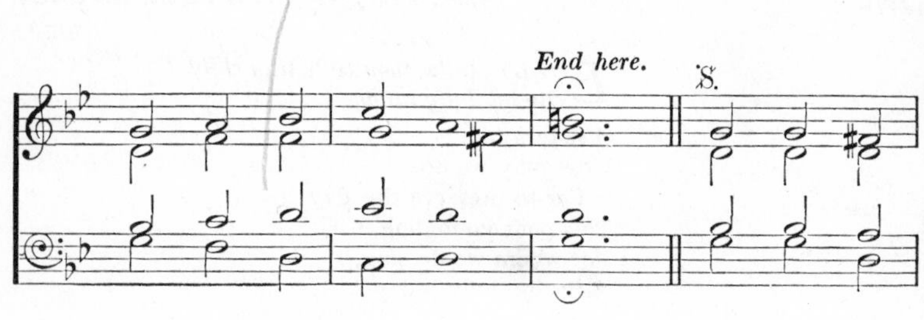

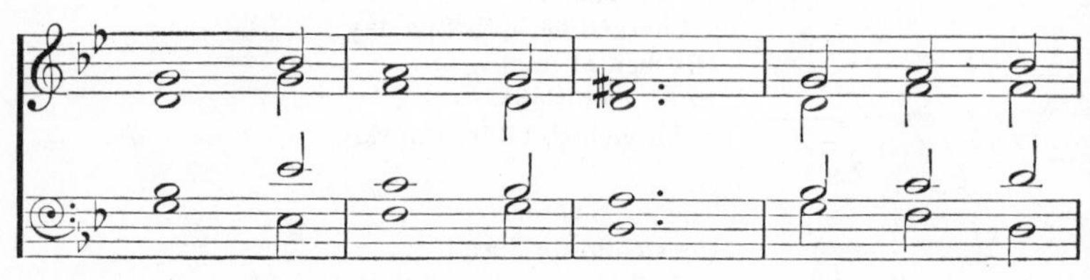

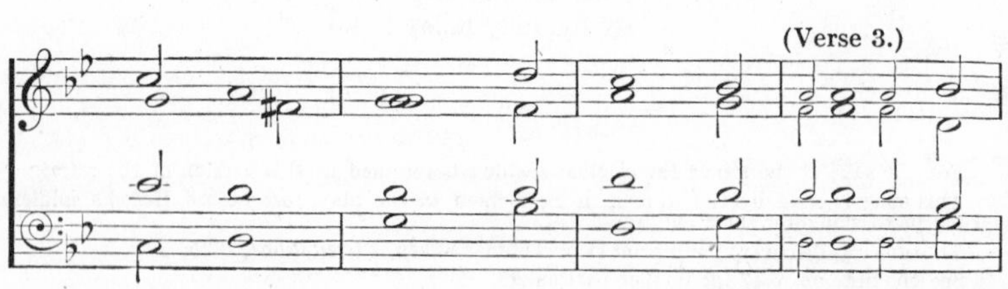

After 3rd verse, sing Refrain again.

Dal 𝄋

1591 (*Modern Version*). *Pageant of the Shearmen and Tailors, 15th century.*

LULLY, lulla, thou little tiny child,
By by, lully lullay.

O sisters too,
How may we do
For to preserve this day
This poor youngling,
For whom we do sing,
By by, lully lullay?

2 Herod, the king,
In his raging,
Chargèd he hath this day
His men of might,
In his own sight,
All young childrén to slay.

3. That woe is me,
Poor child for thee!
And ever morn and day,
For thy parting
Neither say nor sing
By by, lully lullay!

The text is that of Robert Croo, 1534, reprinted by E. Rhys, *Everyman and other Plays*. The Coventry plays were witnessed by Margaret, Queen of Henry VI, in 1456, by Richard III in 1484, by Henry VII in 1492, and we hear of the Smith's play being performed in 1584, which brings us near to the date where the tune appears.

See the note on p. 45.

23 MAKE WE JOY

(CHRISTMAS: EPIPHANY)

(M. S.)

15th century. *Ibid.*

MAKE *we joy now in this feast*
In quo Christus natus est :
Eya !

A Patre unigenitus
Through a maiden is come to us:
Sing we of him and say, 'Welcome,
Veni Redemptor gentium.'

2 *Agnoscat omne seculum :*
A bright star made three Kingès come,
For to seek with their presénts
Verbum supernum prodiens :

3 *A solis ortus cardine,*
So mighty a Lord was none as he :
He on our kind his peace hath set,
Adam parens quod polluit :

4 *Maria ventre concipit,*
The Holy Ghost was ay her with :
In Bethlehem yborn he is,
Consors paterni luminis :

5. *O lux beata, Trinitas !*
He lay between an ox and ass,
And by his mother, maiden free.
Gloria tibi, Domine !

1. *In quo Christus,* &c.] On which Christ was born. *A Patre,* &c.] From the Father only-begotten. *Veni Redemptor,* &c.] Come. Redeemer of the nations (*English Hymnal,* 14). 2. *Agnoscat,* &c.] Let every age acknowledge (thee). *Verbum,* &c.] The celestial word proceeding (*E. H.* 2). 3. *A solis,* &c.] Risen from the quarter of the sun (*E. H.* 18). *Adam parens,* &c.] Which the parent Adam defiled. 4. *Maria ventre,* &c.] Mary conceived in her womb. *Consors,* &c.] Consort of the Father's light. 5. *O lux,* &c.] O blessed light, O Trinity (*E. H.* 164). *Gloria,* &c.] Glory to thee, O Lord.

Words (slightly altered in third lines of verses 3 and 5) and melody from the Selden MS., B. 26 (Southern English, *c.* 1450), which came to the Bodleian *c.* 1659.

24 SUSSEX CAROL

Verses 1, 2, & 4.
(CHRISTMAS)
VOICES IN UNISON.
(R. V. W.)
On Christ-mas night all Chris-tians sing, To hear the news the
HARMONY, ad lib.
an - gels bring. On Christ-mas night all Chris-tians sing, To hear the news the
UNISON.
an - gels bring—
HARMONY, ad lib.
Traditional.
Ibid.

ON Christmas night all Christians sing,
To hear the news the angels bring—
News of great joy, news of great mirth,
News of our merciful King's birth.

2 Then why should men on earth be so sad,
Since our Redeemer made us glad,
When from our sin he set us free,
All for to gain our liberty.

4. All out of darkness we have light,
Which made the angels sing this night;
'Glory to God and peace to men,
Now and for evermore. Amen.'

24

SUSSEX CAROL

(CHRISTMAS)

(R. V. W.)

Verse 3.

When sin de - - - parts be - - -
When sin de - - - - parts be - - - -
When sin de - parts be - fore...... his grace, Then
When sin de - - - parts be - - - -

- fore his grace,............ When sin de- parts be -
- fore his grace, Then life and
life and health come in its place, Then life and
- fore his grace, Then......... life and

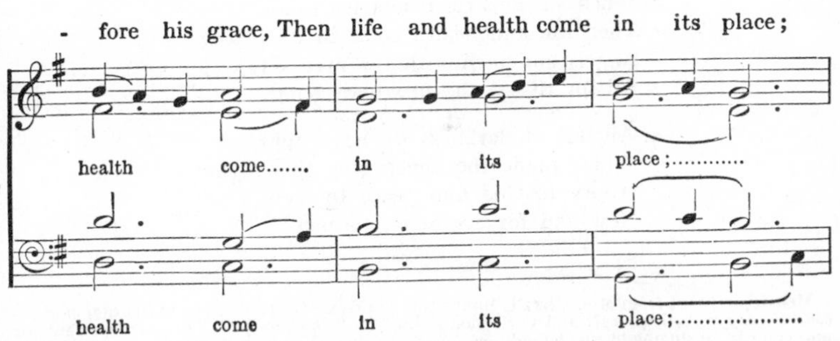
- fore his grace, Then life and health come in its place;
health come....... in its place ;............
health come in its place ;......................

An - gels and men with joy may sing,
An gels...................... may sing,...........
All for to see the new - born King.

Traditional. *Ibid.*

ON Christmas night all Christians sing,
To hear the news the angels bring—
News of great joy, news of great mirth,
News of our merciful King's birth.

2 Then why should men on earth be so sad,
Since our Redeemer made us glad,
When from our sin he set us free,
All for to gain our liberty.

3 When sin departs before his grace,
Then life and health come in its place;
Angels and men with joy may sing,
All for to see the new-born King.

4. All out of darkness we have light,
Which made the angels sing this night;
'Glory to God and peace to men,
Now and for evermore. Amen.'

Melody and text from Mrs. Verrall, Monks Gate, Sussex. Other versions in *Journal of Folk-song Society*, vol. ii, p. 127, and Cecil Sharp, *English Folk-Carols*, No. X. Arrangement for unaccompanied singing in *Eight Traditional English Carols* (Vaughan Williams). Stainer & Bell.

25 A GALLERY CAROL

(CHRISTMAS: EPIPHANY)

(M. S.)

Church-gallery Book. *Ibid.*

REJOICE and be merry in songs and in mirth!
O praise our Redeemer, all mortals on earth!
For this is the birthday of Jesus our King,
Who brought us salvation—his praises we'll sing!

2 A heavenly vision appeared in the sky;
Vast numbers of angels the Shepherds did spy,
Proclaiming the birthday of Jesus our King,
Who brought us salvation—his praises we'll sing!

3 Likewise a bright star in the sky did appear,
Which led the Wise Men from the east to draw near;
They found the Messiah, sweet Jesus our King,
Who brought us salvation—his praises we'll sing!

4. And when they were come, they their treasures unfold,
And unto him offered myrrh, incense, and gold.
So blessèd for ever be Jesus our King,
Who brought us salvation—his praises we'll sing!

The words and tune, from an old church-gallery book, discovered in Dorset, like No. 20, by the Rev. L. J. T. Darwall.

26

SAINT STEPHEN

(DEC. 26 AND OTHER OCCASIONS)

(M. S.)
He spar - ed not, in
He spar - ed not, in
He spar - ed not, in
He spar - ed not, in

Traditional. *Ibid.*

SAINT Stephen was a holy man,
Endued with heavenly might,
And many wonders he did work
Before the people's sight;
And by the blessed Spirit of God,
Which did his heart inflame,
He sparèd not, in every place,
To preach God's holy name:

O man, do never faint nor fear,
When God the truth shall try,
But mark how Stephen, for Christ's sake,
Was willing for to die.

2 Before the elders was he brought
His answer for to make;
But they could not the spirit withstand,
Whereby this man did speak.
Whilst this was told, the multitude,
Beholding him aright,
His comely face began to shine
Most like an angel bright:

3 Then Stephen did put forth his voice,
And he did first unfold
The wondrous works which God hath wrought,
Even for their fathers old;
That they thereby might plainly know
Christ Jesus should be he,
That from the burden of the law
Should quit us frank and free:

4 'But, O,' quoth he, 'you wicked men!
Which of the prophets all
Did not your fathers persecute
And keep in woeful thrall?'
But when they heard him so to say,
Upon him they all ran,
And then without the city gates
They stoned this holy man:

5. There he most meekly on his knees
To God did pray at large,
Desiring that he would not lay
This sin unto their charge;
Then yielding up his soul to God,
Who had it dearly bought,
He lost his life, whose body then
To grave was seemly brought:

Both the tune and words of this carol were preserved by Sandys, from whom we have taken the last two verses; the rest are exactly as in the older and slightly different version of Gilbert: but we have shortened the original, which is in eight verses.

27 THE FIRST NOWELL

(EPIPHANY : CHRISTMAS)

Verses 1, 2, 4, 5, 7, 8, & 9. (M. S.)

* It is suggested that the organ remain silent until the Refrain in one or more verses.

Verses 3 & 6.
S.
3 And by the light of
6 Then en - tered in those
A.
3 And by........ the light of that same
6 Then en - tered in those Wise Men
T.
3 And by.... the light of that same star, Three
6 Then en - tered in those Wise Men three, Fell
B.
Now - ell,.. Now - ell, Now -
that same star, Three Wise Men came from far; To
Wise Men three, Fell rev - 'rent - ly on knee, And
star, Three Wise Men came from coun - try far;............
three, Fell rev - 'rent - ly up - on their knee,............
Wise Men came from coun - try far; To seek for a
rev - 'rent - ly up - on their knee, And of - fered
- ell, Now - ell, Now - ell,........................ Now - ell, Now -

seek for a king was their in - tent, And to fol - low the
of - fered there in his pres - ence Both gold and
Now - ell, Now - ell, Now - ell, Now - ell, Now-
king was their in - tent, And to fol-low the star where-so-
there in his pres - ence Both gold and myrrh and
- ell,
star where-so - ev - er it went:
myrrh and frank - in cense:
Now - ell, Now - ell, Now-
- ell, Now - ell, Now - ell, Now-
ev - er it went:
frank - in - cense:
Now - ell, Now - ell, Now - ell, Now-
Now - ell,

- ell, Now - ell, Now - ell, Now - ell.
- ell, Now - ell, Now - ell, Now - ell, Now - ell.
- ell, Born is the King of Is - ra - el.
Now - ell, Now - ell, Now - ell, Now - ell.

Traditional. *Ibid.*

THE first Nowell the angel did say
Was to certain poor shepherds in fields as they lay;
In fields where they lay, keeping their sheep,
In a cold winter's night that was so deep:

Nowell, Nowell, Nowell, Nowell,
Born is the King of Israel!

2 *They lookèd up and saw a star,
Shining in the east, beyond them far;
And to the earth it gave great light,
And so it continued both day and night:

3 And by the light of that same star,
Three Wise Men came from country far;
To seek for a king was their intent,
And to follow the star wheresoever it went:

4 This star drew nigh to the north-west;
O'er Bethlehem it took its rest,
And there it did both stop and stay
Right over the place where Jesus lay:

5 *Then did they know assuredly
Within that house the King did lie:
One entered in then for to see,
And found the babe in poverty:

6 Then entered in those Wise Men three,
Fell reverently upon their knee,
And offered there in his presénce
Both gold and myrrh and frankincense:

7 *Between an ox-stall and an ass
This child truly there born he was;
For want of clothing they did him lay
All in the manger, among the hay:

8 Then let us all with one accord
Sing praises to our heavenly Lord,
That hath made heaven and earth of naught,
And with his blood mankind hath bought:

9. *If we in our time shall do well,
We shall be free from death and hell;
For God hath preparèd for us all
A resting place in general:

As in Sandys, 1833 (except 'certain' for 'three' in v. 1), with tune. Gilbert (1822) is rougher. The carol cannot be later than the seventeenth century. We have restored the verses omitted by Bramley in 1871, marking them with an asterisk: they are good, and will be sometimes very useful, for this carol makes a fine processional in the Epiphany season. Verse 2 is not quite historical: the carol is more for Epiphany than Christmas.

GREENSLEEVES

(NEW YEAR)

The Treble sings the words, the Alto, Tenor & Bass hum. (M. S.)

Let's mer - ry
The Alto, Tenor & Bass take up the words here.
be this day, &c.

'Greensleeves.' 1642.

THE old year now away is fled,
The new year it is enterèd;
Then let us now our sins down-tread,
And joyfully all appear:
Let's merry be this day,
And let us now both sport and play:
Hang grief, cast care away!
God send you a happy New Year!

2 The name-day now of Christ we keep,
Who for our sins did often weep;
His hands and feet were wounded deep,
And his blessèd side with a spear;
His head they crowned with thorn,
And at him they did laugh and scorn,
Who for our good was born:
God send us a happy New Year!

3. And now with New Year's gifts each friend
Unto each other they do send:
God grant we may all our lives amend,
And that the truth may appear.
Now, like the snake, your skin
Cast off, of evil thoughts and sin,
And so the year begin:
God send us a happy New Year!

A Waits' carol. There are three more verses, appealing to 'Jack, Tom, Dick, Bessy, Mary, and Joan', and also to the dame of the house, rather pathetically pleading for good cheer. From *New Christmas Carols*, 1642 ('to the tune of Greensleeves'), in the unique black-letter collection of Antony à Wood, now in the Bodleian. We have had to alter some words for the sake of choral singing.

29 THIS NEW CHRISTMAS CAROL

(CHRISTMAS: EPIPHANY)

Traditional. *Ibid.*

THIS new Christmas Carol
Let us cheerfully sing,
To the honour and glory
Of our heavenly King,
Who was born of a virgin,
Blessèd Mary by name;
For poor sinners' redemption
To the world here he came.

2 Now the proud may come hither
And perfectly see
The most excellent pattern
Of humility;
For instead of a cradle,
Decked with ornaments gay,
Here the great king of glory
In a manger he lay.

3 As the shepherds were feeding
Of their flocks in the field,
The sweet birth of our Saviour
Unto them was revealed
By blest angels of glory,
Who those tidings did bring,
And directed the shepherds
To their heavenly King.

4 *When the wise men discovered
The bright heavenly star,
Then with gold and rich spices
Straight they came from afar,
In obedience to worship
With a heavenly mind,
Knowing that he was born
For the good of mankind.

5. *Let us learn of those sages,
Who were wise, to obey.
Nay, we find through all ages
They have honoured this day,
Ever since our Redeemer's
Blest nativity,
Who was born of a virgin
To set sinners free.

In Gilbert, 1822; in Sandys with tune, 1833. A new version, with the melody of the third phrase a tone lower, will be found in *The English Carol Book* (Mowbray's), No. 10.

LUTE-BOOK LULLABY

(NATIVITY)

(G. S.)

Sweet was the song the Vir - gin sang,
When
When she to Beth - lem Ju - da came And
she to Beth - lem Ju - - da came
was de - liv - ered of a son, That bless - ed
Je - sus hath to name: 'Lul - la, lul - la,

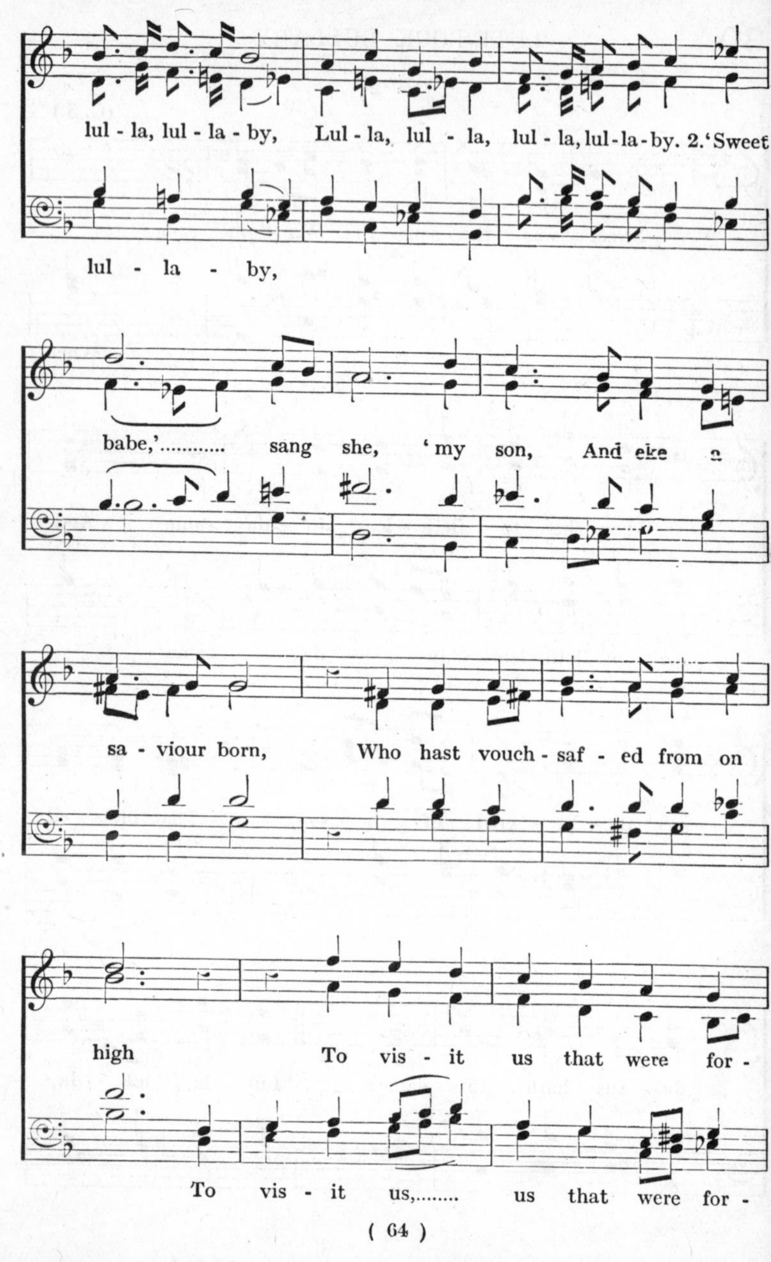

lul - la, lul - la - by,
Lul - la, lul - la, lul - la, lul - la - by. 2. 'Sweet
lul - la - by,
babe,' .... sang she, 'my son, And eke a
sa - viour born, Who hast vouch - saf - ed from on
high To vis - it us that were for -
To vis - it us, ... us that were for -

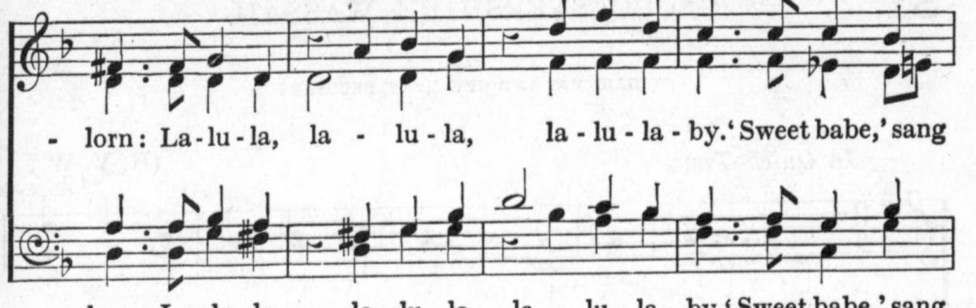
- lorn : La - lu - la, la - lu - la, la - lu - la - by.' Sweet babe,' sang
- lorn : La - lu - la, la - lu - la, la - lu - la - by,' Sweet babe,' sang

she, And rocked him sweet - - - ly on her knee.

W. Ballet, 17th century. *Ibid.*

SWEET was the song the Virgin sang,
When she to Bethlem Juda came
And was delivered of a son,
That blessèd Jesus hath to name :
' Lulla, lulla, lulla, lulla-by,
Lulla, lulla, lulla, lulla-by.

2. 'Sweet babe,' sang she, 'my son,
And eke a saviour born,
Who hast vouchsafèd from on high
To visit us that were forlorn :
Lalula, lalula, lalula-by.'
'Sweet babe,' sang she,
And rocked him sweetly on her knee.

From the MS. *Lute Book* by William Ballet, early seventeenth century, Trinity College, Dublin. We do not know that this Lullaby was ever in traditional use, but it belongs more to our First Part than to any other.

31 GLOUCESTERSHIRE WASSAIL

(CHRISTMAS AND NEW YEAR, SECULAR)

In Quick Time. (R. V. W.)

WASSAIL, Wassail, all over the town!
Our toast it is white, and our ale it is brown,
Our bowl it is made of the white maple tree;
With the wassailing bowl we'll drink to thee.

2 So here is to Cherry and to his right cheek,
Pray God send our master a good piece of beef,
And a good piece of beef that may we all see;
With the wassailing bowl we'll drink to thee.

3 And here is to Dobbin and to his right eye,
Pray God send our master a good Christmas pie,
And a good Christmas pie that may we all see;
With our wassailing bowl we'll drink to thee.

4 So here is to Broad May and to her broad horn,
May God send our master a good crop of corn,
And a good crop of corn that may we all see;
With the wassailing bowl we'll drink to thee.

5 And here is to Fillpail and to her left ear,
Pray God send our master a happy New Year,
And a happy New Year as e'er he did see;
With our wassailing bowl we'll drink to thee.

6 *And here is to Colly and to her long tail,
Pray God send our master he never may fail
A bowl of strong beer; I pray you draw near,
And our jolly wassail it's then you shall hear.

7 *Come, butler, come fill us a bowl of the best,
Then we hope that your soul in heaven may rest;
But if you do draw us a bowl of the small,
Then down shall go butler, bowl and all.

8. *Then here's to the maid in the lily white smock,
Who tripped to the door and slipped back the lock!
Who tripped to the door and pulled back the pin,
For to let these jolly wassailers in.

Wassail, Wes hal, Old English, 'Be thou whole' (hale); a form of salutation, and hence a festive occasion. Cf. 'wassail bowl', cup, or horn.

Cherry and Dobbin are horses. Broad May, Fillpail, and Colly are cows.

Sung by an old person in the county to R. Vaughan Williams. A variant was taken from Mr. William Bayliss at Buckland, Glos., and (5, 6, 7) from Mr. Isaac Bennett at Little Sodbury, Glos., by Cecil Sharp, *English Folk-Carols*, Novello. Collated with Sandys, &c. Other versions in Cecil Sharp's *Folk Songs from Somerset*, Nos. 128–30. Also found in Hone and in Chappell's *Collection of Anc. Eng. Melodies.* Brand recorded a hundred and thirty years ago that it was sung in Gloucestershire by wassailers carrying a great bowl dressed up with garlands and ribbon; Husk, that it was sung in 1864 in Over, near Gloucester, by a troop of wassailers from the neighbouring village of Minsterworth.

32 SOMERSET WASSAIL

(CHRISTMAS AND NEW YEAR, SECULAR)

Traditional. *Ibid.*

WASSAIL, and wassail, all over the town!
The cup it is white and the ale it is brown;
The cup it is made of the good ashen tree,
And so is the malt of the best barley:

For it's your wassail, and it's our wassail!
And it's joy be to you, and a jolly wassail!

2 O master and missus, are you all within?
Pray open the door and let us come in;
O master and missus a-sitting by the fire,
Pray think upon poor travellers, a-travelling in the mire:

3 O where is the maid, with the silver-headed pin,
To open the door, and let us come in?
O master and missus, it is our desire
A good loaf and cheese, and a toast by the fire:

4 There was an old man, and he had an old cow,
And how for to keep her he didn't know how,
He built up a barn for to keep his cow warm,
And a drop or two of cider will do us no harm:

No harm, boys, harm; no harm, boys, harm;
And a drop or two of cider will do us no harm.

5. The girt dog of Langport he burnt his long tail,
And this is the night we go singing wassail:
O master and missus, now we must be gone;
God bless all in this house till we do come again.

For it's, &c.

This Wassail was noted about twenty years ago by Cecil Sharp from the Drayton wassailers in Somerset, and we print it separately because of its fine tune and distinctive words. Sharp thought that the great dog of Langport was a reference to the Danes whose invasion of Langport is not yet forgotten in that town.

33 WHILE SHEPHERDS WATCHED

(CHRISTMAS)

Traditional. *Nahum Tate*, 1652–1715.

WHILE shepherds watched their flocks by night,
All seated on the ground,
The Angel of the Lord came down,
And glory shone around.
'Fear not,' said he (for mighty dread
Had seized their troubled mind);
'Glad tidings of great joy I bring
To you and all mankind.

2 'To you in David's town this day
Is born of David's line
A Saviour, who is Christ the Lord;
And this shall be the sign:
'The heavenly Babe you there shall find
To human view displayed,
All meanly wrapped in swathing bands,
And in a manger laid.'

3. Thus spake the Seraph: and forthwith
Appeared a shining throng
Of angels praising God, who thus
Addressed their joyful song:
'All glory be to God on high,
And to the earth be peace;
Good-will henceforth from heaven to men
Begin and never cease.'

This carol, which is better known as a hymn because of its inclusion in all the hymnals, is here printed for the sake of the traditional tune proper to the words. It is, of course, now usually sung to 'Winchester Old' from *Este's Psalter* of 1592. The words first appeared in the *Supplement* to the *New Version*, the metrical version of the Psalms called 'Tate and Brady', by our forefathers, which appeared in 1696 and was 'allowed' by the King in Council, in place of the *Old Version* of 1556 ('Sternhold and Hopkins'); the earliest *Supplement* was in 1700, and contained 'While shepherds watched'; the *Supplement* of 1782 added 'Hark the herald' and four others. Soon after 1807, 'Jesus Christ is risen to-day' and 'Glory to thee, my God, this night' were added.

34 POVERTY

(NATIVITY)

(DR. CARADOG ROBERTS.)

[*By permission of the Caniedydd Committee, Welsh Congregational Union.*]

Welsh. *Tr. K. E. Roberts.*

ALL poor men and humble,
All lame men who stumble,
Come haste ye, nor feel ye afraid ;
For Jesus, our treasure,
With love past all measure,
In lowly poor manger was laid.

2 Though wise men who found him
Laid rich gifts around him,
Yet oxen they gave him their hay :
And Jesus in beauty
Accepted their duty ;
Contented in manger he lay.

3. Then haste we to show him
The praises we owe him ;
Our service he ne'er can despise :
Whose love still is able
To show us that stable
Where softly in manger he lies.

A free translation of the Welsh Carol O Deued Pob Cristion

35

SANS DAY CAROL

(NATIVITY: PASSIONTIDE TO EASTERTIDE)

(M. S.)

Cornish. *Ibid.*

NOW the holly bears a berry as white as the milk,
And Mary bore Jesus, who was wrapped up in silk:

And Mary bore Jesus Christ our Saviour for to be,
And the first tree in the greenwood, it was the holly, holly!
holly!
And the first tree in the greenwood, it was the holly.

2 Now the holly bears a berry as green as the grass,
And Mary bore Jesus, who died on the cross:

3 Now the holly bears a berry as black as the coal,
And Mary bore Jesus, who died for us all:

4. Now the holly bears a berry, as blood is it red,
Then trust we our Saviour, who rose from the dead:

The Sans Day or St. Day Carol has been so named because the melody and the first three verses were taken down at St. Day in the parish of Gwennap, Cornwall. St. Day or St. They was a Breton saint whose cult was widely spread in Armorican Cornwall. We owe the carol to the kindness of the Rev. G. H. Doble, to whom Mr. W. D. Watson sang it after hearing an old man, Mr. Thomas Beard, sing it at St. Day. A version in Cornish was subsequently published ('Ma gron war'n gelinen') with a fourth stanza, here translated and added to Mr. Beard's English version.

36

THE SALUTATION CAROL

(NATIVITY)

(R. V. W.)

Now - ell, Now - ell, Now - ell, Now - ell! This is the sal - u -
- ta - tion of the an - gel Ga - bri - el. Tid - ings true there
be come new, Sent from the Trin - i - ty By Ga - bri - el to
Naz - a - reth, Ci - ty of Gal - i - lee............ 'A
clean mai - den, a pure vir - gin, By her hu - mil - i - ty Shall

now con-ceive the Per - son Se-cond in de - i - ty.'

15*th century.* *Ibid.*

NOWELL, Nowell, Nowell, Nowell!
This is the salutation of the angel Gabriel.

Tidings true there be come new,
Sent from the Trinity
By Gabriel to Nazareth,
City of Galilee.
'A clean maidén, a pure virgín,
By her humility
Shall now conceive the Person
Second in deity.'

2 When that he presented was
Before her fair viságe,
In most demure and goodly wise
He did to her homáge;
And said, 'Lady, from heaven so high,
That Lordés heritage,
For he of thee now born will be;
I'm sent on his messáge.

3 'Hail, virgin celestiál,
The meek'st that ever was!
Hail, temple of the Deity!
Hail, mirror of all grace!
Hail, virgin pure! I thee ensure,
Within a little space
Thou shalt conceive, and him receive
That shall bring great soláce.'

4. Then bespake the maid again
And answered womanly,
'Whate'er my Lord commandeth me
I will obey truly.'
With '*Ecce sum humillima*
Ancilla Domini;
Secundum verbum tuum.'
She said, '*Fiat mihi.*'

Salutation] an old name for the Annunciation. 2. demure] in its earlier sense of 'grave, sober'. 4. '*Ecce sum*', &c.] 'Lo, I am the most humble handmaid of the Lord. According to thy word,' she said, 'be it done to me.'

In Richard Hill's *Commonplace Book* (Balliol MS. 354). For musical reasons in v. 1 'divinity' is altered to 'deity', in v. 4, 'virgin' to 'maid'. The tune is in the Sloane MS. 2593, which dates from the earlier part of the fifteenth century, and is considered by Wright to be the song-book of a minstrel (but this is doubted by Sir Edmund Chambers), perhaps the Johannes Bardel (or Bradel) whose name is on the last folio; but, alas, he only preserved the one tune, and this he allots to 'Bring us in good ale', though he calls it 'The Salutation of the Angel Gabriel'. Such parodies were common: Gaston Paris (*Romania*, xxi) gives a thirteenth century one of the sequence 'Laetabundus', in which ale is the *Les miranda* that makes men sing Alleluya.

Richard Hill's MS. has been printed (so far as the verse is concerned) by R. Dyboski for the Early English Text Society, *Extra Series*, c. 1, 1908. It was discovered *c.* 1850, having been concealed behind a bookcase for a great number of years. Our carols, Nos. 39, 118, 120, 169, 172, occur in it, and other versions of Nos. 19, 38, 61 (and 184), 70, 116.

Richard Hill was 'servant' or apprentice of John Wyngar, grocer, who became an alderman of the City of London in 1493 and mayor in 1504. Hill married in 1518 Margaret, daughter of Harry Wyngar, haberdasher. The earliest part of the book was written before 1504, the latest date in it is 1536; the carols seem all to have been transcribed together about 1504. This precious MS. contains also English, French, and Latin poems, romances, extracts from Gower, &c., mixed with commercial entries, tables of weights, prices, dates of fairs, medical and cooking recipes (including a 'medicen for a doge that is poysent', and 'a good medycyne for a cutt' which begins 'Take a pynte of good ale'), a form for making letters of attorney, a list of diaper table-cloths, &c., for the mayor's annual feast at the Guildhall, rules for purchase of land, the bread assize, a treatise on wine, dates of his children, pious ejaculations and reflections, notes on the breaking in of horses, the 'crafte to brewe bere', forms for business letters in English and French, riddles, puzzles, with many humorous and satirical verses.

37 THE ANGEL GABRIEL

(NATIVITY : ANNUNCIATION)

(M. S.)

Traditional. *Ibid.*

THE Angel Gabriel from God
Was sent to Galilee,
Unto a virgin fair and free,
Whose name was called Mary.
And when the Angel thither came,
He fell down on his knee,
And looking up in the virgin's face,
He said, All hail, Mary :

Then sing we all, both great and small,
Nowell, Nowell, Nowell ;
We may rejoice to hear the voice
Of the Angel Gabriel.

2 Mary anon looked him upon,
And said, ' Sir, what are ye ?
I marvel much at these tidings
Which thou hast brought to me.
Married I am unto an old man,
As the lot fell unto me ;
Therefore, I pray, depart away,
For I stand in doubt of thee ' :

3 ' Mary,' he said, ' be not afraid,
But do believe in me :
The power of the Holy Ghost
Shall overshadow thee ;
Thou shalt conceive without any grief,
As the Lord told unto me :
God's own dear Son from Heaven shall come,
And shall be born of thee ' :

4 *This came to pass as God's will was,
Even as the Angel told,
About midnight an angel bright
Came to the Shepherds' fold,
And told them then both where and when
Born was the child our Lord,
And all along this was their song,
' All glory be given to God ' :

5. Good people all, both great and small,
The which do hear my voice,
With one accord let's praise the Lord,
And in our hearts rejoice ;
Like sister and brother, let's love one another
Whilst we our lives do spend,
Whilst we have space let's pray for grace,
And so let my carol end :

As in Sandys, 1833 ; Stainer gives the tune from Devonshire. The 'lot' in v. 2 is an allusion to the apocryphal Gospel of the Birth of Mary where Joseph is chosen out from the other suitors by the budding of his rod ; the legend is introduced into the tenth play (Mary's Betrothal) of the so-called *Ludus Coventriæ*, and is familiar in pictures, e.g. in Raphael's *Sposalizio* in the Brera.

THE HOLLY AND THE IVY

(NATIVITY: LENT: AUTUMN)

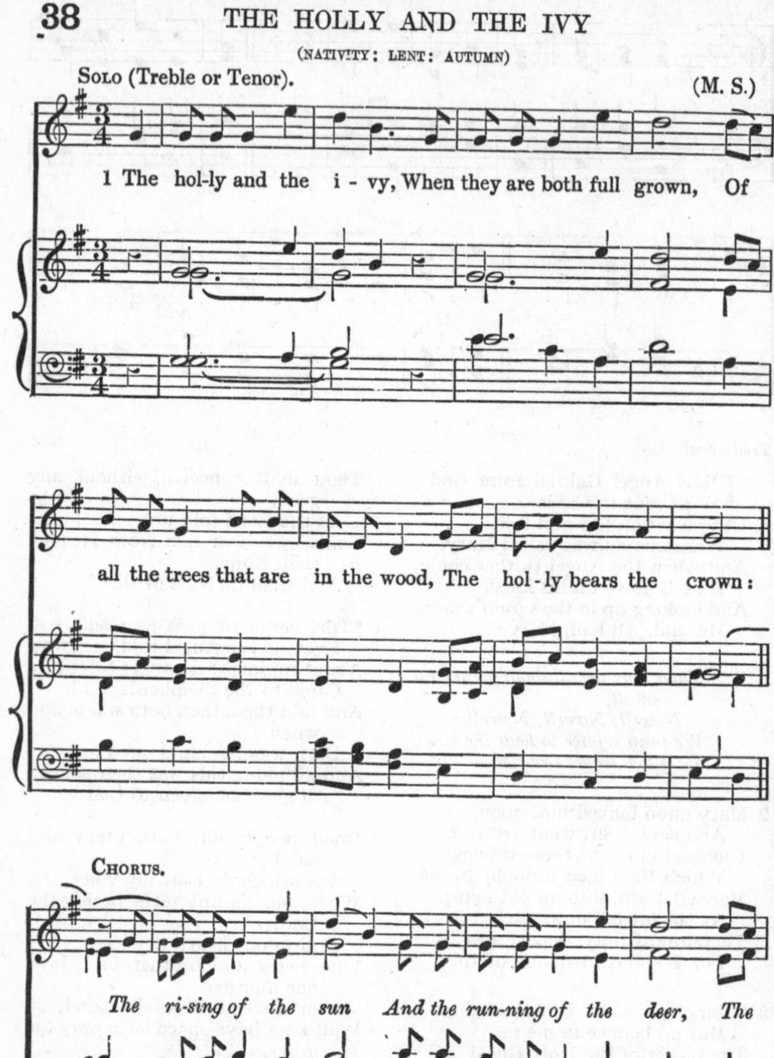
Solo (Treble or Tenor).
(M. S.)
1 The hol-ly and the i - vy, When they are both full grown, Of
all the trees that are in the wood, The hol-ly bears the crown:
Chorus.
The ri-sing of the sun And the run-ning of the deer, The
(Small notes, Organ.)

May be sung with or without accompaniment.

play-ing of the mer-ry or - gan, Sweet sing-ing in the choir.

Traditional. *Ibid.*

THE holly and the ivy,
When they are both full grown,
Of all the trees that are in the wood,
The holly bears the crown :

The rising of the sun
And the running of the deer,
The playing of the merry organ,
Sweet singing in the choir.

2 The holly bears a blossom,
As white as the lily flower,
And Mary bore sweet Jesus Christ,
To be our sweet Saviour :

3 The holly bears a berry,
As red as any blood,
And Mary bore sweet Jesus Christ
To do poor sinners good :

4 The holly bears a prickle,
As sharp as any thorn,
And Mary bore sweet Jesus Christ
On Christmas day in the morn :

5 The holly bears a bark,
As bitter as any gall,
And Mary bore sweet Jesus Christ
For to redeem us all :

6. The holly and the ivy,
When they are both full grown,
Of all the trees that are in the wood,
The holly bears the crown :

Cf. Nos. 35 and 63. Words and melody taken from Mrs. Clayton at Chipping Campden, Glos. (supplemented by words from Mrs. Wyatt, East Harptree, Somerset), by Cecil Sharp, *English Folk-Carols* (Novello). Another version is in Bramley and Stainer, and in the *English Carol Book* (Mowbray's) set to a French carol tune. 'Joshua Sylvester', in his *Christmas Carols*, 1861, was the first to publish the text in a collection ; he took it from 'an old broadside, printed a century and a half since', i.e. *c.* 1710. Husk stated in 1868 that it was still retained in the broadsides printed at Birmingham. These two versions differ in the second line, 'Now are both well grown'. There is another carol of the Holly and the Ivy ('Holy berith beris') in Richard Hill's MS., another in the Harleian MS. ('Nay, Ivy, nay'), and others, for which Dyboski gives references. The subject is probably of pagan origin, and symbolized the masculine (holly) and the feminine (ivy) elements, as the tribal chorus developed into dialogue, all such songs being sung as a dance between the lads and the maids. 'The merry organ' occurs in Chaucer in the Nonne Preestes Tale: 'Chauntecleer's crowing had no peer— | His voice was merrier than the merry organ | On mass-days that in the churche gon.'

39 THIS ENDRIS NIGHT

(NATIVITY)

(R. V. W.)

This tune will be sung twice through, without pause, for the second and following verses.

FA-BURDEN

(M. S.)

It is suggested that this Fa-Burden be sung to—(*a*) the second half of ver. 3; (*b*) the whole of ver. 5 (sing F. B. twice); (*c*) the whole of ver. 7 (sing F. B. twice). The carol may then be shortened, if necessary, by the omission of verses 5 and 6.

THIS endris night
 I saw a sight,
A star as bright as day;
 And ever among,
 A maiden sung,
'Lullay, by by, lullay.'

2 This lovely lady sat and sung,
 And to her child did say:
'My son, my brother, father, dear,
 Why liest thou thus in hay?
My sweetest bird, thus 'tis required,
 Though thou be king veray;
But nevertheless I will not cease
 To sing, By by, lullay.'

3 The child then spake in his talking,
 And to his mother said:
'Yea, I am known as heaven-king,
 In crib though I be laid;
(*Fa-Burden.*)
For angels bright down to me light:
 Thou knowest 'tis no nay:
And for that sight thou may'st
 delight
 To sing, By by, lullay.'

4 'Now sweet son, since thou art a
 king,
 Why art thou laid in stall?
Why dost not order thy bedding
 In some great kingès hall?
Methinks 'tis right that king or
 knight
 Should lie in good array:
And then among, it were no wrong
 To sing, By by, lullay.'

(*Fa-Burden.*)
5 *'Mary mother, I am thy child,
 Though I be laid in stall;
For lords and dukes shall worship
 And so shall kingès all. [me,
Ye shall well see that Kingès three
 Shall come on this twelfth day.
For this behest give me thy breast,
 And sing, By by, lullay.'

6 *'Now tell, sweet son, I thee do
 pray,
 Thou art my love and dear—
How should I keep thee to thy pay,
 And make thee glad of cheer?
For all thy will I would fulfil—
 Thou knowest well, in fay;
And for all this I will thee kiss,
 And sing, By by, lullay.'

(*Fa-Burden.*)
7 *'My dear mother, when time it be,
 Take thou me up on loft,
And set me then upon thy knee,
 And handle me full soft;
And in thy arm thou hold me warm,
 And keep me night and day,
And if I weep, and may not sleep,
 Thou sing, By by, lullay.'

8. *'Now sweet son, since it is come so,
 That all is at thy will,
I pray thee grant to me a boon,
 If it be right and skill,—
That child or man, who will or can
 Be merry on my day,
To bliss thou bring—and I shall
 Lullay, by by, lullay.' [sing,

1. This endris] ('thys ender' in the MS. Add. 31922, 'this endurs' in the MS., Advocates' Lib., Edinburgh), the other night, a few nights ago. ever among] every now and then. 2. veray true. 3. light] alight. no nay] not to be denied. 6. pay] satisfaction. fay] faith. 8. skill] reasonable.

Was not new when it was written out in the Bodleian MS., Eng. Poet., e. 1, which is dated between 1460 and 1490. It is in the MS. of Richard Hill, the grocer (cf. No. 36). Four versions are given by Dyboski in the Early English Text Society, Extra Series, c. 1, p. 174. Wright's version, from the Sloane MS. 2593 (see nos. 174, 182), Percy Society, 1841, is reprinted in Julian's *Dictionary of Hymnology* (p. 209) by Helmore. Two of the versions are in Chambers and Sidgwick, pp. 119 and 121. The tune is used in the *English Hymnal* (20) and *Songs of Praise* (47): it is in the fifteenth or sixteenth century MS., B.M., Royal Appendix 58, set for three voices, with melody in the tenor.

WONDER TIDINGS

(NATIVITY)

(M. S.)

15th century; School of J. Dunstable. *Ibid.*

WHAT tidings bringest thou, messenger,
Of Christès birth this jolly day?
A babe is born of high natúre,
The Prince of peace that ever shall be;
Of heaven and earth he hath the cure
His lordship is eternity:
Such wonder tidings ye may hear,
That man is made now Goddès peer,
Whom sin had made but fiendès prey.

2 A wonder thing is now befall;
That King that formèd star and sun,
Heaven and earth and angels all,
Now in mankind is new begun:
Such wonder tidings ye may hear,
An infant now of but one year,
That hath been ever and shall be ay.

3 That seemeth strange to us to see,
This bird that hath this babe yborn
And Lord conceived of high degree
A maiden is, and was beforn:
Such wonder tidings ye may hear,
That maiden and mother is one in fere,
And she a lady of great array.

4. That loveliest gan greet her child,
'Hail, son! Hail, brother! Hail, father dear!'
'Hail, daughter! Hail, sister! Hail, mother mild!'
This hailing was on quaint mannere:
Such wonder tidings ye may hear,
That hailing was of so good cheer
That mannés pain is turned to play.

1. cure] charge. 3. bird] girl. beforn] before. in fere] together. 4. quaint] (from 'coint', 'cognitus', 'known'), had several shades of meaning in the fifteenth century—'strange', 'curiously wrought', 'dainty', 'graceful'.

Words and tune from a MS. at Cambridge (T.C.C., O. 3. 58), edited by Fuller-Maitland & Rockstro, *English Carols of the Fifteenth Century*. Eitner and others are inclined to think that the tune is actually by Dunstable. In this carol an opening challenge is preserved, both in words and music. We can imagine, with Sir Edmund Chambers, how 'the chanted question comes nearer and nearer along the crooked medieval street': or we can picture a company singing in a hall round the crackling yule logs; the door opens, and the Messenger enters; the company sings 'What tidings . . .', and the Messenger answers with the first stanza, and a choir perhaps takes up the refrain, which changes as the tidings are told out. The same might be done to-day in a parish-hall; or in church, the Messenger, wearing a gown and carrying a staff, like a verger, might walk up the middle alley, the choir beginning 'What tidings' as he approaches the chancel. He would proceed as far as the midst of the chancel, and then, turning west, would sing his verses. (See p. xi.).

41 RIGHTEOUS JOSEPH

(NATIVITY: ADVENT)

(M. S.)

Cornish. *Ibid.*

WHEN righteous Joseph wedded was
To Israel's Hebrew maid,
The angel Gabriel came from Heaven,
And to the Virgin said:
'Hail, blessèd Mary, full of grace,
The Lord remain on thee;
Thou shalt conceive and bear a son,
Our Saviour for to be':

Then sing you all, both great and small,
Now well, now well, now well!
We may rejoice to hear the voice
Of the angel Gabriel.

2 *Then Joseph thought to shun all shame
And Mary to forsake;
But God's dear angel in a dream
His mind did undertake:
'Fear not, old Joseph, she's thy wife,
She's still a spotless maid;
There's no conceit or sin at all
Against her can be laid':

3 Thus Mary and her husband kind
Together did remain,
Until the time of Jesus' birth,
As Scripture doth make plain.
As mother, wife, and virtuous maid,
Our Saviour sweet conceived;
And in due time to bring us him,
Of whom we were bereaved:

4. Sing praises all, both young and old,
To him that wrought such things;
And all without the means of man,
Sent us the King of kings,
Who is of such a spirit blest,
That with his might did quell
The world, the flesh, and by his death
Did conquer death and hell:

As in Davies Gilbert, 1822 (with seven verses); but v. 2 from the less corrupt version of Miss Hocking. The tune has been kindly communicated by the Rev. G. H. Doble, who noted it from Elizabeth Hocking, at Redruth, Cornwall. Miss Hocking was then 84 (1920), and had learnt it from her mother as a very small child, i.e. *c.* 1840.

REMEMBER

(LENT: CHRISTMAS)

(THOS. RAVENSCROFT, 1611.)

T. Ravenscroft, 1611. *Melismata*, 1611.

REMEMBER, O thou man,
O thou man, O thou man,
Remember, O thou man,
Thy time is spent:
Remember, O thou man,
How thou cam'st to me then,
And I did what I can,
Therefore repent.

2 *Remember God's goodness,
O thou man, O thou man,
Remember God's goodness
And promise made:
Remember God's goodness,
How his only Son he sent,
Our sins for to redress:
Be not afraid.

3 The angels all did sing,
O thou man, O thou man,
The angels all did sing,
On Sion hill:
The angels all did sing
Praise to our heavenly King,
And peace to man living,
With right good will.

4 To Bethlem did they go,
O thou man, O thou man,
To Bethlem did they go,
This thing to see:
To Bethlem did they go,
To see whether it was so,
Whether Christ was born or no
To set us free.

5 In Bethlem was he born,
O thou man, O thou man,
In Bethlem was he born,
For mankind dear:
In Bethlem was he born
For us that were forlorn,
And therefore took no scorn,
Our sins to bear.

6. Give thanks to God always,
O thou man, O thou man,
Give thanks to God always,
With hearts most jolly:
Give thanks to God always
Upon this blessèd day;
Let all men sing and say,
Holy, holy.

The words, which are probably of the sixteenth century, are set to music in Ravenscroft's *Melismata*. Four verses omitted will be found in Bullen. Mr. Thomas Hardy gives another version in *Under the Greenwood Tree*. For Lent, vv. 1, 2, 3, 5 are suitable.

43 THE SEVEN VIRGINS

(THE PASSION)

[*Copyright, 1920, by Stainer & Bell, Ltd.*]

Traditional. *Ibid.*

ALL under the leaves, the leaves of life,
I met with virgins seven,
And one of them was Mary mild,
Our Lord's mother from heaven.

2 'O what are you seeking, you seven fair maids,
All under the leaves of life?
Come tell, come tell me what seek you
All under the leaves of life.'

3 'We're seeking for no leaves, Thomas,
But for a friend of thine;
We're seeking for sweet Jesus Christ,
To be our guide and thine.'

4 ‘ Go you down, go you down to yonder town,
And sit in the gallery ;
And there you’ll find sweet Jesus Christ,
Nailed to a big yew-tree.’

5 So down they went to yonder town,
As fast as foot could fall,
And many a grievous bitter tear,
From the virgins’ eyes did fall.

6 ‘ O peace, mother, O peace, mother,
Your weeping doth me grieve ;
O I must suffer this,’ he said,
‘ For Adam and for Eve.’

7 ‘ O how can I my weeping leave,
Or my sorrows undergo,
Whilst I do see my own Son die,
When sons I have no mo’ ? ’

8 ‘ Dear mother, dear mother, you must take John,
All for to be your son,
And he will comfort you sometimes,
Mother, as I have done.’

9 ‘ O, come, thou John Evangelist,
Thou’rt welcome unto me,
But more welcome my own dear son,
That I nursed upon my knee.’

10 Then he laid his head on his right shoulder,
Seeing death it struck him nigh :
‘ The Holy Ghost be with your soul,—
I die, mother dear, I die.’

11 Oh the rose, the rose, the gentle rose,
And the fennel that grows so green !
God give us grace in every place,
To pray for our king and queen.

12. Furthermore for our enemies all
Our prayers they should be strong.
Amen, Good Lord ! your charity
Is the ending of my song.

Melody and a version of Text from Mrs. Whatton and Mrs. Loveridge, The Homme, Dilwyn. From *Twelve Traditional Carols from Herefordshire* (Leather and Vaughan Williams), Stainer & Bell. Cf. *Popular Carols*, by F. Sidgwick (Sidgwick & Jackson). This fine example of the way in which a mystical vision is created by the best folk-poetry appeared in the Staffordshire *A Good Christmas Box*, 1847. Sylvester (1861) printed a version of it from an ‘ old Birmingham broadside ’. Sir A. Quiller-Couch included it in the *Oxford Book of English Verse*, and Mr. De la Mare in *Come Hither*.

44 THE LAMB OF GOD

(THE PASSION : EASTER : NEW YEAR)

(M. S.)
in the
year, So God send you all much joy........ in the year.

AWAKE, Awake, ye drowsy souls,
And hear what I shall tell;
Remember Christ, the Lamb of God,
Redeemed our souls from hell.
He's crowned with thorns, spit on with scorn,
His friends have hid themselves:
So God send you all much joy in the year.

2 They bound Christ's body to a tree,
And wounded him full sore;
From every wound the blood ran down,
Till Christ could bleed no more;
His dying wounds, all rent and tore,
Were covered with pearly gore:

3 And when his foes had murdered Christ
And shown their cruel spite,
The sun and moon did hide their heads
And went in mourning straight;
The heavens stood amazed, and angels gazed,
And the earth was darkened quite:

4. *And when Christ's soul departed
And from his body fled,
The rocks did rend, the graves did ope,
And then appeared the dead;
All they that were there did quake for fear—
''Twas the Son of God,' they said:

PART 2.

(EASTER, &C.)

5 It was early in the morning
That Mary did him seek;
She saw two angels sitting
At Jesus' head and feet:
Mary shed tears while Christ appeared,
And he said: 'Why dost thou weep?'

6 Then Christ he called Thomas,
And bid him: 'Come and see,
And put thy fingers in the wounds
That are in my body;
And be not faithless, but believe,
And happy shalt thou be:'

7 Then Christ called his disciples,
Divided by his death,
And said: 'All powers are given to you
In heaven and on earth;
Go forth and teach all nations;
Despise them not,' he saith:

8. *'Go seek you every wandering sheep
That doth on earth remain,
Till I myself have paid your debts
And turned you back again;
Come all ye heavy laden,
I'll ease you of your pain:'

PART 3.

(GOOD WISHES)

9 *God bless the ruler of this house
And send him long to reign;
Let many a good and happy year
Go over his head again,
And all his godly family
That serveth the Lord so dear:

10. *God bless the mistress of this house,
With peace unto her breast,
And, let her body be asleep or awake,
Lord send her soul to rest,
And all her godly family
That serveth the Lord so dear:

The melody and the first and last verses were taken down by Cecil Sharp at Donnington Wood, Shropshire; the refrain as noted was 'So God send you all a joyful New Year', and v. 5 comes after v. 8. We have substituted 'friends' in v. 1 and 'foes' in v. 3 for 'Jews'; vv. 4 and 7 seem to be corrupt in the original, and we have slightly amended them. The carol is printed in *A Good Christmas Box*, 1847, and in an undated chap-book printed by J. Bates, New Town, Bilston. It is given in Cecil Sharp's *English Folk-Carols*, and is evidently a Passiontide and Easter carol, not perfectly remembered, and adapted to the Christmas-Epiphany season to which carol-singing came to be restricted.

45 'SUSSEX MUMMERS' CAROL

(LENT: THE PASSION)

(L. E. B.)

Slow.
And crown - ed with the thorn.
ALTERNATIVE HARMONIZATION.
(R. V. W.)

And crown - ed with the thorn.

Traditional. ***Ibid.***

O MORTAL man, remember well,
When Christ our Lord was born,
He was crucified between two thieves,
And crownèd with the thorn.

2 O mortal man, remember well,
When Christ died on the rood,
'Twas for our sins and wicked ways
Christ shed his precious blood.

3 O mortal man, remember well,
When Christ was wrapped in clay,
He was taken to a sepulchre
Where no man ever lay.

4 *God bless the mistress of this house
With gold chain round her breast ;
Where e'er her body sleeps or wakes,
Lord, send her soul to rest.

5 *God bless the master of this house
With happiness beside ;
Where e'er his body rides or walks
Lord Jesus be his guide.

6. God bless your house, your children too,
Your cattle and your store ;
The Lord increase you day by day,
And send you more and more.

Sung by Christmas Mummers from the neighbourhood of Horsham, *c.* 1876–81. Collected by Lucy E. Broadwood. See Broadwood's *Sussex Songs* (Stanley Lucas and Weber, later Leonard & Co.); L. E. Broadwood's *English Traditional Songs and Carols* (Boosey & Co.) and her *Christmas Carols for Children* (A. and C. Black), in all of which the original opening verse, describing the Annunciation, is retained.

UNISON SETTING FOR LAST VERSE.
(R. V. W.)
ff
God bless your house, your chil-dren too, Your cat - tle and your
ff ORGAN.
store; The Lord in-crease you day by day, And send you more and
more,........ And send........... you more........ and more.

46 THE BELLMAN'S SONG

(GENERAL: THE PASSION)

(M. S.)

TENOR { v. 3 When shall my sor-rows end, that I may see.
v. 5 We ne'er shall do for Christ as he for us.

Traditional. *The tenor will sing the small notes in verses* 1, 2, 4, *and* 6. *Ibid.*

THE moon shines bright, and the stars give a light:
A little before it was day
Our Lord, our God, he called on us,
And bid us awake and pray.

2 Awake, awake, good people all;
Awake, and you shall hear,
Our Lord, our God, died on the cross
For us whom he loved so dear.

3 O fair, O fair Jerusalem,
When shall I come to thee?
When shall my sorrows have an end,
Thy joy that I may see.

4 The fields were green as green could be,
When from his glorious seat
Our Lord, our God, he watered us,
With his heavenly dew so sweet.

5 And for the saving of our souls
Christ died upon the cross;
We ne'er shall do for Jesus Christ
As he hath done for us.

6. The life of man is but a span
And cut down in its flower;
We are here to-day, and to-morrow are gone,
The creatures of an hour.

This carol is common in the old broadsides, and some of its verses have strayed into other folk-carols (e.g. into the May Carol from Hertfordshire, printed in Hone's *Every-day Book*, 1821, cf. No. 47). The longer version, in ten verses, is printed by Sandys, Husk, Bullen, and others; it includes the 'With one turf' verse, and concludes with New Year wishes (like those of No. 47, with 'here' and 'Year', instead of 'stay' and 'May'); but the song is clearly a Passion carol or Atonement carol, of the type that became common in the later carol era. We have used Hush's form of v. 6. V. 3 is a variant of the first verse of 'Jerusalem, my happy home' (see No. 132), the twenty-six verses of which are in the *English Hymnal* and *Songs of Praise*. The old tune has been familiar since its publication by Bramley & Stainer in 1871. It might perhaps be some version of this carol to which Shakespeare refers in the pages' song, 'It was a lover and his lass', in *As You Like It*—

This carol they began that hour,
With a hey, and a ho, and a hey nonino,
How that a life was but a flower,
In the spring time, the only pretty ring time.

47 MAY CAROL

(R. V. W.)

Slow.
1. A - wake, a-wake, good peo - ple all, A -
- wake! and you shall hear— That Christ has di - ed for our sins For he
lov - ed us so dear.................. 2. So ....
1st time.
Last time.
p
pp

* Crotchet in vv. 1 & 4. † Crotchet in verse 1 only. ‡ Crotchet in vv. 3, 4, & 5.

VERSION FOR UNACCOMPANIED SINGING.

N.B.—Soprano Part * in vv. 2, 3, & 5; † in vv. 2, &c.; ‡ in vv. 3, 4, & 5.

Traditional. *Ibid.*

AWAKE, awake, good people all,
Awake! and you shall hear—
That Christ has diėd for our sins
For He lovėd us so dear.

2 So dearly, so dearly has Christ lovėd us,
And for our sins was slain;
Christ bids us leave off our wickedness
And turn to the Lord again.

3 *The early cock so early crows,
That is passing the night away,
For the trumpet shall sound and the dead shall be raised,
Lord, at the great judgement day.

4 A branch of may I have brought to you,
And at your door it stands;
It is but a sprout, but it's well budded out
By the work of our Lord's hands.

5. Now my song, that is done, and I must be gone,
No longer can I stay;
So God bless you all, both great and small,
And I wish you a joyful May.

The melody and the text (exactly as here, except that 'was' has been put instead of 'were' in v. 2, and 'but' added in v. 4) were taken from Mr. Flack, Fowlmere, Cambs., and printed in *Eight Traditional English Carols* (Vaughan Williams), Stainer & Bell. Cecil Sharp and Miss Broadwood have collected other versions. V. 1 is a variant of the second verse in the Bellman's song, 'The moon shines bright', No. 46. (See also *English County Songs*, and the *Journal of the Folk-song Society*, i. 180.) The Worcestershire version collected by Sharp has the 'fields were green' verse of the Bellman's Song.

MAY-DAY GARLAND

(MAY)

(M. S.)

Traditional. *Ibid.*

I'VE brought you here a bunch of may!
Before your door it stands:
It 's well set out, and well spread about,
By the work of our Lord's hands:
It's well set out, &c.

2 This morning is the first of May,
The primest of the year:
So ladies all, both great and small,
I wish you a joyful cheer:
So ladies all, &c.

3 Then take your Bible in your hand,
And read the scriptures through;
And when the day of Judgement comes,
The Lord will remember you:
And when the day, &c.

4. The clock 's struck one! I must be gone!
No longer can I stay.
If I should live to carry again,
I'll call another May:
If I should live, &c.

This (or 46, or 47) might be sung in church at May-time, when Evensong is over, by one or two girls carrying a branch of may.

The words and tune were taken by Geoffrey and Martin Shaw from an English girl (now Mrs. Betambeau), in the Boro' Polytechnic, London, *c.* 1917; she had brought them from Northamptonshire.

A May carol from Hitchin is printed by Robert Bell in *Songs of the Peasantry*, 1857, of which verses 1 and 2 are the 1 and 2 of the Furry Day Carol; v. 3 is v. 4 of our May Carol and 1 of our Garland; and verses 4, 6, 7 are 4, 6, and 1 of the Bellman's Song.

49 FURRY DAY CAROL

(MAY)

(M. S.)

With Ho - lan - to
Ho - lan - to, Ho - lan - to, sing mer - - ry,
Ho - lan - to,

Traditional. *Ibid.*

REMEMBER us poor Mayers all !
And thus we do begin-a
To lead our lives in righteousness,
Or else we die in sin-a :

With Holan-to, sing merry, O,
With Holan-to, sing merry,
With Holan-to, sing merry, O,
With Holan-to, sing merry !

2 *We have been rambling half the night,
And almost all the day-a,
And now, returnèd back again,
We've brought you a branch of may-a :

3 O, we were up as soon as day,
To fetch the summer home-a ;
The summer is a coming-on,
And winter is agone-a :

4 Then let us all most merry be,
And sing with cheerful voice-a ;
For we have good occasion now
This time for to rejoice-a :

5 *Saint George he next shall be our song :
Saint George, he was a knight-a ;
Of all the men in Christendom
Saint George he was the right-a :

6. God bless our land with power and might,
God send us peace in England ;
Pray send us peace both day and night,
For ever in merry England :

This Furry Day Carol is distinct, both in words and tune, from the Furry Day Song, annually sung at the Spring festival in Helston in Cornwall (the tune of which is given by Gilbert), though there is some resemblance. We are indebted to Mr. Henry Jenner, F.S.A., for much kind information about the Helston festivities, and about the Furry Day Song, which includes references to Robin Hood and the Spaniards—doubtless of the Armada period. The tune of the Carol is given in Duncan's *Story of the Carol*, where he includes also a Robin Hood verse. (For the May verses cf. No. 48, *n.*) The tendency to confine carols to Christmas led to a Christmas version, which must be later. *Furry* is a corruption of the Latin *feria*, holiday (though in its ecclesiastical use it came to mean an unoccupied day and not a holy day). In Chaucer it is (through the Old French *feire, foire*) ' faire', and hence our ' village fair '.

50 NOS GALAN

(WINTER)

(M. S.)

(104)

Welsh. *Pr. K. E. Roberts.*

NOW the joyful bells a-ringing
All ye mountains, praise the Lord!
Lift our hearts, like birds a-winging,
All ye mountains, praise the Lord!
Now our festal season, bringing
Kinsmen all, to bide and board,
Sets our cheery voices singing :
All ye mountains, praise the Lord!

2 Dear our home as dear none other ;
Where the mountains praise the Lord!
Gladly here our care we smother ;
Where the mountains praise the Lord!
Here we know that Christ our brother
Binds us all as by a cord :
He was born of Mary mother
Where the mountains praise the Lord!

3. Cold the year, new whiteness wearing,
All ye mountains praise the Lord!
Peace, goodwill to us a-bearing,
All ye mountains praise the Lord!
Now we all God's goodness sharing
Break the bread and sheathe the sword :
Bright our hearths the signal flaring
All ye mountains, praise the Lord!

Words based on the Welsh New Year's Eve secular Carol, Nos Galan. On New Year's Eve or Day v. 3, l. 5 may be 'Now we all the New Year sharing'.

51 THE SINNERS' REDEMPTION

(GENERAL)

(R. V. W.)

ALL you that are to mirth inclined,
Consider well and bear in mind
What our good God for us hath done,
In sending his belovèd Son.

2 Let all our songs and praises be
Unto his heavenly majesty ;
And evermore amongst our mirth,
Remember Christ our Saviour's birth.

3 Moreover, let us every one
Call unto mind and think upon
His righteous life, and how he died,
To have poor sinners justified.

4 He in the Temple daily taught,
And many wonders strange he wrought.
He gave the blind their perfect sight,
And made the lame to walk upright.

5 He raisèd Lazarus from the grave,
And to the sick their health he gave,
But yet for all these wonders wrought,
The priests his dire destruction sought :

6 With vile reproachful taunts and scorns
They crowned him with a wreath of thorns :
Then to the cross through hands and feet
They nailed our blest Redeemer sweet ;

7. Thus have you seen and heard aright,
The love of Christ, the Lord of might ;
And how he shed his precious blood,
Only to do us sinners good.

One of the most popular carols ; some verses of it used to be reprinted annually on the broadsides. The tune was noted from Mr. Hall of Castleton, Derbyshire, with the first verse only. The late Rev. W. H. Shawcross published other verses in his *Old Castleton Christmas Carols*, but these are nearly identical with those in Husk, who notes the appearance of the carol on a music-sheet of 1775. Gilbert, 1822, prints a west-country version—some of the opening Christmas verses, but with a refrain and a different tune. Our tune is from *Eight Traditional Carols* (Vaughan Williams), Stainer & Bell. Cecil Sharp prints a different text and tune in his *English Folk-Carols*, VIII.

We have gone back to the earliest known original, and have selected from the twenty-eight verses in '*The Garland of Good-Will*, containing many Pleasant Songs and Poems—T—— D—— London : Printed for *G. Conyers* at the Sign of the *Golden-Ring* in *Little-Britain*' (not dated, except in pencil, 'printed about 1699'). Thomas Deloney was a famous ballad-writer and poet of the people, and one of the earliest of story-writers in English (his works were published by the Clarendon Press, ed. F. O. Mann, 1912). He first published in 1583 and died c. 1600. The *Garland* was first published in 1593, but without our carol. To all editions of later date new poems, not by Deloney, were added (this among them, some time after 1631) down to 1709, or later.

52

ANGELUS AD VIRGINEM

(GENERAL, MEDIEVAL: ANNUNCIATION)

(A. G.)

14th *century.* *Ibid.*

ANGELUS ad Virginem
Subintrans in conclave,
Virginis formidinem
Demulcens, inquit, 'Ave!
Ave regina virginum;
Coeli terraeque Dominum
Concipies
Et paries
Intacta
Salutem hominum;
Tu porta coeli facta,
Medela criminum.'

2 'Quomodo conciperem
Quae virum non cognovi?
Qualiter infringerem
Quod firma mente vovi?'
'Spiritus Sancti gratia
Perficiet haec omnia;
Ne timeas,
Sed gaudeas,
Secura
Quod castimonia
Manebit in te pura
Dei potentia.'

3 *Ad haec virgo nobilis
Respondens inquit ei:
'Ancilla sum humilis
Omnipotentis Dei.
Tibi coelesti nuntio,
Tanti secreti conscio,
Consentiens,
Et cupiens
Videre
Factum quod audio;
Parata sum parere,
Dei consilio.'

4. *Eia mater Domini,
Quae pacem reddidisti
Angelis et homini,
Cum Christum genuisti;
Tuum exora filium
Ut se nobis propitium
Exhibeat,
Et deleat
Peccata:
Praestans auxilium
Vita frui beata
Post hoc exsilium.

Chaucer mentions this early carol, or rather sequence, in the *Milleres Tale*: Nicholas, the Clerk of Oxenford, sang it in the evening to the accompaniment of his 'gay sautrye'.—

'On which he made a nightes melodye
So swetely, that al the chambre rong,
And *Angelus ad virginem* he song.'

It is in the Dublin Troper of *c.* 1360, a MS. now at Cambridge (Add. 710), and in an early fourteenth-century MS. in the British Museum (Arundel 248), with the lovely tune. We suggest that it is best sung in the original Latin, and, even thus, one verse is here omitted. There is a modern rendering by Gabriel Gillett in the *English Carol Book* (Mowbray's). The fourteenth-century translation is more difficult: here is the first verse:

Gabriel from evene King, Sent to the maide swete, Broute hire blisful tiding, And faire he gan hire greten: Heil be thu ful of grace arith, For godes sone this evene lith For mannes loven Wile man becomen And taken Fles of the maiden brith, Maken fre for to maken Of sene and deules mith.

53 THE CARNAL AND THE CRANE

(GENERAL, LEGENDARY)

(R. V. W.)

Traditional. *Ibid.*

AS I passed by a river-side,
  And there as I did rein,
In argument I chanced to hear
  A carnal and a crane.

2 The carnal said unto the crane,
  'If all the world should turn,
Before we had the Father,
  But now we have the Son.'

3 'From whence does the Son come?
  From where and from what place?'
He said: 'In a manger,
  Between an ox and ass.'

4 'I pray thee,' said the carnal,
  'Tell me before thou go,
Was not the mother of Jesus
  Conceived by the Holy Ghost?'

5 'She was the purest virgin,
  And the cleanest from sin;
She was the handmaid of our Lord,
  And mother of our King.'

6 'Where is the golden cradle
  That Christ was rockèd in?
Where are the silken sheets
  That Jesus was wrapt in?'

7. 'A manger was the cradle
  That Christ was rockèd in;
The provender the asses left,
  So sweetly he slept on.'

1. rein ('reign')] renne, run.

Cf. No. 54 and No. 55. The ballad of 'The Carnal and the Crane' (The Crow and the Crane) contains four subjects: (1) The conversation between the two birds; (2) The legend of Herod and the Cock (No. 54); (3) of The Lovely Lion (four verses); (4) of The Miraculous Harvest (No. 55). Imperfect versions of various portions have been taken down by Cecil Sharp, Miss Broadwood, and Vaughan Williams: these have been here collated with Sandys, and with Frank Sidgwick in *Popular Carols*. See F. C. Child's *Ballads*, ii, p. 7; and also *The Folk Song Society's Journal*, i. 183; iv. 22. *Carnal* seems to be from the French *corneille*, a crow, but *N.E.D.* leaves it with a query.

Melody and part of text from Mr. Hirons, Haven, Dilwyn, *Twelve Traditional Carols from Herefordshire* (Leather and Vaughan Williams), Stainer & Bell.

54 KING HEROD AND THE COCK

(GENERAL, LEGENDARY)

Traditional. *Ibid.*

THERE was a star in David's land,
So bright it did appear
Into King Herod's chamber,
And brightly it shined there.

2 The Wise Men soon espied it,
And told the king on high,
A princely babe was born that night
No king could e'er destroy.

3 'If this be true,' King Herod said,
'As thou hast told to me,
This roasted cock that lies in the dish
Shall crow full fences three.'

4. The cock soon thrustened and feathered well,
By the work of God's own hand,
And he did crow full fences three,
In the dish where he did stand.

3. fences or 'sences'] times. 4. thrustened] (Early Mid. Eng.), pressed, thrust out.

Cf. No. 53 and No. 55. Words and tune from Mrs. Plumb, Armscote, Worcestershire (*Cecil Sharp; by permission of Novello & Co., Ltd.*). The cock story is also in a ballad of St. Stephen, and is told of others: it has been traced to *c.* 1200 in Prior's *Ancient Danish Ballads.*

THE MIRACULOUS HARVEST

(GENERAL, LEGENDARY)

(R. V. W.)

Traditional. *Ibid.*

'RISE up, rise up, you merry men all,
See that you ready be :
All children under two years old
Now slain they all shall be.'

2 Then Jesus, aye, and Joseph,
And Mary that was unknown,
They travelled by a husbandman,
Just while his seed was sown.

3 'God speed your work,' said Jesus,
'Throw all your seed away,
And carry home as ripened corn,
What you have sown this day ;

4 'For to keep your wife and family
From sorrow, grief, and pain,
And keep Christ in remembrance
Till seed-time comes again.'

5 The husbandman fell on his knees,
Even upon his face ;
'Long time hast thou been lookèd for
But now thou art come at last.

6 *' And I myself do now believe,
Thy name is Jesus called ;
Redeemer of mankind thou art,
Though undeserving all.'

7 After that there came King Herod,
With his train so furiously,
Enquiring of the husbandman,
Whether Jesus had passed by.

8 ' Why, the truth it must be spoke,
And the truth it must be known,
For Jesus he passed by this way,
Just as my seed was sown.

9 ' But now I have it reapen,
And some laid in my wain,
Ready to fetch and carry
Into my barn again.'

10 *' Turn back,' then says the Captain,
' Your labour and mine 's in vain ;
It 's full three quarters of a year
Since he his seed has sown.'

11 *So Herod was deceivèd
By the work of God's own hand :
No further he proceeded
Into the Holy Land.

12. There 's thousands of children young,
Which for his sake did die ;
Do not forbid those little ones,
And do not them deny.

The tune here set to *The Miraculous Harvest* was noted by Miss Lucy Broadwood from some gypsies of the name of Goby in 1893. They sang it to the following words, which are an interesting example of the way old ballads become confused among illiterate singers. The illiterate, however, often preserve in their own way what the educated lose : King Pharim (Pharaoh), for instance, may go back to the apocryphal *Gospel of the Infancy* (the Holy Family ' went down to Memphis, and having seen Pharaoh, they stayed three years in Egypt, and the Lord Jesus wrought many miracles there '). These apocryphal legends seem to have got into ballads through the preaching Friars. See Miss Broadwood's *English Traditional Songs and Carols* (Boosey), and *Journal of the Folk-Song Society* (1910), iv. 24, for further information.

King Pharim : 1. King Pharim sat a-musing, A-musing all alone ; There came a blessed Saviour, And all to him unknown. 2. 'Say, where did you come from, good man, O where did you then pass ? ' ' It is out of the land Egypt, Between an ox and ass.' 3. ' O, if you come out of Egypt, man, One thing I fain I known, Whether a blessed Virgin Mary Sprung from an Holy Ghost ? 4. For if this is true, is true, good man, That you've been telling to me, That the roasted cock do crow three times In the place where they did stand.' 5. ' O, it's straight away the cock did fetch, And feathered to your own hand, Three times a roasted cock did crow, On the place where they did stand. 6. Joseph, Jesus and Mary Were travelling for the West, When Mary grew a-tired She might sit down and rest. 7. They travelled further and further, The weather being so warm, Till they came unto some husbandman A-sowing of his corn. 8. ' Come, husbandman,' cried Jesus, ' From over speed and pride, And carry home your ripened corn That you've been sowing this day. 9. For to keep your wife and family From sorrow, grief and pain, And keep Christ in your remembrance Till the time comes round again.'

56 THE HOLY WELL

(GENERAL, LEGENDARY)

(E. M.)

Traditional. *Ibid.*

AS it fell out one May morning,
And upon a bright holiday,
Sweet Jesus asked of his dear mother
If he might go to play.
'To play, to play, sweet Jesus shall go,
And to play now get you gone;
And let me hear of no complaint
At night when you come home.'

2 Sweet Jesus went down to yonder town,
As far as the Holy Well,
And there did see as fine childrén
As any tongue can tell.
He said, 'God bless you every one,
And your bodies Christ save and see!
And now, little children, I'll play with you,
And you shall play with me.'

3 But they made answer to him, 'No!
Thou art meaner than us all;
Thou art but a simple fair maid's child,
Born in an ox's stall.'
Sweet Jesus turned him round about,
Neither laughed, nor smiled, nor spoke;
But the tears came trickling from his eyes
Like waters from the rock.

4 Sweet Jesus turned him round about,
To his mother's dear home went he,
And said, 'I have been in yonder town,
As after you may see:
I have been down in yonder town,
As far as the Holy Well;
There did I meet with as fine childrén
As any tongue can tell.

5 'I said, "God bless you every one,
And your bodies Christ save and see!
And now, little children, I'll play with you,
And you shall play with me."
But they made answer to me "No";
They were lords' and ladies' sons,
And I the meanest of them all,
Born in an ox's stall.'

6 'Though you are but a maiden's child,
Born in an ox's stall,
Thou art the Christ, the King of Heaven,
And the Saviour of them all!
Sweet Jesus, go down to yonder town,
As far as the Holy Well,
And take away those sinful souls,
And dip them deep in hell.'

7. 'Nay, nay,' sweet Jesus smiled and said;
'Nay, nay, that may not be,
For there are too many sinful souls
Crying out for the help of me.'
Then up spoke the angel Gabriel,
Upon a good set steven,
'Although you are but a maiden's child,
You are the King of Heaven!'

3. simple] *orig.* 'silly': see note to No. 2. 7. steven] voice, an Anglo-Saxon word; it occurs in Spenser and still survives in dialect. Sometimes corrupted to 'our good Saint Stephen'.

Two Herefordshire versions collated with Sandys, 1833, and with the fine version printed by Frank Sidgwick. Melody from Sandys.

57 DIVES AND LAZARUS

(GENERAL)

[*Copyright*, 1920, *by Stainer & Bell, Ltd.*] (R. V. W.)

This carol may also be sung to the second tune of No. 60 ('Come all you worthy Christian men').

* This bar must be all quavers in verse 14.

Traditional. *Ibid.*

AS it fell out upon one day,
Rich Dives made a feast,
And he invited all his friends
And gentry of the best.

2 Then Lazarus laid him down and down,
And down at Dives' door:
'Some meat and drink, brother Diverus,
Bestow upon the poor.'

3 'Thou'rt none of my brothers, Lazarus,
That liest begging at my door;
No meat, nor drink will I give thee,
Nor bestow upon the poor.'

4 *Then Lazarus laid him down and down,
All under Dives' wall:
'Some meat, some drink, brother Diverus,
For hunger starve I shall.'

5 *'Thou'rt none of my brothers, Lazarus,
That liest begging at my wall;
No meat, nor drink will I give thee,
For hunger starve you shall.'

6 *Then Lazarus laid him down and down,
And down at Dives' gate:
'Some meat! some drink! brother Diverus,
For Jesus Christ his sake.'

7 *' Thou'rt none of my brothers, Lazarus,
That liest begging at my gate ;
No meat, no drink will I give thee,
For Jesus Christ his sake.'

8 *Then Dives sent out his hungry dogs,
To bite him as he lay ;
They hadn't the power to bite one bite,
But licked his sores away.

9 *Then Dives sent to his merry men,
To worry poor Lazarus away ;
They'd not the power to strike one stroke,
But flung their whips away.

10 As it fell out upon one day,
Poor Lazarus sickened and died ;
There came two angels out of heaven,
His soul therein to guide.

11 ' Rise up ! rise up ! brother Lazarus,
And go along with me ;
For you've a place prepared in heaven,
To sit on an angel's knee.'

12 And it fell out upon one day,
Rich Dives sickened and died ;
There came two serpents out of hell,
His soul therein to guide.

13 ' Rise up ! rise up ! brother Diverus,
And come along with me ;
There is a place provided in hell
For wicked men like thee.'

14 *Then Dives looked up with his eyes
And saw poor Lazarus blest ;
' Give me one drop of water, brother Lazarus,
To quench my flaming thirst.

15. *' O, was I now but alive again
The space of one half hour !
O, that I had my peace again
Then the devil should have no power ! '

V. 13, l. 4. In some versions 'To sit upon a serpent's knee', which is generally preferred by choirs. The text is the result of a collation of the two Herefordshire texts mentioned below with the help of other versions. A version of eighteen verses is given by Mr. F. Sidgwick in his *Popular Carols*. The various recurring words (such as 'Dives ' (Divus), 'upon one day', &c.) have been made to conform with the version associated with the melody. The following verses are taken entirely from the other versions—2, 3, 11, 12, 13, 14, 15.

Melody from Mr. John Evans, Dilwyn. Text from Mr. John Evans and Mrs. Harris, Eardisley, &c. From *Twelve Traditional Carols from Herefordshire* (Leather and Vaughan Williams), Stainer & Bell.

The Elizabethan dramatist, Fletcher, mentions 'the merry ballad of Dives and Lazarus' in his *Monsieur Thomas*. Sylvester in 1861 claims to be the first to include it in a collection, giving it (but he was not a scrupulous transcriber) from an old Birmingham broadside. Hone includes it in his list, 1822 ; and Husk prints it from an eighteenth-century Worcester sheet. See also F. C. Child's *Ballads*, ii, p. 10.

58 JACOB'S LADDER

(GENERAL)

Traditional. *Ibid.*

AS Jacob with travel was weary one day,
At night on a stone for a pillow he lay;
He saw in a vision a ladder so high,
That its foot was on earth and its top in the sky:

Alleluya to Jesus, who died on the tree,
And hath raised up a ladder of mercy for me.

2 This ladder is long, it is strong and well-made,
Has stood hundreds of years and is not yet decayed;
Many millions have climbed it and reached Sion's hill,
And thousands by faith are climbing it still:

3 Come let us ascend! all may climb it who will;
For the angels of Jacob are guarding it still:
And remember, each step that by faith we pass o'er,
Some prophet or martyr hath trod it before:

4. And when we arrive at the haven of rest,
We shall hear the glad words, 'Come up hither, ye blest,
Here are regions of light, here are mansions of bliss.'
O, who would not climb such a ladder as this?

This is apparently a carol to which new words were fitted under the influence of the Methodist revival. It is printed here with its traditional melody, which Stainer made familiar in 1871.

WELSH CAROL

(GENERAL : WHITSUNTIDE)

(Dr. Caradog Roberts.)

[*By permission of the Caniedydd Committee, Welsh Congregational Union.*]

Welsh. *Pr. K. E. Roberts.*

AWAKE were they only, those shepherds so lonely,
On guard in that silence profound :
When colour had faded, when night-time had shaded
Their senses from sight and from sound,
Lo, then broke a wonder, then drifted asunder
The veils from the splendour of God,
When light from the Holy came down to the lowly,
And heaven to the earth that they trod.
[*Repeat last four lines.*]

2. May light now enfold us, O Lord, for behold us
Like shepherds, from tumult withdrawn,
Nor hearing, nor seeing, all other care fleeing,
We wait the ineffable dawn.
O Spirit all-knowing, thou source overflowing,
O move in the darkness around,
That sight may be in us, true hearing to win us
Glad tidings where Christ may be found.
[*Repeat last four lines.*]

A paraphrase of the Welsh Carol, 'Roedd yn y wlad honno'.

60

JOB

FIRST TUNE

Traditional (*2 tunes*).

Ibid.

COME all you worthy Christian men
That dwell upon this land,
Don't spend your time in rioting;
Remember you're but man.
Be watchful for your latter end;
Be ready for your call. [world;
There are many changes in this
Some rise while others fall.

2 Now, Job he was a patient man,
The richest in the East:
When he was brought to poverty,
His sorrows soon increased.
He bore them all most patiently;
From sin he did refrain;
He always trusted in the Lord;
He soon got rich again.

60 JOB

SECOND TUNE.

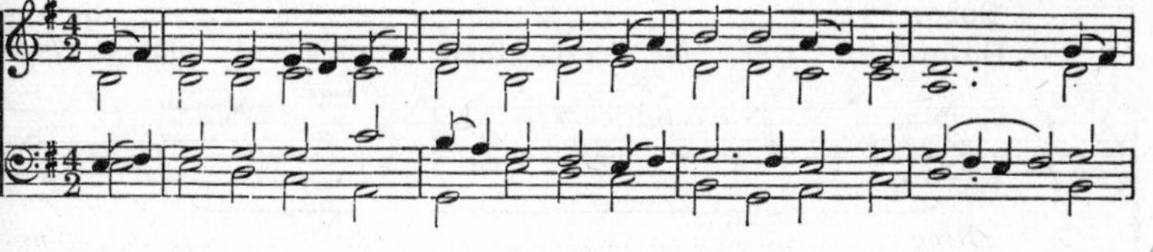

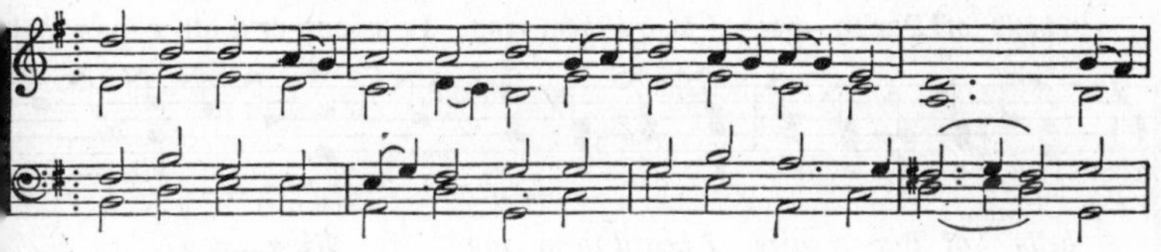

(When sung to the 2nd tune the last 4 lines should be repeated.)

3 Come all you worthy Christian men
That are so very poor,
Remember how poor Lazarus
Lay at the rich man's door,
While begging of the crumbs of bread
That from his table fell.
The Scriptures do inform us all
That in heaven he doth dwell.

4. The time, alas, it soon will come
When parted we shall be ;
But all the difference it will make
Is in joy and misery ;
And we must give a strict account
Of great as well as small.
Believe me, now, dear Christian friends,
That God will judge us all.

Taken by Cecil Sharp from Mrs. Woodberry, Ash Priors, Somerset, *Folk Songs from Somerset*, No. 88 (*by permission of Novello & Co., Ltd.*). The second tune was noted by the late A. J. Hipkins in Westminster and printed in *English County Songs* to the words of 'Dives and Lazarus', but it probably belongs to 'Job'. It belongs more properly, however, to the above words.

61 DOWN IN YON FOREST

(GENERAL)

(R. V. W.)

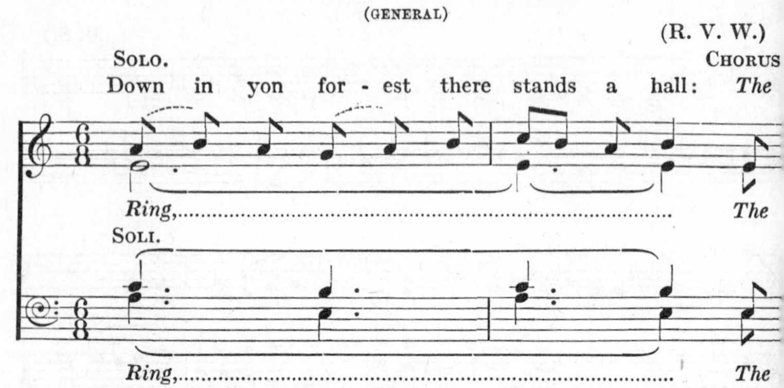

NOTE.—It is suggested that the Solo portion be sung without harmony in the opening verses; also that the Solo portion be divided among various voices (male and female).

Traditional. *Ibid.*

DOWN in yon forest there stands a hall:
The bells of Paradise I heard them ring:
It's covered all over with purple and pall:
And I love my Lord Jesus above anything.

2 In that hall there stands a bed:
It's covered all over with scarlet so red:

3 At the bed-side there lies a stone:
Which the sweet Virgin Mary knelt upon:

4 Under that bed there runs a flood:
The one half runs water, the other runs blood:

5 At the bed's foot there grows a thorn:
Which ever blows blossom since he was born:

6.*Over that bed the moon shines bright:
Denoting our Saviour was born this night:

Melody and text taken from Mr. Hall, Castleton, Derbyshire, by R. Vaughan Williams *Eight Traditional Carols*), Stainer & Bell. Text unaltered except for (4) *flood* for 'river', 5) *bed's foot* for 'foot of the bed'.

Cf. another folk version in No. 184. The earliest version is one only found in Richard Hill's MS. (cf. No. 36), and is printed below; it is in a different metre, but the hall, the bed, the knight of No. 184, the maid, and the stone are all there, and the words 'Corpus Christi' are written on the stone; the mystical meaning of the fifteenth-century original was therefore ucharistic, the altar and the sacrifice, while the thorn (not in the Hill MS.) and other allusions f this and the other two versions point to an interweaving of the legend of the Holy Grail. ee F. Sidgwick, *Notes and Queries* (1905), iv. 181; *Folk-Song Soc. J.* (1910), iv. 52.

The text of the carol in the Hill MS. (*c.* 1500), printed by Dyboski and others is: *Lully, lulley, ully, lulley! The falcon hath borne my make away.* 1. He bare him up, he bare him down, He bare him in to an orchard brown [*Refrain*]. 2. In that orchard there was an hall, That was anged with purple and pall. 3. And in that hall there was a bed, It was hanged with gold so ed. 4. And in that bed there lieth a knight, His wounds bleeding day and night. 5. By that ed's side kneeleth a may, And she weepeth both night and day. 6. And by that bed's side here standeth a stone, 'Corpus Christi' written thereon.

ALL AND SOME

(GENERAL, MEDIEVAL)

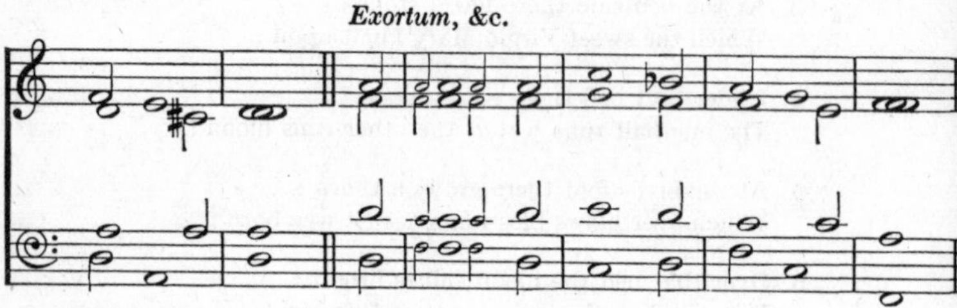

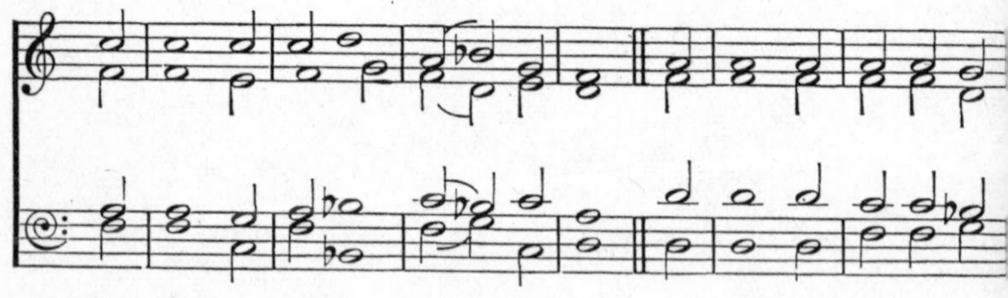

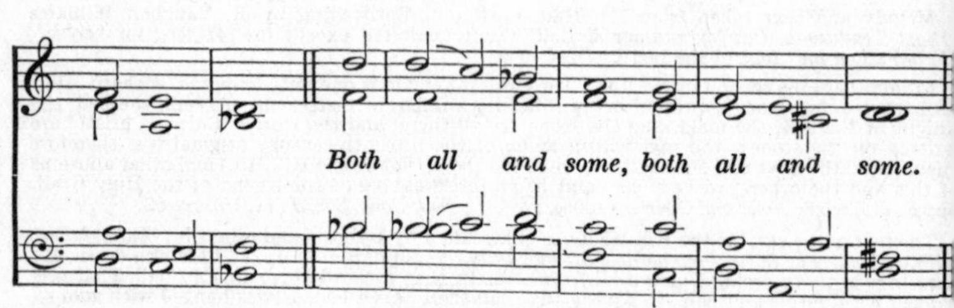

The Nowell refrain may be sung again after the last verse.

c. 1450. *Ibid.*

NOWELL sing we, both all and some,
Now Rex pacificus is ycome.
Exortum est in love and lysse.
Now Christ his gree he gan us gysse,
And with his body us brought to bliss,
Both all and some.

2 *De fructu ventris* of Mary bright,
Both God and man in her alight,
Out of disease he did us dight :

3 *Puer natus* to us was sent,
To bliss us bought, fro bale us blent,
And else to woe we had ywent :

4 *Lux fulgebit* with love and light,
In Mary mild his pennon pight,
In her took kind with manly might :

5. *Gloria tibi*, ay, and bliss,
God unto his grace he us wysse,
The rent of heaven that we not miss :

1. *Exortum est*] it is risen up. lysse] comfort, joy. gree (in MS. 'gre he')] favour. gysse] to prepare, attire (=guise). 2. *De fructu*, &c.] of the fruit of the womb. disease ('dysese')] dis-ease, discomfort, misery. dight] orig. dictate; prepare, hence make ready, array (revived by Walter Scott in the last sense). 3. *Puer natus*] a boy born. fro] from. bale] sorrow. blent] blenched, turned aside. ywent] gone. 4. *Lux*, &c.] the light will shine. pight] pitched. kind] nature. 5. *Gloria tibi*] glory to thee. wysse] guide. rent] tenure.

This carol from the Selden MS. (B. 26), *c.* 1450 (printed (not quite correctly) in *Early Bodleian Music*), where it is preserved with its original music. Alteration of its interesting archaisms would have meant rewriting; we have therefore only modernized the spelling.

63 GREEN GROW'TH THE HOLLY

(GENERAL)

(M. T.)

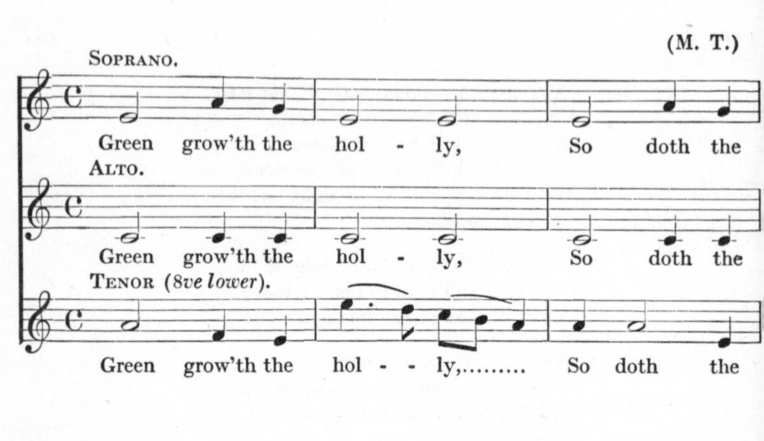

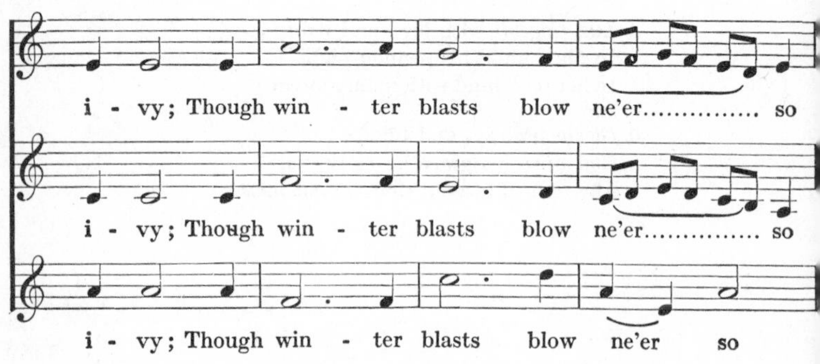

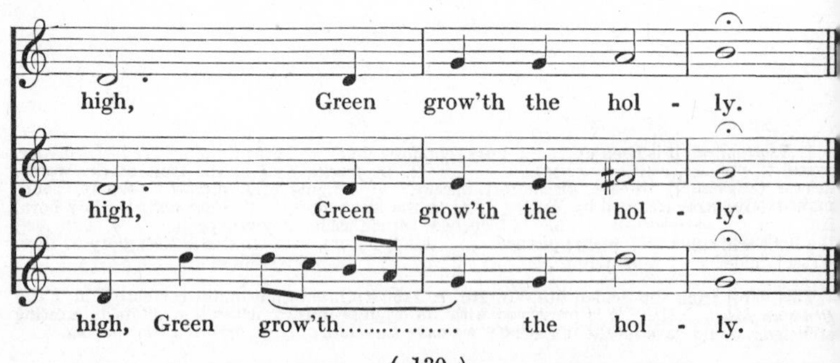

16th century. *O.B.C. version.*

GREEN grow'th the holly,
So doth the ivy;
Though winter blasts blow ne'er so high,
Green grow'th the holly.

2 Gay are the flowers,
Hedgerows and ploughlands;
The days grow longer in the sun,
Soft fall the showers.

3 Full gold the harvest,
Grain for thy labour;
With God must work for daily bread,
Else, man, thou starvest.

4 Fast fall the shed leaves,
Russet and yellow;
But resting-buds are snug and safe
Where swung the dead leaves.

5. Green grow'th the holly,
So doth the ivy;
The God of life can never die,
Hope! saith the holly.

The music, one of the sixteenth-century songs attributed to Henry VIII, has survived in this refrain, 'Green grow'th the holly', &c. (attached to a love-song in a different metre and with no tune extant); it has been transcribed by Lady Mary Trefusis, and other verses have been added in the metre of the old melody.

64 A NEW DIAL

(GENERAL)

(M. S.)

Traditional. 1625.

IN those twelve days let us be glad,
For God of his power hath all things made.
What are they that are but one?
What are they that are but one?
One God, one Baptism, and one Faith,
One Truth there is, the scripture saith:

2 What are they that are but two?
Two Testaments, the old and new,
We do acknowledge to be true:

3 What are they that are but three?
Three Persons are in Trinity
Which make one God in unity:

4 What are they that are but four ?
Four sweet Evangelists there are,
Christ's birth, life, death, which do declare :

5 *What are they that are but five ?
Five Senses, like five kings, maintain
In every man a several reign :

6 *What are they that are but six ?
Six Days to labour is not wrong,
For God himself did work so long :

7 *What are they that are but seven ?
Seven Liberal Arts hath God sent down
With divine skill man's soul to crown :

8 *What are they that are but eight ?
Eight Beatitudes are there given ;
Use them aright and go to heaven :

9 *What are they that are but nine ?
Nine Muses, like the heavens' nine spheres,
With sacred tunes entice our ears :

10 *What are they that are but ten ?
Ten Statutes God to Moses gave,
Which, kept or broke, do spill or save :

11 *What are they that are but eleven ?
Eleven thousand Virgins did partake,
And suffered death for Jesus' sake :

12. *What are they that are but twelve ?
Twelve are attending on God's Son ;
Twelve make our Creed. The Dial's done :

In an almanack of 1625, in the Bagford collection. Gilbert (1822) prints a version too rough to be sung without constant mispronunciation and alteration of the music ; this version is smoothed by Sandys, but is still almost unsingable. The refrain (from Gilbert) is not given in the almanack, but was probably then known. This 1625 version is evidently by a scholar working on a much older carol ; and it is curious to see how the scholarly parts are absent from the folk-version of 1822. Two verses (and the tune) are from Sandys : v. 8 (Gilbert's singer gave 'Altitudes' instead of 'Beatitudes') where the Almanack has, 'Eight in Noah's Ark alive were found, When (in a word) the World lay drown'd'; and v. 11 (the same, but more confused, in Gilbert), where the Almanack rejects the Virgins of Cologne, only to give a duplicate Apostle verse, 'Eleven with Christ in Heaven do dwell, The Twelfth for ever burns in Hell'.

The Seven Liberal Arts (changed in Gilbert to 'Seven Days in week') and the Eleven thousand Virgins point to a medieval origin for both verses. V. 5, We now know that there are more than five senses. V. 7, The Seven Liberal arts (the *Trivium* and *Quadrivium* of thirteenth-century schoolmen, and of St. Augustine, Boethius, and Cassiodorus) were—grammar, rhetoric, and dialectic, arithmetic, geometry, astronomy, and music. V. 9, The Nine Muses of the Greeks were—Calliope (epic song), Clio (history), Euterpe (lyric song), Thalia (comedy), Melpomene (tragedy), Terpsichore (dancing), Erato (erotic poetry), Polymnia (sacred songs), Urania (astronomy). V. 11, There are various explanations of the extravagant legend of St. Ursula and the Eleven Thousand Virgins (familiar through the paintings of Memlinc and Carpaccio) : one is that it originated in an inscription to 'Ursula et Undecimilla, virgines', another that there were originally Ursula and eleven Martyrs, the MM. being read as 'thousand'. V. 12, The Twelve Apostles, and the twelve articles of the Apostles' Creed ; each article is sometimes represented in art on a scroll held by an Apostle.

65 THE DECREE

FIRST TUNE.

(GENERAL)

(M. S.)

FA-BURDEN (Melody in the Bass).

Traditional (2 *tunes*). ***Ibid.***

LET Christians all with one accord rejoice,
And praises sing, with heart as well as voice,
To God on high, for glorious things he 's done,
In sending us his best-belovèd Son.

2 What pains and labours did not Christ endure
To save our souls and happiness secure!
Was always doing good, to let us see
By his example what we ought to be.

3 He made the blind to see, the lame to go,
He raised the dead, which none but he could do:
He cured the lepers of infected evils,
And by his mighty power he cast out devils.

4 But yet for all the wonders that he wrought,
Ungrateful men still his destruction sought:
Then to a cross the Saviour of mankind
Was led, an harmless Lamb, as was designed.

5. Thus blessèd Jesus freely did resign
His precious soul to save both thine and mine;
Then let us all his mercies highly prize,
Who for our sins was made a sacrifice.

Selected verses from the long carol of twenty-three, rather oddly called 'The Black Decree' (from a line about the massacre of the Innocents), in the Dudley collection, *A Good Christmas Box*, 1847, which preserved the words. The verses were evidently written by one author, and not earlier than the eighteenth century, perhaps to replace some older folk-carol which had been associated with the tune. Stainer restored the second traditional melody; the first melody, also proper to the words, was noted by Cecil Sharp in an unpublished MS.

THE DECREE

SECOND TUNE.

(GENERAL)

(M. S.)

Traditional (2 *tunes*). *Ibid.*

LET Christians all with one accord rejoice,
And praises sing, with heart as well as voice,
To God on high, for glorious things he 's done,
In sending us his best-belovèd Son.

2 What pains and labours did not Christ endure
To save our souls and happiness secure!
Was always doing good, to let us see
By his example what we ought to be.

3 He made the blind to see, the lame to go,
He raised the dead, which none but he could do:
He cured the lepers of infected evils,
And by his mighty power he cast out devils.

4 But yet for all the wonders that he wrought,
Ungrateful men still his destruction sought:
Then to a cross the Saviour of mankind
Was led, an harmless Lamb, as was designed.

5. Thus blessèd Jesus freely did resign
His precious soul to save both thine and mine;
Then let us all his mercies highly prize,
Who for our sins was made a sacrifice.

See note to No. 65 on p. 135.

66 THE CHERRY TREE CAROL

Part I

(GENERAL, LEGENDARY)

Traditional (*3 tunes*). *Ibid.*

JOSEPH was an old man,
And an old man was he,
When he wedded Mary
In the land of Galilee.

2 Joseph and Mary walked
Through an orchard good,
Where was cherries and berries
So red as any blood.

3 *Joseph and Mary walked
Through an orchard green,
Where was berries and cherries
As thick as might be seen.

4 O then bespoke Mary,
With words so meek and mild,
'Pluck me one cherry, Joseph,
For I am with child.'

5 *O then bespoke Joseph,
With answer most unkind,
'Let him pluck thee a cherry
That brought thee now with child.'

6 *O then bespoke the baby
Within his mother's womb—
'Bow down then the tallest tree
For my mother to have some.'

7 Then bowed down the highest tree,
Unto his mother's hand.
Then she cried, 'See, Joseph,
I have cherries at command.'

8 *O then bespake Joseph—
'I have done Mary wrong;
But now cheer up, my dearest
And do not be cast down.

9 'O eat your cherries, Mary,
O eat your cherries now,
O eat your cherries, Mary,
That grow upon the bough.'

10 *Then Mary plucked a cherry,
As red as any blood;
Then Mary she went homewards
All with her heavy load.

Part II

(CHRISTMAS EVE)

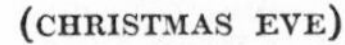

(M. S.)

Last verse of Part II begins here.

11 As Joseph was a-walking,
He heard an angel sing:
'This night there shall be born
On earth our heavenly King;

12 'He neither shall be born
In housen nor in hall,
Nor in the place of Paradise,
But in an ox's stall.

13 'He neither shall be clothèd
In purple nor in pall,
But all in fair linen
As wear the babies all.

14 'He neither shall be rockèd
In silver nor in gold,
But in a wooden cradle
That rocks upon the mould.

15 'He neither shall be christened
In white wine nor red,
But with fair spring water
As we were christenèd.'

Part III

(LENT : PASSIONTIDE)

(M. S.)

16 Then Mary took her young son,
And set him on her knee :
Saying, 'My dear son, tell me,
Tell how this world shall be.'

17 'O I shall be as dead, mother,
As stones are in the wall ;
O the stones in the streets, mother,
Shall sorrow for me all.

18. 'On Easter-day, dear mother,
My rising up shall be ;
O the sun and the moon, mother,
Shall both arise with me.'

This was one of the most popular carols, and was printed in broadsides in all parts of England. Hone gives a version, 1822, and Sandys another, 1833, identical down to v. 8 with Bullen's. The same legend, with a dialogue no less 'unkind', occurs in *The Coventry Mystery Plays*. Our first tune is from Husk, our second was preserved by Fyfe in his *Carols* of 1860, our third is also traditional. The whole story of carol-music is summed up in an incident related by Baring-Gould: about 1865 he was teaching carols to a party of mill-girls in the West Riding; 'and amongst them that by Dr. Gauntlett—" Saint Joseph was a walking "—when they burst out with "Nay! we know one a great deal better nor yond"; and, lifting up their voices, they sang'.

67 SONG OF THE NUNS OF CHESTER

(GENERAL: MEDIEVAL)

Chester MS. (*c.* 1425). *Ibid.*

(arr. J. H. ARNOLD.)

TWO BOYS.
CHORUS.
Qui cre - a - vit coe - lum, Lul - ly, lul - ly, lu,............
(*Softly throughout.*)

BOYS.
CHORUS.
Nas - ci - tur in stab - u - lo, By, by, by, by, by,........

BOYS.
CHORUS, &c.
Rex qui re - git sec - u - lum, Lul - ly, lul - ly, lu..........

2. Jo - seph e - mit pa - nic - u - lum, Lul-ly, lul - ly, lu,.......
Ma - ter in - vol-vit pu - er - um, By, by, by, by, by,......
Et po - nit in prae - se - pi - o, Lul-ly, lul - ly, lu,........

3. In - ter an - i - ma - li - a, Lul - ly, lul - ly, lu,............
Ja - cent mun-di gau - di - a, By, by, by, by, by,........
Dul - cis su - per om - ni - a, Lul - ly, lul - ly, lu,..........

4. Lac-tat ma-ter do-mi-ni, Lul-ly, lul-ly, lu,.........
5. Ro-ga ma-ter fi-li-um, Lul-ly, lul-ly, lu,.........
Os-cu-la-tur par-vu-lum, By, by, by, by, by,..........
Ut det no-bis gau-di-um, By, by, by, by, by,..........
Et a-do-rat do-mi-num, Lul-ly, lul-ly, lu.........
In pe-ren-ni glo-ri-a, Lul-ly, lul-ly, lu.........

6. In sem-pi-ter-na sae-cu-la, Lul-ly, lul-ly, lu..........
In e-ter-num et ul-tra, By, by, by, by, by,.........
Det no-bis su-a gau-di-a, Lul-ly, lul-ly, lu..........

This lullaby, in which the nuns of St. Mary's gave vent to their womanly instincts, would only lose by translation. The text and music are from the Processional of the nunnery of St. Mary, Chester (printed by the Henry Bradshaw Society), and we give it just as it stands, with the addition of Mr. Arnold's harmonies.

THE TRUTH FROM ABOVE

(GENERAL)

Andante sostenuto. (R. V. W.)

1 This is the truth sent from a - bove, The
first thing which I do re - late
truth of God, the God of love, There - fore don't turn me
Is that God did man cre - ate ; The next thing which to
from your door, But hearken all both rich and poor............ 2 The
you I'll tell— Wo-man was made with man to dwell........
1st time.
1st time.
p

2nd time.
.... 3 And we were heirs to end-less woes, Till
.... at that sea-son of the year Our
2nd time.
God the Lord did in-ter-pose; And so a pro-mise soon did run That
blest Re-deem-er did ap-pear; He here did live, and here did preach, And
1st time.
he would re-deem us by his Son.................... 4 And
ma-ny thou-sands
1st time.

2nd time.
he did teach..................... 5. Thus he in love to
2nd time.
cres.
f
us be-haved, To show us how we must be saved; And
molto rall.
if you want to know the way, Be pleas'd to hear what he did say.
colla voce.

Version for Unaccompanied Singing.

THIS is the truth sent from above,
The truth of God, the God of love,
Therefore don't turn me from your door,
But hearken all both rich and poor.

2 The first thing which I do relate
Is that God did man create ;
The next thing which to you I'll tell—
Woman was made with man to dwell.

3 And we were heirs to endless woes,
Till God the Lord did interpose ;
And so a promise soon did run
That he would redeem us by his Son.

4 And at that season of the year
Our blest Redeemer did appear ;
He here did live, and here did preach,
And many thousands he did teach.

5. Thus he in love to us behaved,
To show us how we must be saved ;
And if you want to know the way,
Be pleased to hear what he did say.

Melody and part of text from Mr. W. Jenkins, Kings Pyon, Herefordshire. Melody included by permission of Mrs. Leather. From *Eight Traditional English Carols* (Vaughan Williams), Stainer & Bell. For notes on the text and melody see the *Journal of the Folk-Song Society*, iv. 17.

For another tune and different version of text see Sharp, *English Folk-Carols*, xviii. The vers'on in *A Good Christmas Box* has sixteen verses.

69 THE SAVIOUR'S WORK

(GENERAL : NATIVITY)

(E. M.)

Traditional. *Ibid.*

THE babe in Bethlem's manger laid
In humble form so low;
By wondering angels is surveyed
Through all his scenes of woe:

Nowell, Nowell, now sing a Saviour's birth,
All hail his coming down to earth
Who raises us to Heaven!

2 A Saviour! sinners all around
Sing, shout the wondrous word;
Let every bosom hail the sound,
A Saviour! Christ the Lord:

3 For not to sit on David's throne
With worldly pomp and joy,
He came on earth for sin to atone,
And Satan to destroy:

4 To preach the word of life divine,
And feed with living bread,
To heal the sick with hand benign
And raise to life the dead:

5 *He preached, he suffered, bled and died
Uplift 'twixt earth and skies;
In sinners' stead was crucified,
For sin a sacrifice:

6. *Well may we sing a Saviour's birth,
Who need the grace so given,
And hail his coming down to earth,
Who raises us to Heaven:

In the Staffordshire *A Good Christmas Box*, 1847, without the chorus, which is given, with the tune, in Rimbault's *Old English Carols*, 1865.

70 JOYS SEVEN

(GENERAL)

Traditional. *Ibid.*

THE first good joy that Mary had,
It was the joy of one;
To see the blessèd Jesus Christ
When he was first her son:

When he was first her son, good man:
And blessèd may he be,
Both Father, Son, and Holy Ghost,
To all eternity.

2 The next good joy that Mary had,
It was the joy of two ;
To see her own son, Jesus Christ
To make the lame to go :

3 The next good joy that Mary had,
It was the joy of three ;
To see her own son, Jesus Christ
To make the blind to see :

4 The next good joy that Mary had,
It was the joy of four ;
To see her own son, Jesus Christ
To read the Bible o'er :

5 The next good joy that Mary had,
It was the joy of five ;
To see her own son, Jesus Christ
To bring the dead alive :

6 The next good joy that Mary had,
It was the joy of six ;
To see her own son, Jesus Christ
Upon the crucifix :

7. The next good joy that Mary had,
It was the joy of seven ;
To see her own son, Jesus Christ
To wear the crown of heaven :

2. Adding 'To make the lame to go, good man', and so on in all verses.

Some versions have for v. 6 'to bear the crucifix'. The version in Hill's MS., in another metre, gives the seeing Jesus on the rood as the third joy: his five are the Annunciation, Nativity, Crucifixion, Harrowing of Hell, Ascension. The Sloane MS. 2593 of the fifteenth century also gives the witnessing of the Crucifixion as a 'joy of great might'. This carol was one of the most popular and was annually reprinted in eighteenth-century broadsides all over England. In late eighteenth-century and nineteenth-century sheets it is sometimes extended to twelve. A melody was noted by Cecil Sharp with a Ten Joy version (8, 'To bring the croked straight', 9, 'Turn water into wine', 10, 'Bring up ten gentlemen') from Mrs. Duddridge at Mark, Somerset—*Folk Songs from Somerset* (No. 125) and *English Folk Carols*. A Gloucestershire version gives Twelve Joys (10, 'To write with a golden pen', 11, 'To have the keys of heaven', 12, 'To have the keys of hell'); Husk gives Twelve from a Newcastle sheet, with many variants (e.g. 10, 'To write without a pen'). The Seven Joy versions are older and less corrupt descendants of the Seven Joys of the Sloane MS. Bramley & Stainer (1871) printed the traditional air here given. W. J. Phillips in *Carols* (*c.* 1890) stated that he remembered the unemployed, *c.* 1850, tramping with shovels through the London snow and singing to the tune, 'We've got no work to do-oo-oo'. We can corroborate this for a later period, *c.* 1890, only they sang, 'We're all froze out'.

71 MY DANCING DAY

(GENERAL)

(M. S.)

Traditional. Ibid.

TO-MORROW shall be my dancing day:
I would my true love did so chance
To see the legend of my play,
To call my true love to my dance:

Sing O my love, O my love, my love, my love;
This have I done for my true love.

2 Then was I born of a virgin pure,
Of her I took fleshly substánce;
Thus was I knit to man's natúre,
To call my true love to my dance:

3 In a manger laid and wrapped I was,
So very poor, this was my chance,
Betwixt an ox and a silly poor ass,
To call my true love to my dance:

4 Then afterwards baptized I was;
The Holy Ghost on me did glance,
My Father's voice heard from above,
To call my true love to my dance:

Part II

(LENT: PASSIONTIDE)

5 Into the desert I was led,
Where I fasted without substánce;
The devil bade me make stones my bread,
To have me break my true love's dance:

6 The Jews on me they made great suit,
And with me made great variance,
Because they loved darkness rather than light,
To call my true love to my dance:

7 For thirty pence Judas me sold,
His covetousness for to advance;
'Mark whom I kiss, the same do hold,'
The same is he shall lead the dance:

Part III

(PASSIONTIDE: EASTER: ASCENSION)

8 Before Pilate the Jews me brought,
Where Barabbas had deliveránce;
They scourged me and set me at nought,
Judged me to die to lead the dance:

9 Then on the cross hangèd I was,
Where a spear to my heart did glance;
There issued forth both water and blood,
To call my true love to my dance:

10 Then down to hell I took my way
For my true love's deliverance,
And rose again on the third day,
Up to my true love and the dance:

11. Then up to heaven I did ascend,
Where now I dwell in sure substánce,
On the right hand of God, that man
May come unto the general dance:

Words and melody from Sandys, 1833. In many broadsides. This is probably based on a secular song, but the interweaving of the two love motives is as ancient and widespread as the association of religion with the dance. The text seems to go back earlier than the seventeenth century.

72 WONDROUS WORKS

(GENERAL)

(M. S.)

Traditional. *Ibid.*

WHEN Jesus Christ was twelve years old,
As holy Scripture plainly told,
He then disputed brave and bold
Amongst the learnèd doctors:

Then praise the Lord both high and low,
'Cause he his wondrous works doth shew,
That we at last to heaven might go,
Where Christ in glory reigneth.

2 At thirty years he then began
To preach the Gospel unto man,
And all Judaea wondered then
To hear his heavenly doctrine :

3 The woman's son, that dead did lie,
When Christ our Saviour passèd by,
He rose to life immediately,
To her great joy and comfort :

4 Likewise he healed the lepers ten,
Whose bodies were full filthy then ;
And there returnèd back but one
Him humble thanks to render :

5 *More of his heavenly might to shew,
Himself upon the sea did go ;
And there was none that e'er did so,
But only Christ our Saviour :

Part II

(PASSIONTIDE : EASTER : ASCENSION)

6 When they bereaved his life so good,
The moon was turnèd into blood,
The earth and temple shaking stood,
And graves full wide did open :

7 Then some of them that stood thereby
With voices loud began to cry :
'This was the Son of God truly,'
Without any fear or doubting :

8 For, as he said, it came so plain,
That in three days he rose again ;
Although he suffered bitter pain,
Both heaven and earth he conquered :

9. Then afterwards ascended he
To Heaven in glorious majesty ;
With him God grant us all to be
In Heaven with him rejoicing :

As in Gilbert, 1822 (15 verses), with two corrections from Sandys (1833), who also gives the tune.

II. FOREIGN CAROLS

73 DUTCH CAROL

(CHRISTMAS)

(arr. JULIUS RÖNTGEN.)

mf
f
A - mor, a - mor, a - mor, a - mor, a - mor, quam dul - cis est a - mor!

Dutch, 1599. *Tr. R. C. Trevelyan*

A CHILD is born in Bethlehem
Awaiteth him all Jerusalem.
Amor! quam dulcis est amor!

2 The Son took upon him humanity,
That to the Father thus draws nigh:

3 The angels above were singing then,
Below were rejoicing the shepherd men:

4. Now let us all with the angels sing,
Yea, now let our hearts for gladness spring:

1. *Amor*, &c.] Love! how sweet is love!
We owe the original of this carol, 'Een kint gheboren in Bethlehem' to the kindness of Professor Röntgen in Holland.

74 FLEMISH CAROL

(CHRISTMAS AND NEW YEAR)

(arr. JULIUS RÖNTGEN.)

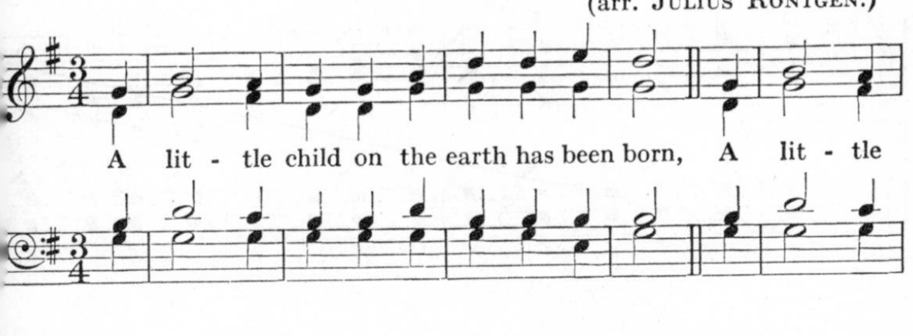
A lit - tle child on the earth has been born, A lit - tle

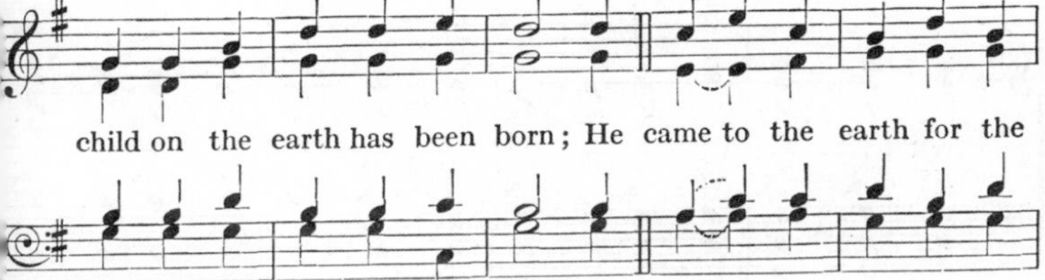
child on the earth has been born; He came to the earth for the

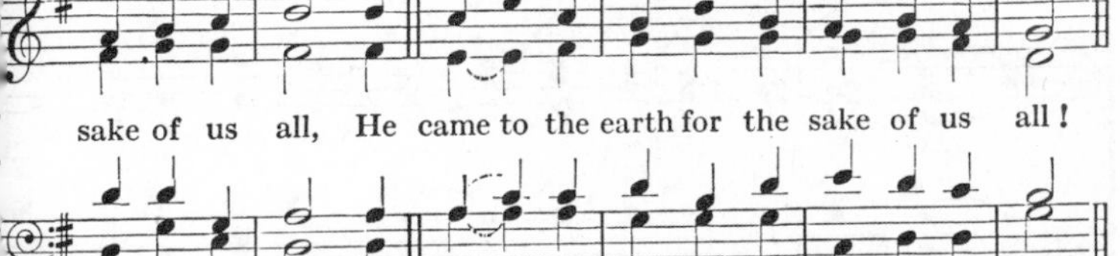
sake of us all, He came to the earth for the sake of us all!

Old Flemish. *Tr. R. C. Trevelyan.*

A LITTLE child on the earth has been born;
He came to the earth for the sake of us all!

2 He came to earth but no home did he find,
He came to earth and its cross did he bear.

3. He came to earth for the sake of us all
And wishes us all a happy New Year.

As in the case of No. 73, we owe the original, 'Er is een kindeken geboren op d'aard', to Professor Röntgen.

75

BETHLEHEM

(CHRISTMAS)

(arr. CHARLES GOUNOD.)

French. *Fléchier, Tr. Maurice F. Bell.*

DANS cette étable
Que Jésus est charmant,
Qu'il est aimable
Dans cet abaissement !
Que d'attraits à la fois !
Tous les palais des rois
N'ont rien de comparable
Aux charmes que je vois
Dans cette étable !

2 Que sa puissance
Paraît bien en ce jour,
Malgré l'enfance
Où l'a réduit l'amour !
Notre ennemi dompté,
L'enfer déconcerté,
Font voir qu'en sa naissance
Rien n'est si redouté
Que sa puissance.

3 Sans le connaître,
Dans sa divinité
Je vois paraître
Toute sa majesté :
Dans cet enfant qui naît,
À son aspect qui plaît,
Je découvre mon maître
Et je sens ce qu'il est
Sans le connaître.

4. *Plus de misère !
Un Dieu souffre pour nous
Et de son père
Apaise le courroux ;
C'est en notre faveur
Qu'il naît dans la douleur ;
Pouvait-il pour nous plaire
Unir à sa grandeur
Plus de mièsre ?

In that poor stable
How charming Jesus lies,
Words are not able
To fathom his emprise!
No palace of a King
Can show so rare a thing
In history or fable
As that of which we sing
In that poor stable.

2 See here God's power
In weakness fortifies
This infant hour
Of Love's epiphanies !
Our foe is now despoiled,
The wiles of hell are foiled ;
On earth there grows a flower
Pure, undefiled, unsoiled—
See here God's power !

3 Though far from knowing
The babe's divinity,
Mine eyes are growing
To see his majesty ;
For lo ! the new-born child
Upon me sweetly smiled,
The gift of faith bestowing ;
Thus I my Lord descry,
Though far from knowing.

4. No more affliction !
For God endures our pains ;
In crucifixion
The Son victorious reigns.
For us the sufferer brings
Salvation in his wings ;
To win our souls' affection
Could he, the King of kings,
Know more affliction ?

We give the original as well as a translation of this French carol, which is often called Gounod's Bethlehem' because the traditional tune was arranged by C. F. Gounod (1818-93).

76 ES IST EIN' ROS'

(CHRISTMAS)

In moderate time. (arr. MICHAEL PRAETORIUS.)

The barring of this tune is necessarily irregular. But its performance will be found to be easy if it is remembered that the time-value of a crotchet is the same throughout.

German, 15th century. *Ibid*

Es ist ein' Ros' entsprungen
  Aus einer Wurzel zart,
Als uns die Alten sungen :
  Aus Jesse kam die Art ;
    Und hat ein Blümlein bracht,
      Mitten im kalten Winter,
    Wohl zu der halben Nacht.

2 Das Röslein, das ich meine,
  Davon Jesaias sagt,
Ist Maria die reine,
  Die uns dies Blümlein bracht ;
    Aus Gottes ew'gem Rat
      Hat sie ein Kindlein g'boren,
    Ist blieb'n ein' reine Magd.

3. Wir bitten dich von Herzen,
  Maria, Rose zart,
Durch dieses Blümlein's Schmerzen,
  Die er empfunden hat,
    Wollst uns behülflich sein,
      Dass wir ihm mögen machen
    Ein' Wohnung hübsch und fein !

This carol is here printed with the original German words, because our book would not be complete without it. English words have been set to the tune in the *English Hymnal* (19) and *Songs of Praise* (46).

The fifteenth-century words and melody are in the *Speierschen Gesangbuch*, Cologne, 1600; the setting by Praetorius in *Musae Sioniae*, 1609.

77 SONG OF THE CRIB

(CHRISTMAS)

Moderately fast. VOICES IN UNISON. (R. V. W.)

Jo - seph dear - est, Jo - seph mine, Help me cra - dle the
child di - vine; God re-ward thee and all that's thine In
Par - a - dise, So prays the mo - ther Ma - ry.

CHORUS.
He came a-mong us at Christ-mas tide, At Christ-mas tide, In
Beth-le-hem; Men shall bring him from far and wide Love's
di-a-dem: Je-sus, Je-sus,

Lo, he comes, and loves, and saves, and frees us!

German, 15th century. Tr. N. S. T.

JOSEPH dearest, Joseph mine,
Help me cradle the child divine;
God reward thee and all that's
In Paradise, [thine
So prays the mother Mary.

2 Gladly, dear one, lady mine,
Help I cradle this child of thine;
God's own light on us both shall
In Paradise, [shine
As prays the mother Mary.

CHORUS

He came among us at Christmas tide,
At Christmas tide,
In Bethlehem; [*wide*
Men shall bring him from far and
Love's diadem:
Jesus, Jesus, [*and frees us!*
Lo, he comes, and loves, and saves,

3 *Servant* (1)
Peace to all that have goodwill!
God, who heaven and earth doth
fill,
Comes to turn us away from ill,
And lies so still
Within the crib of Mary.

4 *Servant* (2)
All shall come and bow the knee;
Wise and happy their souls shall be,
Loving such a divinity,
As all may see
In Jesus, Son of Mary.

5 *Servant* (3)
Now is born Emmanuel,
Prophesied once by Ezekiel,
Promised Mary by Gabriel—
Ah, who can tell
Thy praises, Son of Mary!

6 *Servant* (4)
Thou my lazy heart hast stirred,
Thou, the Father's eternal Word,
Greater than aught that ear hath
Thou tiny bird [heard,
Of love, thou Son of Mary.

7 *Servant* (1)
Sweet and lovely little one, [Son,
Thou princely, beautiful, God's own
Without thee all of us were undone;
Our love is won
By thine, O Son of Mary.

8. *Servant* (2)
Little man, and God indeed,
Little and poor, thou art all we
need;
We will follow where thou dost lead,
And we will heed
Our brother, born of Mary.

'Joseph lieber, Joseph mein, Hilf mir wiegen mein Kindelein' occurs in a MS. at Leipzig University, *c.* 1500, as part of a mystery play acted in church around the crib. It would make to-day a beautiful little Christmas play for children, Mary and Joseph singing vv. 1 and 2, and then the children singing the chorus. In the old arrangement the chorus was not sung after every verse; the remaining verses can be sung by one or more men and women (servants of the inn), each verse (or the alternate verses) being followed by the chorus. There are versions in German and Latin ('Resonet in lauaibus'), some without the chorus, in Johann Walther's *Gesangbuch*, 1544, and elsewhere; our version is that of the *Mainzer Cantual*, 1605, the harmonies being those of the *English Hymnal* (612) and *Songs of Praise* (422), 'Resonet in laudibus' being there set to new words.

78 PERSONENT HODIE

(CHRISTMAS : EPIPHANY)

Moderato maestoso.
(arr. GUSTAV HOLST.)
f
f
1 Per - so - nent
2 In mun - do
3 Ma - gi tres
4. Om - nes cle -
Women
Men
ho - di - e Vo - ces pu - - er - u - lae,
nas - ci - tur, Pan - nis in - - vol - vi - tur,
ve - ne - runt, Par - vu - lum in - qui - runt,
- ric - u - li, Par - i - ter pu - e - ri,
Lau - dan - tes ju - cun - dè Qui no - bis est
Prae - se - pi po - ni - tur Sta - bu - lo bru -
Par - vu - lum in - qui - runt, Stel - lu - lam se -
Can - tent ut an - ge - li: Ad - ven - is - ti

na - - - tus, Sum - mo De - o
- to - - - rum, Rec - tor su - per -
- quen - - - do, Ip - sum a - do -
mun - - - do, Lau - des ti - bi
ff
da - - tus, Et de vir - - vir - - vir,
- no - - rum. Per - di - dit, dit, dit,
- ran - - do, Au - rum, thus, thus, thus,
fun - - do. Id - e - o - - o - - o,
R.H.
ff R.H. L.H.
sf
Et de vir - - - vir - - vir, Et de vir -
Per - di - dit, dit, dit, Per - di - dit
Au - rum, thus, thus, thus, Au - rum, thus,
Id - e - o - - o - - o, Id - e - o
sf
sf

- gi - ne - o ven - tre pro - cre - a - tus.
spo - li - a prin - ceps in - fer - no - rum.
et myrr - ham e - i of - fe - ren - do.
glo - ri - a in ex - cel - sis De - o!
sf

German, 1360. *Piae Cantiones*, 1582.

PERSONENT hodie
Voces puerulae,
Laudantes jucundè
Qui nobis est natus,
Summo Deo datus,
Et de virgineo ventre procreatus.

2 In mundo nascitur,
Pannis involvitur,
Praesepi ponitur
Stabulo brutorum,
Rector supernorum.
Perdidit spolia princeps infernorum.

3 Magi tres venerunt,
Parvulum inquirunt,
Parvulum inquirunt,
Stellulam sequendo,
Ipsum adorando,
Aurum, thus, et myrrham ei offerendo.

4. Omnes clericuli,
Pariter pueri,
Cantent ut angeli :
Advenisti mundo,
Laudes tibi fundo.
Ideo gloria in excelsis Deo !

This carol is here printed with its original Latin words from *Piae Cantiones*, 1582, to make our book more complete. English words have been set to the tune in *Songs of Praise*, 425. Ver. 1, in the original book, 'virgineo' is printed 'vir ij ij gineo' under the music to show the repetition at the end of each verse.

QUEM PASTORES

(CHRISTMAS: EPIPHANY)

German, 14th century. *Ibid.*

QUEM pastores laudavere,
Quibus angeli dixere,
Absit vobis jam timere,
Natus est rex gloriae.

2 Ad quem magi ambulabant,
Aurum, thus, myrrham portabant,
Immolabant haec sincere
Nato regi gloriae.

3. Christo regi, Deo nato,
Per Mariam nobis dato,
Merito resonet vere
Laus, honor et gloria.

This carol also is printed with its original Latin words because of its importance. English words have been set to the tune in *The English Hymnal* (598) and *Songs of Praise* (429), from which books the harmonies are taken. The carol occurs in V. Triller, 1555, *Leisentritt*, 1567, in Schein's *Cantionale*, 1627, and elsewhere.

80

THREE KINGS

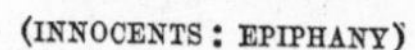

(INNOCENTS : EPIPHANY)

(M. S.)

With tambours, etc.

Flemish. *Tr. Robert Graves.*

THREE Kings are here, both wealthy and wise,
Come riding far over the snow-covered ice ;
Royal in throng,
Noble in song,
They search for the Child, the Redeemer of wrong ;
With tambours and drums they go sounding along.

2 God's angel speaks Saint Joseph anigh :
' With Jesus thy charge into far Egypt fly.
Stay not nor stand ;
Herod 's at hand.'
The ass hastens panting ; the hot desert sand
Has rescued our Saviour from Herod's ill band.

3. Herod betrays these innocent lives
Both younger and elder to lances and knives.
Who can dare tell
Murder so fell ?
These pretty young children in anguish of hell
Were martyred together his anger to quell.

A translation of 'De Drie Koningen', an old Flemish carol.

---

81 TORCHES

(CHRISTMAS)

Allegro moderato. (arr. from PEDRELL.)

Galician. *Tr. J. B. Trend.*

TORCHES, torches, run with torches
All the way to Bethlehem !
Christ is born and now lies sleeping ;
Come and sing your song to him !

2 Ah, Ro-ro, Ro-ro, my baby,
Ah, Ro-ro, my love, Ro-ro ;
Sleep you well, my heart's own darling,
While we sing you our Ro-ro.

3. Sing, my friends, and make you merry,
Joy and mirth and joy again ;
Lo, he lives, the King of heaven,
Now and evermore, Amen.

A Spanish carol from Galicia, 'Villancico de Navidad'. The melody is from Pedrell, *Cancionero musical*; the words are translated from the *Cancionero popular gallego* by J. Pérez Ballesteros. The second verse may be repeated at the end.

82 PATAPAN

(CHRISTMAS)

Verses 1 & 3. (M. S.)

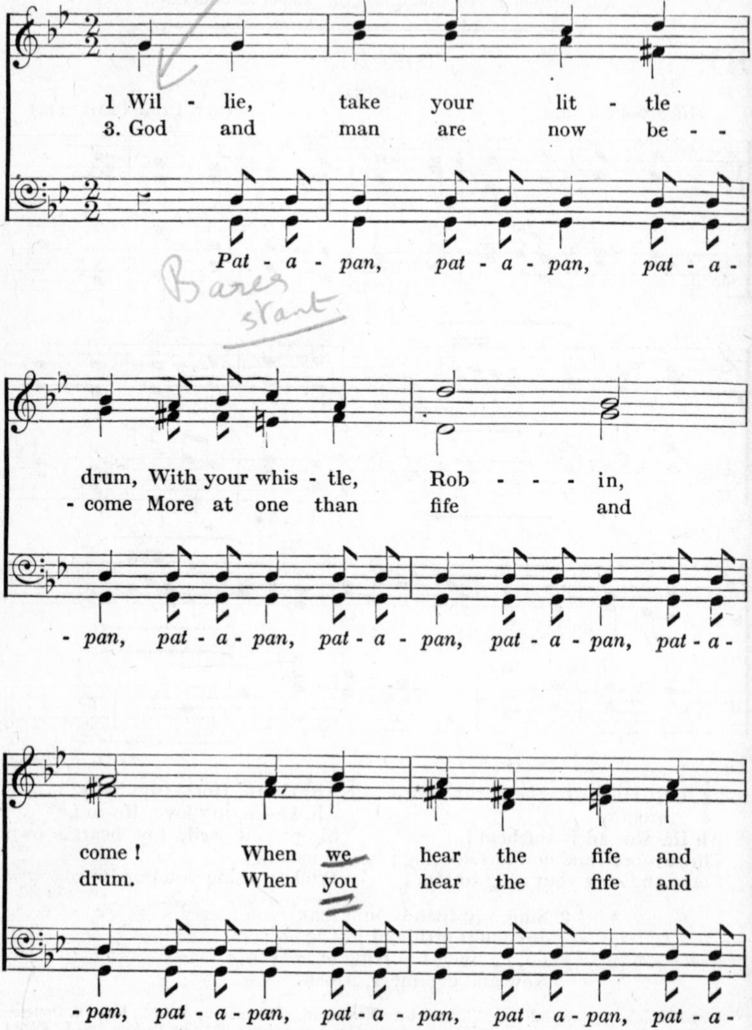

1 Wil - lie, take your lit - tle
3. God and man are now be - -
Pat - a - pan, pat - a - pan, pat - a-
drum, With your whis - tle, Rob - - - in,
- come More at one than fife and
- pan, pat - a - pan, pat - a - pan, pat - a - pan, pat - a-
come ! When we hear the fife and
drum. When you hear the fife and
- pan, pat - a - pan, pat - a - pan, pat - a - pan, pat - a-

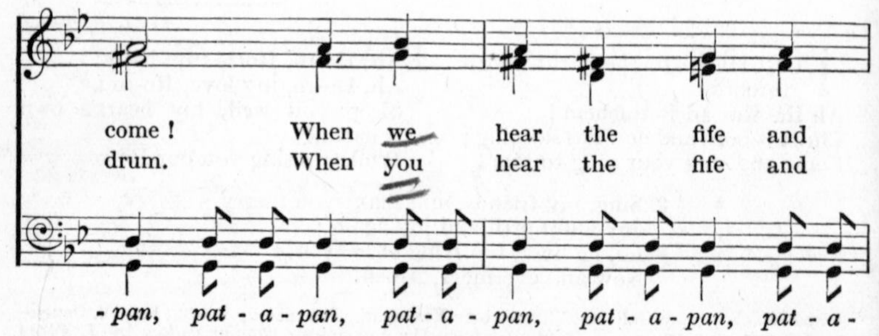

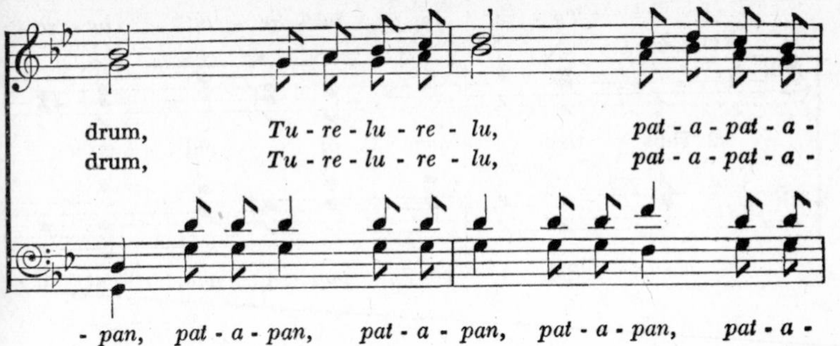

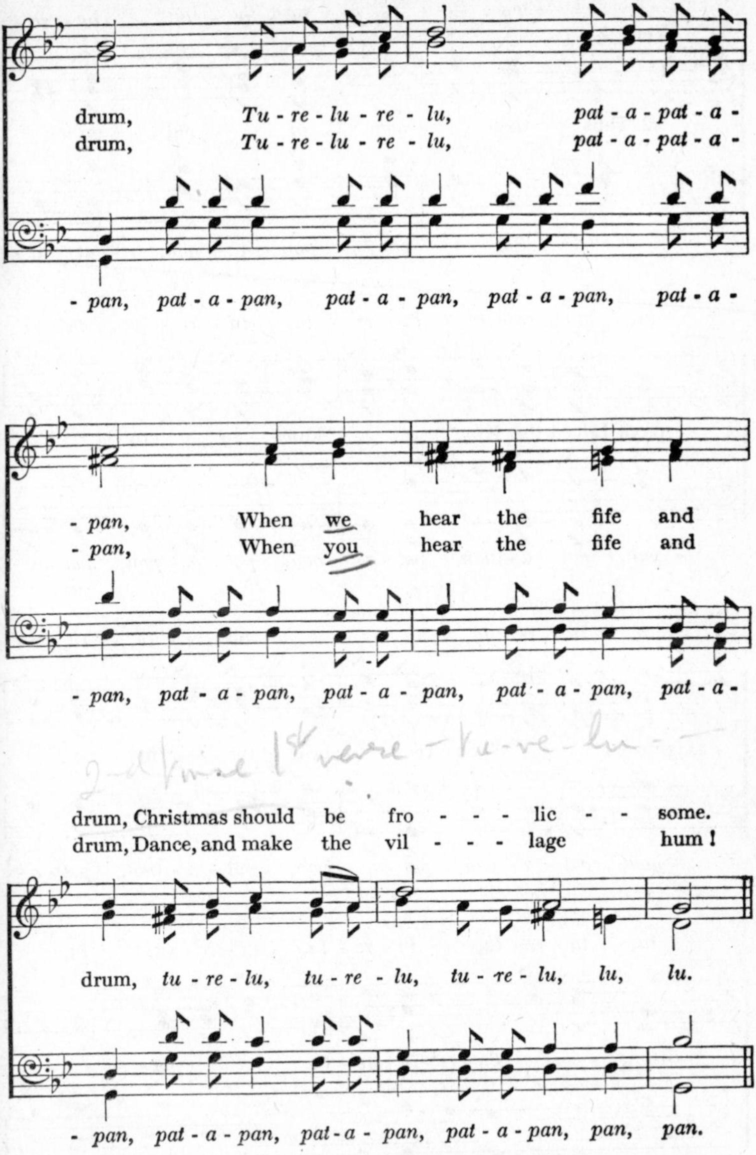

drum, Tu - re - lu - re - lu, pat - a - pat - a -
drum, Tu - re - lu - re - lu, pat - a - pat - a -
- pan, pat - a - pan, pat - a - pan, pat - a - pan, pat - a -
- pan, When we hear the fife and
- pan, When you hear the fife and
- pan, pat - a - pan, pat - a - pan, pat - a - pan, pat - a -
drum, Christmas should be fro - - - lic - - some.
drum, Dance, and make the vil - - - lage hum!
drum, tu - re - lu, tu - re - lu, tu - re - lu, lu, lu.
- pan, pat - a - pan, pat - a - pan, pat - a - pan, pan, pan.

(May be sung a semitone higher.)

Verse 2.
Tu - re - lu, tu - re - lu, tu - re -
2 Thus the men of old - en
Pat - a - pan, pat - a - pan, pat - a -
- lu, tu - re - lu, tu - re - lu, tu - re - lu, tu - re -
days Loved the King of kings to
- pan, pat - a - pan, pat - a - pan, pat - a - pan, pat - a -
- lu, tu - re - lu, tu - re - lu, tu - re - lu, tu - re -
praise : When they hear the fife and
- pan, pat - a - pan, pat - a - pan, pat - a - pan, pat - a -
- lu, tu - re - lu, tu - re - lu, tu - re - lu, lu,
drum, Tu - re - lu - re - lu, pat - a - pat - a -
- pan, pat - a - pan, pat - a - pan, pat - a - pan, pat - a -

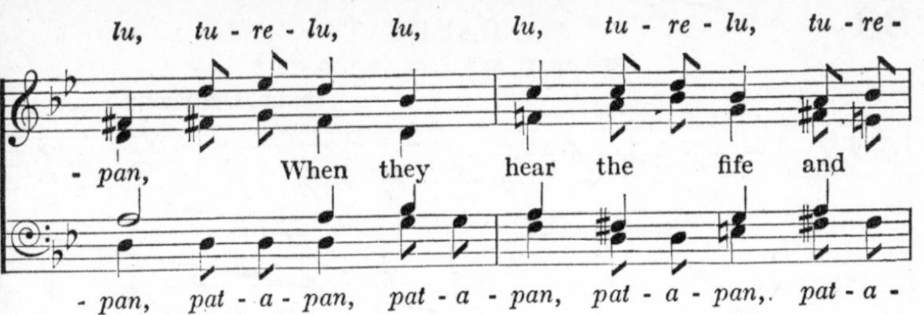

(May be sung a semitone higher.)

Burgundian. *La Monnoye, Tr. O. B. C.*

WILLIE, take your little drum,
With your whistle, Robin, come!
When we hear the fife and drum,
Ture-lure-lu, pata-pata-pan,
When we hear the fife and drum,
Christmas should be frolicsome.

2 Thus the men of olden days
Loved the King of kings to praise:
When they hear the fife and drum,
Ture-lure-lu, pata-pata-pan,
When they hear the fife and drum,
Sure our children won't be dumb!

3. God and man are now become
More at one than fife and drum.
When you hear the fife and drum,
Ture-lure-lu, pata-pata-pan,
When you hear the fife and drum,
Dance, and make the village hum!

It may be worth while to print the first verse of the original dialect noël, which illustrates the genial nature of those old French carols that were not rewritten in an age of less spontaneous faith: 'Guillô, pran ton tamborin. | Toi, pran tai fleùte Rôbin; Au son de cés instruman, | *Turelurelu patapatapan*; Au son de cés instruman. | Je diron Noei gaiman. The carol is printed by F. Fertiault, *Noëls Bourgignons de Bernard de la Monnoye,* 1842. Bernard lived from 1641 to 1728.

The *tambourin* is a small elongated drum, hung from the shoulders, and played originally with the hands.

Sandys got hold of this carol a century ago; and the original words were reprinted, 1907, by H. J. L. Masse and C. Kennedy Scott in their first *Book of Old Carols.* As the tune runs quickly, it may be well to repeat one or more verses.

83 CONGAUDEAT

(CHRISTMAS: NEW YEAR: EPIPHANY)

(harm. GEOFFREY SHAW.)

Piae Cantiones.

Ibid., Tr. Maurice F. Bell.

WITH merry heart let all rejoice in one;
The mother-maid hath now brought forth her son
In Bethlehem.

2 An angel's voice declared the Saviour's birth,
Glory to God, goodwill and peace on earth:

3 The shepherds sped to see this wondrous thing
And found the babe, the which is Christ our King:

4 Both ox and ass, adoring in the byre,
In mute acclaim pay homage to our Sire:

5 As custom was, the babe when eight days old
Received his name of Jesus, long foretold:

6 Three kings bowed low to infant majesty
And brought three gifts to hail the Trinity:

7. Now bless we Christ, eternal glory's King,
And Christ bless us, as to his praise we sing:

The words and melody of 'Congaudeat turba fidelium' occur in the Swedish *Piae Cantiones* (1582); but the tune is much older than this; an early form of it is found in a twelfth-century MS., from Apt, near Avignon, printed in the *Revue du Chant Grégorien* for September 1902.

84 THE CRADLE

(NATIVITY)

(M. S.)

Austrian, 1649.

Tr. Robert Graves.

HE smiles within his cradle,
A babe with face so bright
It beams most like a mirror
Against a blaze of light:
This babe so burning bright.

2 This babe we now declare to you
Is Jesus Christ our Lord;
He brings both peace and hearti-
ness:
Haste, haste with one accord
To feast with Christ our Lord.

3 And who would rock the cradle
Wherein this infant lies,
Must rock with easy motion
And watch with humble eyes,
Like Mary pure and wise.

4. O Jesus, dearest babe of all
And dearest babe of mine,
Thy love is great, thy limbs are
small.
O, flood this heart of mine
With overflow from thine!

Translation of 'Ein Kindlein in der Wiegen'. Words and melody from D. G. Corner's *Geistliche Nachtigal*, Vienna, 1649.

85

PUER NATUS

(NATIVITY)

(M. S.)

In Beth - - - le -
Last verse—And glo - - - - - ry

- hem;..............
bright,............

Al - le - lu - ya, al - le - - - - - - - - - lu - ya.

ALTERNATIVE VERSION (as harmonized by J. S. Bach).

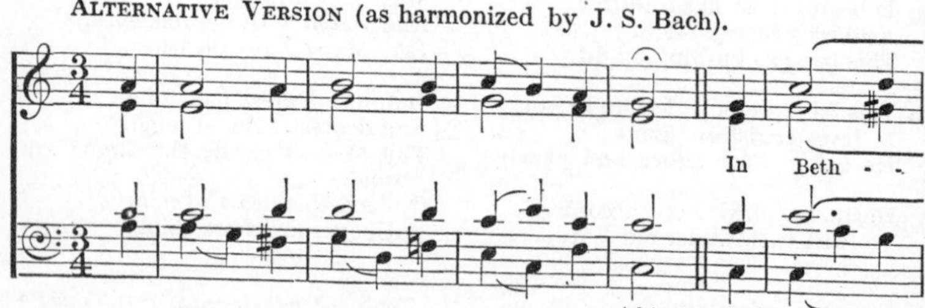
In Beth - -
Last verse—And glo - - -

- - - - - - le - hem;
- - - - - - - ry bright,

Al - le - lu - ya, al - le - - - - - lu - ya.

(If both versions are used together it is suggested that the alternative be sung, slower, to the last verse; the first version being raised a tone.)

German, 16th century. *Tr. N. S. T.*

A BOY was born in Bethlehem
Rejoice for that, Jerusalem!
Alleluya.

2 For low he lay within a stall,
Who rules for ever over all:

3 He let himself a servant be,
That all mankind he might set free:

4 Then praise the Word of God who came,
To dwell within a human frame:

5 And praised be God in threefold might,
And glory bright,
Eternal, good, and infinite!

This melody for 'Ein kind geborn zu Bethlehem' ('Puer natus in Bethlehem') is in L. Lossius's *Psalmodia*, 1553, the Ingolstadt *Obsequiale*, 1570, and in many German books of the seventeenth century: it is really the descant of an older melody which it has supplanted. The words 'in Bethlehem' are repeated, and similarly with the corresponding words in vv. 2, 3, and 4.

IN DULCI JUBILO

(NATIVITY)

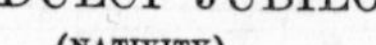

Verses 1, 2, & 3. *Allegro.* (Harm. BARTHOLOMEW GESIUS, 1601.)

The small notes in the last two bars are added to preserve the usual version of the tune, and may be used if preferred.

German, 14th century. *Tr. S. P.*

IN dulci jubilo
Now sing with hearts aglow!
Our delight and pleasure
Lies *in praesepio*,
Like sunshine is our treasure
Matris in gremio.
Alpha es et O!

2 *O Jesu, parvule,*
For thee I long alway ;
Comfort my heart's blindness,
O puer optime,
With all thy loving-kindness,
O princeps gloriae.
Trahe me post te !
3 *O Patris caritas !*
O Nati lenitas !
Deeply were we stainèd
Per nostra crimina ;
But thou for us hast gainèd
Coelorum gaudia.
O that we were there !
4. *Ubi sunt gaudia*
In any place but there ?
There are angels singing
Nova cantica,
And there the bells are ringing
In Regis curia.
O that we were there !
(Setting by J. S. Bach.)
Verse 4. *Maestoso.*
4. *U - bi sunt gau - di - a.................* In an - y place but there ?.....
There are an - gels sing - - ing *No - - va can - ti -*
There are.... an - gels..... sing - ing
- *ca,.......................* And there the bells are ring - ing *In*

1. *In dulci jubilo*] In sweet shouting, or jubilation. *In praesepio*] in a manger. *Matris*, &c.] In his mother's lap. *Alpha*, &c.] Thou art Alpha and Omega. 2. *O Jesu parvule*] O tiny Jesus. *O puer optime*] O best of boys. *O princeps gloriae*] O prince of glory. *Trahe*, &c.] Draw me after thee. 3. *O Patris*, &c.] O love of the Father. *O Nati*, &c.] O gentleness of the Son. *Per nostra*, &c.] Through our crimes. *Coelorum*, &c.] The joys of the heavens. 4. *Ubi sunt*, &c.] Where are joys ? *Nova*, &c.] New songs. *In Regis*, &c.] In the court of the King.

This famous old German macaronic carol was first translated into English by John Wedderburn in his *Gude and Godly Ballates*, c. 1540, ' In dulci jubilo, Now let us sing with mirth and jo[y] ', irregular, in three stanzas. Other translations are—*Lyra Davidica*, 1708, Sir J. Bowring, 1825, &c. R. L. de Pearsall (1795–1856) and G. R. Woodward in the *Cowley Carol Book* follow the tune correctly. The music only allows us to use three of Wedderburn's lines (21 and 28 in part, and 23) in this new rendering.

Because of the importance of this carol, we append the original old German lines : 1. Nu singet und seyt fro : Unsers herzens wonne Leyt : Und leuchtet als die sonne. 2. Nach dir ist mir so we : Tröst mir myn gemüte : Durch aller juncfrawen güte. 3. Wir weren all verloren : So hat er uns erworben : Eya, wär wir da ! 4. Nirgend mer denn da : Da die engel singen : Und die schellen klingen : Eya, wär wir da ! But there are many variants, old and new, e.g. in v. 2 the fifteenth-century line is modernized by Vehe to ' Durch alle deine Güte '.

The fourteenth-century melody occurs, with the words, in a MS. at Leipzig University Library, which belongs to the beginning of the fifteenth century. The developed form of the melody is in Michael Vehe's *Gesangbuch*, Leipzig, 1537, and in Witzel's *Psaltes Ecclesiasticus*, Cologne, 1550. In Babst's *Gesangbuch*, Leipzig, 1545, the last hymn-book produced for Luther and representing his final text-editorship, the third stanza, doubtless by Luther himself, ' O Patris caritas ', is substituted for an earlier one. The melody and versions of the words occur in many other books, including *Piae Cantiones*, 1582, with a Swedish translation.

The original words are said by a fourteenth-century writer to have been sung by angels to Henry Suso (†1366), the mystic, who was drawn in thereby to dance with his celestial visitors.

87 ROCKING

(NATIVITY)

Moderato. (M. S.)

Czech. *Tr. O. B. C.*

LITTLE Jesus, sweetly sleep, do not stir;
We will lend a coat of fur,
We will rock you, rock you, rock you,
We will rock you, rock you, rock you:
See the fur to keep you warm,
Snugly round your tiny form.

2. Mary's little baby, sleep, sweetly sleep,
Sleep in comfort, slumber deep;
We will rock you, rock you, rock you,
We will rock you, rock you, rock you:
We will serve you all we can,
Darling, darling little man.

Translation of the Czech carol, 'Hajej, nynjej'. This carol may well be sung twice.

88 WAKING-TIME

(NATIVITY)

(M. S.)

'Get up, good folk, 'tis wa - king - time!'

French. *Pr. Eleanor Farjeon.*

NEIGHBOUR, what was the sound, I pray,
That did awake me as I lay,
And to their doorways brought the people ?
Every one heard it like a chime
Pealing for joy within a steeple :
'Get up, good folk !
Get up, good folk, 'tis waking-time !'

2 Nay then, young Martin, know you not
That it is this our native spot
Sweet Love has chosen for his dwelling ?
In every quarter rumours hum,
Rumours of news beyond all telling :
‘ Wake up, good folk !
Wake up, good folk, for Christ is come.’

3 Neighbours, and is it really true
True that the babe so small and new
Is lying even now among us ?
What can we lay upon his knees—
He whose arrival angels sung us,
What can we give,
What can we give the child to please ?

4 Dickon shall bring a ball of silk,
Peter his son a pot of milk,
And Tom a sparrow and a linnet,
Robin a cheese, and Ralph the half
Part of a cake with cherries in it,
And jolly Jack,
And jolly Jack a little calf.

5 I think this child will come to be
Some sort of workman such as we,
So he shall have my tools and chattels,
My well-set saw, my plane, my drill,
My hammer that so merry rattles,
And planks of wood,
And planks of wood to work at will.

6 When we have made our offerings,
Saying to him the little things
Whereof all babies born are witting,
Then we will take our leave and go,
Bidding goodnight in manner fitting—
Hush, hush, wee lamb,
Hush, hush, wee lamb, dream sweetly so.

7. And in a stable though he lies,
We in our hearts will soon devise
Such mansions as can never shame him :
There we will house and hold him dear,
And through the world to all proclaim him :
‘ Wake up, good folk !
Wake up, good folk, for Christ is here.’

The tune, with six verses, is in the *Grand Bible des Noëls Angevins*, 1766 ; there are many variants of the tune, in Anjou and elsewhere, and seven more verses are known of ‘ Voisin, d’où venait ce grand bruit ? ’ which is here paraphrased.

89 SION'S DAUGHTER

(NATIVITY)

(M. S.)

Netherland. *Tr. A. G.*

O SION'S daughter, where art thou?
Good news have I to tell thee,
A greater joy I bring thee now
Than ever yet befell thee.

2 A maiden hath brought forth a son;
Great was the gift she gave us;
In Bethlem was that life begun
Of him who came to save us.

3 As through a casement light will flood
That darkness may be ended,
So through her maiden motherhood
The child of God descended.

4. Upon her lap he lay so fair,
She kissed him and caressed him;
Great was the love she did him bear,
As to her heart she pressed him.

A translation of the old Netherland carol, 'Waer is die dochter van Syoen', from *Nederlandsch Volksliederenboek*, by Lange, Riemsdijk, and Kalff, 1896.

90 SONG OF THE SHIP

(NATIVITY)

(Mel. & Harm. 1608.)

German, 1608. *c.* 1470. *Tr. O. B. C.*

THERE comes a ship a-sailing
With angels flying fast;
She bears a splendid cargo
And has a mighty mast.

2 This ship is fully laden,
Right to her highest board;
She bears the Son from heaven,
God's high eternal Word.

3 Upon the sea unruffled
The ship moves in to shore,
To bring us all the riches
She has within her store.

4 And that ship's name is Mary
Of flowers the rose is she,
And brings to us her baby
From sin to set us free.

5. The ship made in this fashion,
In which such store was cast,
Her sail is love's sweet passion,
The Holy Ghost her mast.

The oldest text, in four stanzas (1 and 2 forming one stanza), is in a MS. 1470–80 (Royal Library, Berlin). Sudermann (*Gesänge*, 1626) gives what has become the better known text, and says that it was found among Tauler's writings. The melody is from the version ('Uns kompt ein Schiff gefahren') in the *Andernach Gesangbuch*, 1608. There is much doubt about Tauler's writings; and Sudermann seems to have rewritten the hymns in his collection. The last lines of the 1470 version are: Der segel is die minne, | Der heilig geist der mast.

91 IN THE TOWN

(NATIVITY)

In moderate time. (M. S.)

French, 15th century. *Pr. Eleanor Farjeon.*

Joseph :

TAKE heart, the journey's ended :
 I see the twinkling lights,
Where we shall be befriended
 On this the night of nights.

Mary :

Now praise the Lord that led us
 So safe unto the town,
Where men will feed and bed us,
 And I can lay me down.

Joseph :

2 And how then shall we praise him ?
 Alas, my heart is sore
That we no gifts can raise him
 Who are so very poor.

Mary :

We have as much as any
 That on the earth do live,
Although we have no penny
 We have ourselves to give.

Joseph :
3 Look yonder, wife, look yonder!
An hostelry I see,
Where travellers that wander
Will very welcome be.

Mary :
The house is tall and stately,
The door stands open thus ;
Yet, husband, I fear greatly
That inn is not for us.

Joseph :
4 God save you, gentle master!
Your littlest room indeed
With plainest walls of plaster
To-night will serve our need.

Host :
For lordlings and for ladies
I've lodging and to spare ;
For you and yonder maid is
No closet anywhere.

Joseph :
5 Take heart, take heart, sweet Mary,
Another inn I spy,
Whose host will not be chary
To let us easy lie.

Mary :
Oh aid me, I am ailing,
My strength is nearly gone ;
I feel my limbs are failing,
And yet we must go on.

Joseph :
6 God save you, Hostess, kindly!
I pray you, house my wife,
Who bears beside me blindly
The burden of her life.

Hostess :
My guests are rich men's daughters
And sons, I'd have you know!
Seek out the poorer quarters
Where ragged people go.

Joseph :
7 Good sir, my wife 's in labour,
Some corner let us keep.

Host :
Not I: Knock up my neighbour,
And as for me, I'll sleep.

Mary :
In all the lighted city
Where rich men welcome win,
Will not one house for pity
Take two poor strangers in ?

Joseph :
8 Good woman, I implore you
Afford my wife a bed.

Hostess :
Nay, nay, I've nothing for you
Except the cattle-shed.

Mary :
Then gladly in the manger
Our bodies we will house,
Since men to-night are stranger
Than asses are and cows.

Joseph :
9. Take heart, take heart, sweet Mary,
The cattle are our friends :
Lie down, lie down, sweet Mary,
For here the journey ends.

Mary :
Now praise the Lord that found me
This shelter in the town,
Where I with friends around me
May lay my burden down.

A paraphrase of the touching old dialogue carol, 'Nous voici dans la ville'. The lovely tune is famous and widespread in France ; the words set to it by Lucas Le Moigne ('Or, nous dites Marie') date it as at least not later than *c.* 1450, and the macaronic carol 'Célébrons la naissance' (which is given to the tune together with 'Nous voici' in the *Grande Bible des Noëls* of 1766) is clearly a fifteenth-century work. Other words (not all religious) have been sung to it, e.g. 'Hélas! je l'ai perdue', 'Voulex-vous plaire aux dames', 'Bergère que j'adore', and 'Chantons, je vous en prie'. In 1676 Le Bègue used the melody for an organ prelude ; and its strains upon the organ are often heard creeping into the silence of the consecration at Christmas time in French churches.

We have arranged it in parts ; and it can be sung thus in church, or else as a little play upon the stage.

92 PUER NOBIS

(NATIVITY)

FULL (VOICES IN UNISON). (GEOFFREY SHAW.)

1 Un - to us a boy is born! King of all cre -
a - tion, Came he to a world for - lorn, The
Lord of ev - 'ry na - - - - - - - - - - - - - - - tion.
Ped.

TREBLES.
2 Cra - dled in a stall was he With sleep - y cows and
Senza Ped.

ass - es; But the ve - ry beasts could see That

he all men sur - pas - - - - - - - - - - - - - ses.

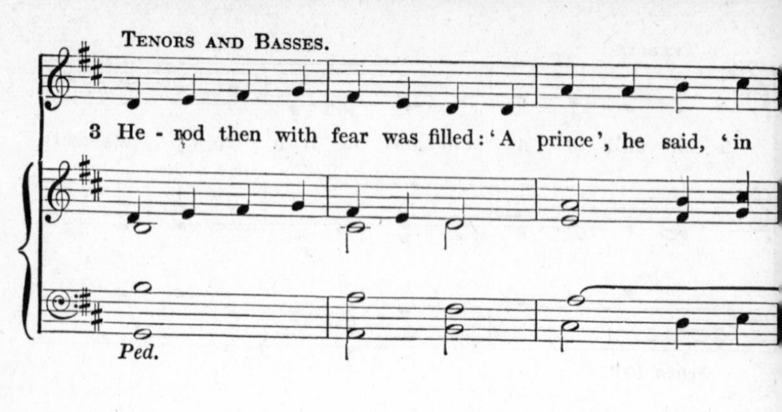
Tenors and Basses.
3 He - rod then with fear was filled: 'A prince', he said, 'in
Ped.

Jew - ry!' All the lit - tle boys he killed At

Beth - lem in his fu - - - - - - - - - - - - - - - ry.

Trebles.
4 Now may Ma - ry's son, who came So long a - go to
Choir.
Great.
love us, Lead us all with hearts a - flame Un -
- - to the joys a - bove.. us.

H

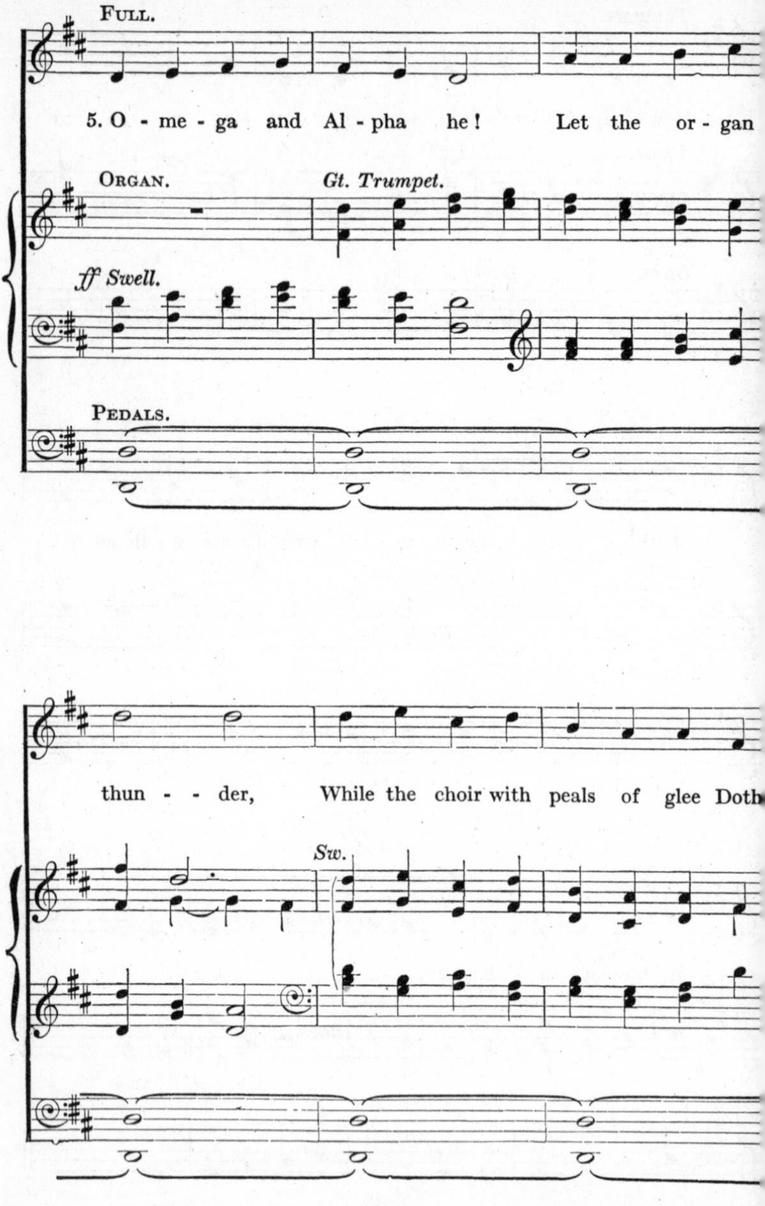

FULL.

5. O - me - ga and Al - pha he! Let the or - gan

ORGAN. *Gt. Trumpet.*

ff Swell.

PEDALS.

thun - - der, While the choir with peals of glee Doth

Sw.

rend the air a - sun - - - - - - - - - - - - - der.
Gt. Trumpet.
Sw.

German. *15th century, tr. O. B. C.*

UNTO us a boy is born!
  King of all creation,
Came he to a world forlorn,
  The Lord of every nation.

2 Cradled in a stall was he
  With sleepy cows and asses;
But the very beasts could see
  That he all men surpasses.

3 Herod then with fear was filled:
  'A prince', he said, 'in Jewry!'
All the little boys he killed
  At Bethlem in his fury.

4 Now may Mary's son, who came
  So long ago to love us,
Lead us all with hearts aflame
  Unto the joys above us.

5. Omega and Alpha he!
  Let the organ thunder,
While the choir with peals of glee
  Doth rend the air asunder.

The words and original melody of 'Puer nobis nascitur' are in a Trier MS. of the fifteenth century. There are many variants, given in Zahn, Dreves, and Baümker; a German translation ('Uns ist geborn ein Kindelein') is printed by Spangenberg, 1544, in the Mainz *Cantual*, 1605, and elsewhere. The melody in this form is in *Piae Cantiones*, 1582, and the words are from the version of Mone (*Lateinische Hymnen*), who prints the Trier form.

93 MARY'S WANDERING

(THE PASSION)

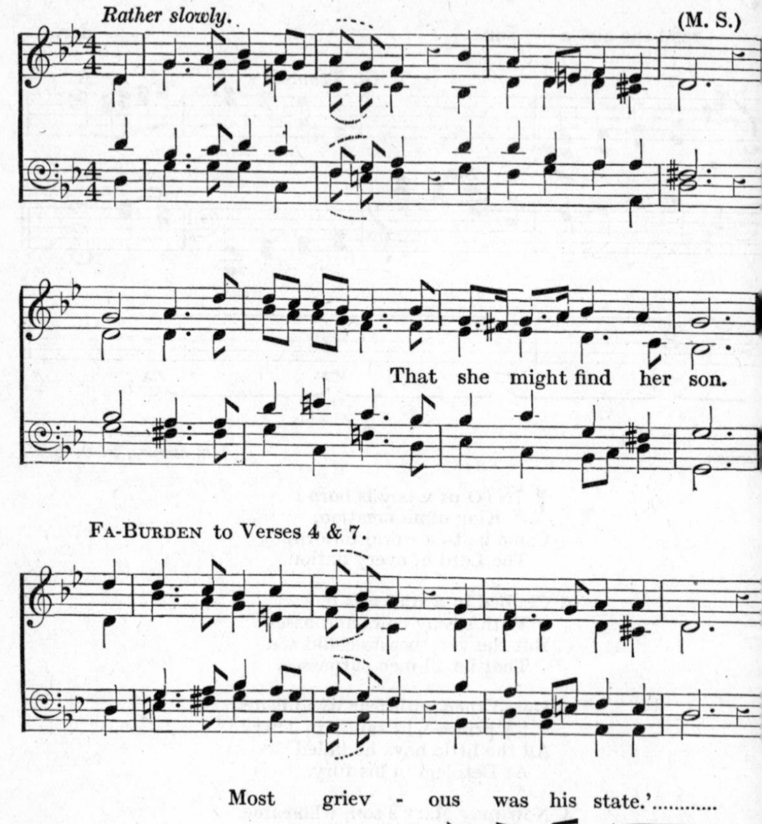

Rather slowly.
(M. S.)
That she might find her son.
FA-BURDEN to Verses 4 & 7.
Most griev - ous was his state.'............

Most griev - ous was his state.'

Most griev-ous was his state, most griev - ous was his state.'

Most griev-ous was his state, most griev - ous was his state.'

But heav'n is won for all, but heav'n is won for all!'

German. *Tr. A. F. D.*

ONCE Mary would go wandering,
To all the land would run,
That she might find her son.

2 Whom met she as she journeyed forth?
Saint Peter, that good man,
Who sadly her did scan.

3 'O tell me have you seen him yet—
The one I love the most—
The son whom I have lost?'

4 'Too well, too well, I've seen thy son
'Twas by a palace-gate,
Most grievous was his state.'

5 'O say, what wore he on his head?'
'A crown of thorns he wore;
A cross he also bore.'

6 'Ah me! and he must bear that cross,
Till he's brought to the hill,
For cruel men to kill.'

7. 'Nay Mary, cease thy weeping, dear:
The wounds they are but small;
But Heaven is won for all!'

'Marias Wanderschaft' ('Maria die wollt' wandern gehn') is one version of this legend, and to it belongs this folk-melody, which was published by Friedlaender. The third line of each verse is repeated.

See No. 179 for Brahms's tune to another version of the ballad.

EASTER EGGS

Eas-ter eggs! Eas-ter eggs! Give to him that begs! (M. S.)

'm... *For Christ the Lord is a -*

- ris - en,.... is a-ris - en. To the poor, o-pen door, something give from your

'm..

FINE.

store ! *For Christ the Lord is a - ris - en,.... is a-ris - en.* Those who

Russian. *Tr. A. F. D*

EASTER eggs! Easter eggs! Give to him that begs!
For Christ the Lord is arisen.
To the poor, open door, something give from your store!
Those who hoard can't afford—moth and rust their reward!
Those who love freely give—long and well may they live!
Easter tide, like a bride, comes, and won't be denied.

Words and Melody from the traditional Easter Song, 'Dalalin, Dalalin, po Yaichenku' in Rimsky-Korsakov's *Russian National Songs*, 1877.

95 NOW GLAD OF HEART

(EASTER: ASCENSION: TRINITY SUNDAY)

(GEOFFREY SHAW.)

German, 16th century. *Tr. A. H. Fox-Strangways.*

NOW glad of heart be every one!
The fight is fought, the day is won,
The Christ is set upon his throne,

2 Who on the rood was crucified,
Who rose again, as at this tide,
In glory to his Father's side,

3 Who baffled death and harrowed hell
And led the souls that loved him well
All in the light of lights to dwell;

4 To him we lift our heart and voice
And in his Paradise rejoice
With harp and pipe and happy noise.

5 Then rise, all Christian folk, with me
And carol forth the One in Three
That was, and is, and is to be,

6. By faith, the shield of heart and mind,
Through love, which suffers and is kind,
In hope, that rides upon the wind.

In some versions of 'Wir wollen alle fröhlich sein', one or more stanzas of *Alleluya* (repeated) are added. This was 'an old song' already in Spangenberg's *Christlichs Gesangbüchlein*, 1568. It is also in the *Gesangbuch der Brüder in Behemen*, Nürnberg, 1544, and elsewhere.

96

HILARITER

(EASTER: SPRING: SUMMER)

Rather quickly. (M. S.)

German, 1623. *Tr. O. B. C.*

THE whole bright world rejoices now,
Hilariter, hilariter ;
The birds do sing on every bough
Alleluya, Alleluya.

2 Then shout beneath the racing skies,
Hilariter, hilariter,
To him who rose that we might rise,
Alleluya, Alleluya.

3 And all you living things make praise,
Hilariter, hilariter ;
He guideth you on all your ways,
Alleluya, Alleluya.

4. He, Father, Son, and Holy Ghost—
Hilariter, hilariter !—
Our God most high, our joy and boast.
Alleluya, Alleluya.

The earliest appearance of 'Die ganze Welt' is in the Cologne *Kirchengesäng*, 1623; it appears later in several other books, e.g. at Mainz, 1628, Prag, 1655, and Strassburg, 1697.

97 THE SECRET FLOWER

(EASTER: WHITSUNTIDE: SAINTS' DAYS) (M. S.)

German, 16th century. *Do., 17th century, Pr. Eleanor Farjeon.*

THIS child was born to men of God:
Love to the world was given;
In him were truth and beauty met,
On him was set
At birth the seal of heaven.

2 He came the Word to manifest,
Earth to the stars he raises:
The teacher's errors are not his,
The Truth he is:
No man can speak his praises.

3 He evil fought and overcame,
He took from death the power;
To all that follow where he goes
At last he shows
The Kingdom's secret Flower.

4 The secret Flower shall bloom on earth
In them that have beholden;
The heavenly Spirit shall be plain
In them again,
As first it was of olden.

5 The Spirit like a light shall shine,
Evil himself dispelling,
The Spirit like a wind shall blow,
And Death shall go
Unfeared in her own dwelling.

6. And by the spirit shall be known
Heroes and Saints and Sages;
Yea, they shall walk in all men's [sight,
Amid the light
God sent to crown the ages.

A paraphrase of 'Gebor'n ist uns ein Kindelein'. Melody in the Mainz *Cantual*, 1605, but certainly of the sixteenth century, and perhaps earlier, says Riemann. Words and melody in the Cologne *Gesangbuch*, 1634.

98

SPRING HAS COME

(SPRING)

(G. S.)

Piae Cantiones, 1582. *Ibid., Tr. Steuart Wilson.*

NOW the spring has come again, joy and warmth will follow ;
Cold and wet are quite forgot, northward flies the swallow ;
Over sea and land and air spring's soft touch is everywhere
And the World looks cleaner ;
All our sinews feel new strung, hearts are light that once were wrung,
Youthful zests are keener.

2 All the woods are new in leaf, all the fruit is budding,
Bees are humming round the hive, done with winter's brooding ;
Seas are calm and blue again, clouds no more foretell the rain,
Winds are soft and tender ;
High above, the kingly sun laughs once more his course to run,
Shines in all his splendour.

3. God is in the midst of her, God commands her duty ;
Earth does but reflect his light, mirrors back his beauty ;
God's the fount whence all things flow, great and small, above, below,
God's their only maker :
We but poorest patterns are of that Mind beyond compare,
God our great Creator.

Neale turned this spring carol, 'In vernali tempore', from *Piae Cantiones*, 1582, into a Christmas carol in 1853 ('O'er the hill and o'er the vale'), as he did also with No. 99.

99 FLOWER CAROL

(SPRING, ETC.)

FA-BURDEN for Verses 2 and 4 (melody in the Tenor).

set the mea - dows danc - - - - - - - - - - - - - ing.

Verses 3 and 5.

3 Thro' each won - der of fair days God him-self ex - press - es;
5. Praise the Mak - er, all ye saints; He with glo - ry girt you,

3 Thro' each wonder of fair days God him - self ex - press -
5. Praise the Mak-er, all ye saints; He with glo - ry girt

3 Thro' each won - der of fair days God him - self ex - press - es;
5. Praise the Mak - er, all ye saints; He with glo - ry girt you,

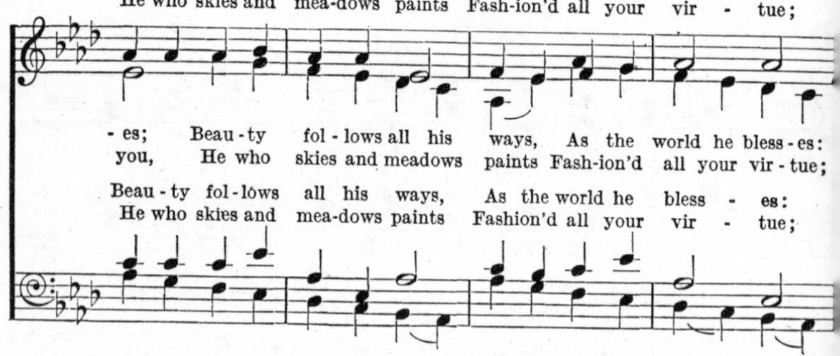
Beau - ty fol - lows all his ways, As the world he bless - es:
He who skies and mea-dows paints Fash-ion'd all your vir - tue;
- es; Beau - ty fol - lows all his ways, As the world he bless - es:
you, He who skies and meadows paints Fash-ion'd all your vir - tue;
Beau - ty fol - lows all his ways, As the world he bless - es:
He who skies and mea-dows paints Fashion'd all your vir - tue;

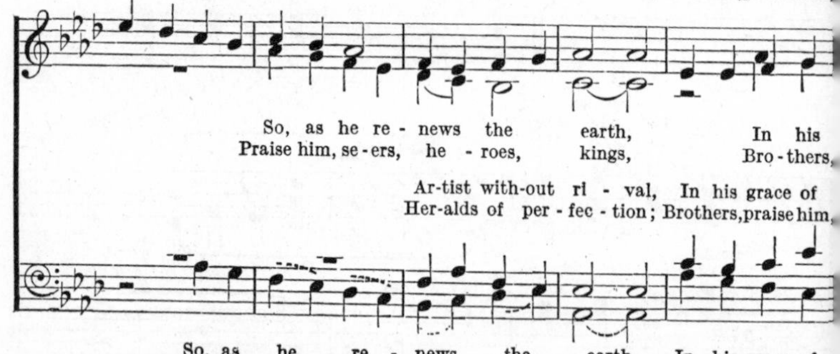
So, as he re-news the earth, Ar - tist with-out ri - val, In his grace of
Praise him, se-ers, he-roes, kings, Her-alds of per - fec - tion; Brothers, praise him,
So, as he re - news the earth, In his
Praise him, se - ers, he - roes, kings, Bro - thers,
Ar-tist with-out ri - val, In his grace of
Her-alds of per - fec - tion; Brothers, praise him,
So, as he re - news the earth, In his grace of
Praise him, se-ers, he -roes, her-alds of per - fec - tion; Brothers, praise him,

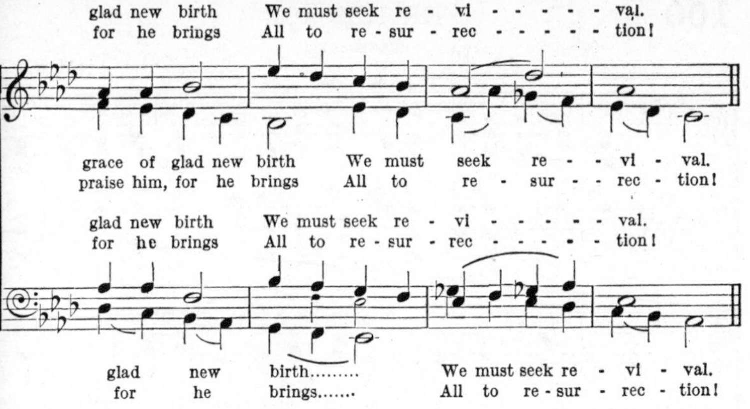
glad new birth We must seek re - vi - - - - - - val.
for he brings All to re - sur - rec - - - - - - tion!
grace of glad new birth We must seek re - - vi - val.
praise him, for he brings All to re - sur - - rec - tion!
glad new birth We must seek re - vi - - - - - - val.
for he brings All to re - sur - rec - - - - - - tion!
glad new birth......... We must seek re - vi - val.
for he brings....... All to re - sur - rec - tion!

Piae Cantiones, 1582. *Ibid., Tr. O. B. C.*

SPRING has now unwrapped the flowers,
Day is fast reviving,
Life in all her growing powers
Towards the light is striving :
Gone the iron touch of cold,
Winter time and frost time,
Seedlings, working through the mould,
Now make up for lost time.

2 Herb and plant that, winter long,
Slumbered at their leisure,
Now bestirring, green and strong,
Find in growth their pleasure :
All the world with beauty fills,
Gold the green enhancing ;
Flowers make glee among the hills,
And set the meadows dancing.

3 Through each wonder of fair days
God himself expresses ;
Beauty follows all his ways,
As the world he blesses :
So, as he renews the earth,
Artist without rival,
In his grace of glad new birth
We must seek revival.

4 Earth puts on her dress of glee ;
Flowers and grasses hide her ;
We go forth in charity—
Brothers all beside her ;
For, as man this glory sees
In the awakening season,
Reason learns the heart's decrees,
And hearts are led by reason.

5. Praise the Maker, all ye saints ;
He with glory girt you,
He who skies and meadows paints
Fashioned all your virtue ;
Praise him, seers, heroes, kings,
Heralds of perfection ;
Brothers, praise him, for he brings
All to resurrection !

This is a free translation, with a doxology, of the words proper to the melody of No. 136 'Tempus adest floridum', the Spring carol which Neale unfortunately turned into a Christmas carol by writing his rendering of the legend of 'Good King Wenceslas'. We have therefore reprinted the proper tune here, with the suggestion that it should be sung as a Spring carol, and that 'Good King Wenceslas' might be gradually dropped.

100 THE MESSAGE

(GENERAL)

(M. S.)

In shi - ning robes and with golden tongue, He
told what should be - tide her:
By God's most high de - cree !

Dutch. *Pr. E. B. G.*

A MESSAGE came to a maiden young;
The angel stood beside her,
In shining robes and with golden tongue,
He told what should betide her:
The maid was lost in wonder—
Her world was rent asunder—
Ah! how could she
Christ's mother be
By God's most high decree!

2 No greater news could a messenger bring;
For 'twas from that young mother
He came, who walked on the earth as a king,
And yet was all men's brother:
His truth has spread like leaven,
'Twill marry earth to heaven,
Till all agree
In charity
To dwell from sea to sea.

3 He came, God's Word to the world here below;
And round him there did gather
A band who found that this Teacher to know
Was e'en to know the Father:
He healed the sick who sought him,
Forgave the foes who fought him;
Beside the Sea
Of Galilee
He set the nations free.

4. And sometimes trumpets from Sion ring out,
And tramping comes, and drumming—
'Thy Kingdom come,' so we cry; and they shout,
'It comes!' and still 'tis coming—
Far, far ahead, to win us,
Yet with us, nay within us;
Till all shall see
That King is he,
The Love from Galilee!

Melody and words of 'De Boodschap van Maria' (Er was een maagdetje) which is freely translated in the first verse. From the *Nederlandsch Volksliederenboek*, 1896.

101 GEMS OF DAY

(GENERAL)

French, 1553. *N. Denisot, Pr. Patrick R. Chalmers.*

ALL the gay gems of day—
Pearls the morning sky adorning,
Manifold gems of gold,
Golder getting now day 's setting,
Are the sun's pretty ones
Of his shining or declining,
Are his joys, birthday toys
These God's Very Babe make merry;

2 When Sir Sun his course done,
Westward stooping home 's gone drooping,
It is naught, look! new wrought
Joy and Beauty bear his duty—
Planets peep down night's deep,
Softly seeming gold and dreaming
Jasmin o'er heaven's door,
Lest God's only Babe fall lonely.

3. Newly born king of morn,
Noon and night time, dark and light time,
Be our light, day and night,
Ne'er withholden, greatlier golden
Than the boon sun at noon,
Than the garland sheen of starland;
Saviour small, light us all—
Light our blindness, of thy kindness!

Paraphrased from 'Le vermeil du soleil', *Cantiques du Premier Advénement de Jésus-Christ*, par Le Comte d'Alsinois (Nicholas Denisot), Paris, 1553. There are twenty verses in the original; nine of them will be found in *A Book of Old Carols*, by H.J.L.J. Massé and Charles Kennedy Scott, 1907, No. 15, p. 24. The melody is stated to be by Marc-Antoine Muret in a MS. note, apparently of the sixteenth century, in the British Museum copy.

102 GABRIEL'S MESSAGE

(GENERAL : EASTER)

(G. S.)

Piae Cantiones, 1582. *Ibid., Tr. J. M. Neale* ‡, 1818–66.

GABRIEL'S message does away
Satan's curse and Satan's sway,
Out of darkness brings our Day :

So, behold,
All the gates of Heaven unfold.

2 He that comes despised shall reign ;
He that cannot die, be slain ;
Death by death its death shall gain :

3 Weakness shall the strong confound ;
By the hands, in grave-clothes wound,
Adam's chains shall be unbound :

4 By the sword that was his own,
By that sword, and that alone,
Shall Goliath be o'erthrown :

5. Art by art shall be assailed ;
To the cross shall Life be nailed ;
From the grave shall hope be hailed :

The words, written by Neale in 1853, to this tune have been slightly altered, to bring them more in accordance with the original of 'Angelus emittitur' upon which they were based; the original refrain is 'Igitur Porta coeli panditur'. Two Christmas verses not in the original are omitted. The earliest known version is in *Piae Cantiones*, 1582.

103 THE BIRDS

Czech. *Tr. O. B. C.*

FROM out of a wood did a cuckoo fly,
Cuckoo,
He came to a manger with joyful cry,
Cuckoo;
He hopped, he curtsied, round he flew,
And loud his jubilation grew,
Cuckoo, cuckoo, cuckoo.

2 A pigeon flew over to Galilee,
Vrercroo,
He strutted, and cooed, and was full of glee,
Vrercroo,
And showed with jewelled wings unfurled,
His joy that Christ was in the world,
Vrercroo, Vrercroo, Vrercroo.

3. A dove settled down upon Nazareth,
Tsucroo,
And tenderly chanted with all his breath
Tsucroo:
"O you,' he cooed, 'so good and true,
My beauty do I give to you—
Tsucroo, Tsucroo, Tsucroo.'

A translation of an unpublished carol, 'Zezulka z lesa vylitla, kuku', which was taken down from a Czech peasant girl in the Christmas of 1921 at Policka, in the hills between Bohemia and Moravia, and kindly communicated by Miss Jakubičková.

104 HOW BRIGHTLY BEAMS

FIRST TUNE.

(GENERAL : EPIPHANY : EASTER)

(harm. J. S. BACH.)

German. (*P. Nicolai?*)

Nicolai and Schlegel.

HOW brightly beams the morning star!
What sudden radiance from afar
Doth glad us with its shining?
Brightness of God, that breaks our night
And fills the darkened souls with light
Who long for truth were pining!
Thy word, Jesus, inly feeds us,
Rightly leads us,
Life bestowing.
Praise, oh praise such love o'erflowing!

104 HOW BRIGHTLY BEAMS

SECOND TUNE.

(GENERAL : EPIPHANY : EASTER)

(harm. F. MENDELSSOHN-BARTHOLDY.)

Rather slow.

2 Through thee alone can we be blest;
Then deep be on our hearts imprest
The love that thou hast borne us;
So make us ready to fulfil
With burning zeal thy holy will,
Though men may vex or scorn us;
Saviour, let us never lose thee,
For we choose thee,
Thirst to know thee;
All we are and have we owe thee!

3. O praise to him who came to save,
Who conquer'd death and burst the grave;
Each day new praise resoundeth
To him the Lamb who once was slain,
The friend whom none shall trust in vain,
Whose grace for ay aboundeth;
Sing, ye Heavens, tell the story,
Of his glory,
Till his praises
Flood with light earth's darkest places!

Three verses of the seven in the recast by J. A. Schlegel (1721–93), 'Wie herrlich strahlt der Morgenstern', of 'Wie schon leuchtet der Morgenstern', which appeared with the tune in Nicolai's *Freudenspiegel*, 1599. The famous tune, to which very soon many city chimes in Germany were set, was published with Nicolai's hymn, and may therefore be by the author and composer of 'Wachet auf'. It may in part have been suggested by earlier melodies, especially by 'Resonet in Laudibus' (No. 77). The translation is almost entirely that of Miss C. Winkworth, 1863.

105 THE GARDEN OF JESUS

(GENERAL)

(GEOFFREY SHAW.)

And
harps, and cym-bals, trum-pets, pipes, And gen - tle flutes............

Dutch, 1633. *Tr. E. B. G.*

LORD Jesus hath a garden, full of flowers gay,
Where you and I can gather nosegays all the day:

There angels sing in jubilant ring,
With dulcimers and lutes,
And harps, and cymbals, trumpets, pipes,
And gentle, soothing flutes.

2 There bloometh white the lily, flower of Purity;
The fragrant violet hides there, sweet Humility:

3 The rose's name is Patience, pruned to greater might;
The marigold's, Obedience, plentiful and bright:

4 And Hope and Faith are there; but of these three the best,
Is Love, whose crown-imperial spreads o'er all the rest:

5 And one thing fairest is in all that lovely maze,
The gardener, Jesus Christ, whom all the flowers praise:

6. O Jesus, all my good and all my bliss! Ah me!
Thy garden make my heart, which ready is for thee!

The Dutch words and melody of 'Jesus' Bloemnof' (beginning 'Heer Jesus heeft een hofken waart vol bloemen staat') occur in *Geestlijke Harmonie* (1633), and were reprinted in *Oude en Nieuwere Kerst-Liederen* (1852). A translation ('Our Master hath a garden') by S. S. Greatheed was printed in *The Ecclesiologist* for February, 1856, and was included by E. Sedding in *Antient Christmas Carols*, 1860, and in *The People's Hymnal*, 1867. It does not, however, quite fit the melody; and therefore, while we have preserved the 'gentle, soothing' flutes, we give a new translation here.

106

SO, BROTHER

(GENERAL)

Moderately quick. (M. S.)

Besançon. *Pr. A. A. Milne.*

NOW brothers lift your voices,
  And laugh and dance and sing,
For all the world rejoices
  That Christ the Lord is King.
With joy in him to arm you
  The Devil cannot harm you:
So, brother, laugh and sing,
  That Christ the Lord is King.

2 Poor Satan, you can hear him,
  Is raging down in hell,
For now there 's none to fear him,
  And none to wish him well.
The fires that he was keeping
  Are on his footsteps creeping
So, brother! laugh and sing
  That Christ the Lord is King.

3 And fiercer now and faster
  The flames come roaring in
On him that was their Master,
  On Satan, prince of sin.
Then, brother, as he lies there,
  Then, brother, as he dies there,
Come laugh and dance and sing—
  That Christ the Lord is King.

A paraphrase of three verses (out of twelve) in the original carol 'Fesans raijouissance' written by Père Christin Prost, a Capuchin friar who died in 1676. His carols were reprinted in *Recueil de Noëls anciens au patois de Besançon*, edited by Th. Belamy, 1842. The old air on which the carol was written was known as 'Je suis dans la tristesse' or 'De turlu turlutu'.

107 PRAISE TO GOD

(GENERAL)

(M. S.)
Moderato e maestoso.
Praise to God in the
Guide and pros-per thy
Melody in Tenor.
FINE.
high - - est! to God, Praise to thee.
na - tions, ru-lers and peo - ple: Praise to thee.

Russian. *Tr. A. F. D.*

PRAISE to God in the highest! Bless us, O Father!
Praise to thee.
Guide and prosper the nations, rulers and people:
May the truth in its beauty flourish triumphant:
May the mills bring us bread, for food and for giving;
May the good be obeyed, and evil be conquered:
Give us laughter, and set us gaily rejoicing:
Peace on earth, and goodwill, be ever amongst us:

'Slava Bogu na nebye' was printed by Yakushkin in 1815, and exists in many variants, as well as in Rimsky-Korsakov, who calls it a Christmas Song, though its many verses, from which we have selected, are all of general national application. The melody was used by Beethoven in his Quartet, Op. 59, No. 2; by Rimsky-Korsakov in his cantata 'Slava'; and by Mussorgsky in the Coronation Scene of 'Boris Godunov'.

108 THE KINGDOM

(GENERAL)

Angevin. *Pr. Patrick R. Chalmers.*

'O I have seen a King's new Baby,'
Susan she said,
'Joy upon his bright, dear birthday be
And his bright head!'
Catherine, her kindly comrade, then did
Say, 'Show me too—
Son of a King must lie so splendid
All gold and blue!'

2 'O the King's Son he lies so sparely,'
Susan she told,
No lace to lappen him so fairly,
No blue and gold.'
'Prince—and he ne'er has fine adorning?'
Catherine cried,
'Prince, and the Sun, my girl, at morning?'
The maid replied.

3 'Where, then 's his mighty Kingdom, say you?'
'Everywhere.'
'So! and how may I know it, pray you?'
'Kindness is there.'
'Kings have bright swords to follow after,
Bugles to ring?'
'Nay, here is only children's laughter,
Here thrushes sing.'

4 'Whom, say now, shall he rule anon? he
Coming to reign?'
'Both bird and beast and man, my bonny,
Mountain and plain.'
'These shall he hold and have securely—
How? Tell me friend?'
'Only by being a servant, surely,
Unto the end.'

5. 'Susan, who'll herald him, this stranger,
This kingly boy?'
'Just a lit star above a manger
Laughing for joy.'
'Still, gossip, I might doubt him, maybe,
Knowing no thing?'
'Dear my heart, would you doubt a Baby
To be a King?'

Words written for the older, modal, melody in Henri Lemeignen, *Vieux Noëls* (Nantes, 1876), and in Grimault, of the Angevin carol, 'Quoi ma voisine', a dialogue between two women, here freely paraphrased.

109 O LITTLE ONE FIRST VERSION.

(GENERAL)

(M. S.)

vv. 1, 3.

German, S. Scheidt, 1650. *Ibid., Tr. O. B. C.*

O LITTLE One sweet, O Little One mild,
Thy Father's purpose thou hast fulfilled;
Thou cam'st from heaven to mortal ken,
Equal to be with us poor men,
O Little One sweet, O Little One mild.

2 O Little One sweet, O Little One mild,
With joy thou hast the whole world filled;
Thou camest here from heaven's domain,
To bring men comfort in their pain,
O Little One sweet, O Little One mild.

3 O Little One sweet, O Little One mild,
In thee Love's beauties are all distilled;
Then light in us thy love's bright flame,
That we may give thee back the same,
O Little One sweet, O Little One mild.

109 O LITTLE ONE SECOND VERSION.

(GENERAL)

(Harm. J. S. BACH.)

4. O Little One sweet, O Little One mild,
Help us to do as thou hast willed.
Lo, all we have belongs to thee !
Ah, keep us in our fealty !
O Little One sweet, O Little One mild.

* If sung in conjunction with the first version the melody rhythm of this bar may be altered for the sake of consistency.

Scheidt's version, 'O Jesulein süss, O Jesulein mild, Dein's Vaters Will'n hast du erfüllt', is in his *Tabulaturbuch*, 1650. Set by J. S. Bach in 1736. The melody appears also in *Seelenharphe* (Halle, 1650) to the words 'Komm, heiliger Geist mit deiner Gnad'.

110 JESUS OF THE MANGER

(GENERAL)

(M. S.)
On a
day, on a day,
On a day, With the
He lay there for us all, us all.
He lay there for us all.
Man's heart on - ly there - for.
God will lodge with us then.

Flemish. *Pr. Patrick R. Chalmers.*

SING, good company, frank and free!
Jesus, when so young was he,
With the little calf shared the stall;
Low he lay
On a day, on a day,
With the little calf in the stall
Low he lay,
He lay there for us all, us all.

2 Rouse, good company, rouse you, rouse!
All the earth to Jesus bows;
Yet the dwelling that he'd implore
Poor must stay,
By my fay, by my fay,
Still the dwelling that he'd implore
Poor must stay—
Man's heart only must serve therefor.

3. Sing, good company, glad and true!
God may lodge with me and you;
So let's love them—all beasts and men,
Kindlily,
As doth he, as doth he;
If we love them—all beasts and men,
Kindlily,
God will lodge with us then, ah then!

Paraphrase of 'Jesus in den Stal', printed in *Chants Populaires Flamands*, by Lootens and Feys, reprinted by E. Duncan, *Story of the Carol*, and by H. J. L. J. Massé and C. Kennedy Scott, *Book of Old Carols*.

111

THE BUILDERS

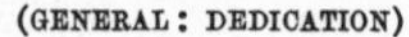

(GENERAL: DEDICATION)

Moderately quick. (M. S.)

Angevin. *Pr. Geoffrey Dearmer.*

SING all good people gathered,
Your voices raise in song
Within this church that fathered
Our ancient faith so strong,
So tried and wrought to fitness
In scorn of fire and sword;
Sing, as these stones bear witness,
Of men who praised the Lord.

2 Each rib from pillars springing
A frozen fountain plays,
Above the chancel singing
In harmony of praise;
Like tall trees ever growing
The differing columns stand
To bear the vault down-throwing
The shadow of God's hand.

3 At all times and unceasing,
Work well and truly done,
In loveliness increasing,
Has mellowed here in one ;
The towers and piers unshaken,
The vaulting finely groined,
Time in his span hath taken
And in one glory joined.

4 Of wealth and fame and power
These masons did not know :
' Let's build,' they said, ' a tower,
Square to the winds that blow ;
We are not men of culture,
Yet we are here to build
Room for a king's sepulture
And worthy of our guild.'

5 So came each beam and rafter,
Each wingèd flight of stone.
Their deathless work lives after,
Their names were never known :
For beauty did they plead not,
Yet beauty they did win,
And, like a child you heed not,
The grace of Heaven crept in.

6 Here, for a workman's wages,
This glass so surely stained
Down the long aisles of ages
In glory has remained.
As brother works with brother
The glaziers worked to paint
The blue robe of the Mother,
The red robe of a saint.

7. Proud heads lie here, disowning
All but a drooping Head ;
Whole hands worked here, atoning
For open Hands that bled ;
Full hearts and living voices
A broken Heart proclaim ;
Life after death rejoices,
And after silence, fame.

Since the original twenty-two verses of ' Venez à Saint-Maurice ' deal in great detail with the characteristics and treasures of Angers Cathedral, the English words have been written for the general idea rather than for the details of the original, and we claim the tune as proper to them only in this most generous and spiritual sense. Topical allusions in the original fix its date as earlier than 1699 and later than 1562. The gay melody has been always attributed to Urbain Renard, but the origin and date of folk-tunes is very doubtful. The carol (which is printed by Grimault in *Noëls Angevins*) very likely grew up from some humble fiddler seeking alms outside the Cathedral of Saint-Maurice.

112 EIA, EIA

(GENERAL)

Cölner Psalter, 1638. *Ibid.*, *Pr. A. G*

TO us in Bethlem city
  Was born a little son;
In him all gentle graces
  Were gathered into one,
    Eia, Eia,
  Were gathered into one.

2 And all our love and fortune
  Lie in his mighty hands;
Our sorrows, joys, and failures,
  He sees and understands,
    Eia, Eia,
  He sees and understands.

3 O Shepherd ever near us,
  We'll go where thou dost lead;
No matter where the pasture,
  With thee at hand to feed,
    Eia, Eia,
  With thee at hand to feed.

4. No grief shall part us from thee,
  However sharp the edge:
We'll serve, and do thy bidding—
  O take our hearts in pledge!
    Eia, Eia,
  Take thou our hearts in pledge

The folk-carol, here paraphrased, 'Zu Bethlehem geboren', appears first in print i the *Cölner Psalter*, 1638. Riemann reprinted this version from Nordstern's *Führer zu Seligkeit*, 1671.

113 SPANISH CAROL

(NATIVITY)

Galician. *Tr. J. B. Trend.*

UP now, laggardly lasses,
  Up, awake and away!
Out and gone before cock-crow,
  On the road before day!
Mary meek and gentle,
  Rose of Jericho,
Bore a babe and laid him
  In a manger low.

2. See the tears in his eyes, now;
  (Sleep, my pretty one, sleep!)
Let him dream when he can, now
  (Sleep, my innocent, sleep!)
Ah, my precious jewel,
  Great the grief and pain,
Suffered through the wide world
  For the sins of men!

'Panxoliña de Nadal', a Spanish carol from Galicia. The melody is from Pedrell, *Cancionero musical*; the words translated from the *Cancionero popular gallego* of J. Pérez Ballesteros. Cf. No. 81.

PART II

114 NO ROOM IN THE INN

(ADVENT)

A Traditional tune.

Words, Traditional

WHEN Caesar Augustus had raised a taxation,
He assessed all the people that dwelt in the nation;
The Jews at that time being under Rome's sway
Appeared in the city their tribute to pay:
Then Joseph and Mary, who from David did spring,
Went up to the city of David their king,
And, there being entered, cold welcome they find.—
From the rich to the poor they are mostly unkind.

2 They sought entertainment, but none could they find,
Great numbers of strangers had fillèd the inn ;
They knockèd and callèd all this at the door,
But found not a friend where in kind they had store ;
Their kindred accounted they come were too soon ;
'Too late,' said the innkeeper, 'here is no room.'
Amongst strangers and kinsfolk cold welcome they find.—
From the rich to the poor they are mostly unkind.

3 Good Joseph was troubled, but most for his dear,
For her blessèd burden whose time now drew near ;
His heart with true sorrow was sorely afflicted
That his virgin spouse was so rudely neglected.
He could get no house-room who houses did frame,
But Joseph and Mary must go as they came.
For little is the favour the poor man can find.—
From the rich to the poor they are mostly unkind.

4 Whilst the great and the wealthy do frolic in hall,
Possess all the ground-rooms and chambers and all,
Poor Joseph and Mary are thrust in a stable
In Bethlehem city, ground inhospitáble,
And with their mean lodging contented they be :
For the minds of the just with their fortunes agree ;
They bear all affronts with their meekness of mind,
And be not offended though the rich be unkind.

5. O Bethlehem, Bethlehem, welcome this stranger
That was born in a stable and laid in a manger ;
For he is a Physician to heal all our smarts—
Come welcome, sweet Jesus, and lodge in our hearts.

This simple and charming carol was probably sung to one of the traditional 'Virgin unspotted' tunes (cf. No. 4). We have chosen the one printed by Sandys in 1833. The text is also from Sandys, very slightly altered.

115 JOSEPH AND MARY

(ADVENT AND CHRISTMAS)

Andante.
(R. V. W.)
mf
1 O, Jo-seph being an old man tru-ly, He married a vir - gin
fair and free ; A pur - er vir - gin could no man see Than he
chose for his wife and his dear - est dear.
pp
2 They liv - ed both in

joy and bliss; But now a strict commandment is, In
Jew - ry - land no man should miss To go a - long with his
1st time.
Last.
dear - est dear,...............
3 Un -

ARRANGEMENT FOR UNACCOMPANIED VOICES.

NOTE—The words to be sung by the Tenors only, the other parts to vocalize.

English Traditional. *Traditional.*

O JOSEPH being an old man truly,
He married a virgin fair and free;
A purer virgin could no man see
Than he chose for his wife and his dearest dear.

2 They livèd both in joy and bliss;
But now a strict commandment is,
In Jewry-land no man should miss
To go along with his dearest dear,

3 Unto the place, where he was born,
Unto the Emperor to be sworn,
To pay a tribute that's duly known,
Both for himself and his dearest dear.

4 And when they were to Bethlehem come,
The inns were filled, both all and some;
For Joseph entreated them, every one,
Both for himself and his dearest dear.

5 Then were they constrained presently
Within a stable all night to lie,
Where they did oxen and asses tie,
With his true love and his dearest dear.

6. The king of all power was in Bethlehem born,
Who wore for our sakes a crown of thorn.
Then God preserve us both even and morn
For Jesus' sake, our dearest dear!

The original words ('There is a fountain') to which Mrs. Esther Smith sung this tune at Weobley were probably not traditional, and were moreover full of the rather unpleasant imagery which is characteristic of much of the eighteenth-century evangelistic verse. They are printed in the *Journal of the Folk-Song Society*, ii. 133 and iv. 21. Rather than omit such a fine tune, the Editors of *Twelve Traditional Carols from Herefordshire* decided to set other words to it—undoubtedly traditional, for which, as far as they know, no tune has been preserved, and we have done the same. These words are taken from Sandys. They seem to reach back to the seventeenth century; but the story of Joseph's doubts (here omitted from the sixteen verses of the original) was familiar in the fourteenth, and occurs in a different carol of the fifteenth century. See E. Rickert, *Ancient English Christmas Carols*, xix. 24–7.

116 A BABE IS BORN

(CHRISTMAS : EPIPHANY)

Nowell, el, el, el,
Now is well, that ever was woe.

(M. S.)

English Traditional. *15th century.*

A BABE is born all of a may,
To bring salvation unto us.
To him we sing both night and day
Veni creator Spiritus.

2 At Bethlehem, that blessèd place,
The child of bliss now born he was;
And him to serve God give us grace,
O lux beata Trinitas.

3 There came three kings out of the East,
To worship the King that is so free,
With gold and myrrh and frankincense,
A solis ortus cardine.

4 The shepherds heard an angel's cry,
A merry song that night sung he.
'Why are ye so sore aghast?'
Jam ortus solis cardine.

5. The angels came down with one cry,
A fair song that night sung they
In the worship of that child:
Gloria tibi Domine.

1. may] maid. *Veni creator*] Come, creator Spirit: the Whitsun hymns, *E.H.* 153, 154, 156. 2. *O lux beata*] O Trinity, blessed light: Evening hymn, *E.H.* 164. 3. *A solis ortus cardine*] Risen from the quarter of the sun: Christmas hymn, *E.H.* 18. 4. Orig. 'The herdes heardyn'. 5. *Gloria tibi Domine*] Glory to thee, O Lord.

Sloane MS. 2593, first half of the fifteenth century. Another version in Richard Hill's MS. (cf. No. 36), 'There is a child born of a may'. We have altered, in v. 1, 'In the savasyoun of us', with Bramley and Stainer, who preserved the tune, and in 4, 'A merye song then sungyn he', and similarly in 5.

117 IMMORTAL BABE

(CHRISTMAS : EPIPHANY)

(M. S.)

German, 16th century. *Bishop Joseph Hall,* 1574–1656.

IMMORTAL Babe, who this dear day
Didst change thine heaven for our clay,
And didst with flesh thy godhead veil,
Eternal Son of God, all hail!

2 Shine, happy star: ye Angels sing
Glory on high to heaven's King:
Run, Shepherds, leave your nightly watch,
See heaven come down to Bethlehem's cratch.

3 Worship, ye Sages of the East,
The King of gods in meanness dressed:
O blessèd Maid, smile and adore
The God thy womb and arms have bore.

4. Star, Angels, Shepherds, and wise Sages,
Thou virgin glory of all ages,
Restorèd frame of heaven and earth,
Joy in your dear Redeemer's birth!

2. cratch] cradle.

From *The Shaking of the Olive Tree*, by Joseph Hall, Bishop of Exeter, 1660. The melody is a German traditional carol tune.

118

SUSANNI

(CHRISTMAS : EPIPHANY)

(M. S.)

German tune. *15th century.*

A LITTLE child there is yborn,
Eia, eia, susanni, susanni, susanni.
And he sprang out of Jesse's thorn,
Alleluya, Alleluya.
To save all us that were forlorn.

2 Now Jesus is the childès name,
And Mary mild she is his dame;
And so our sorrow is turned to game.

3 It fell upon the high midnight,
The stars they shone both fair and bright,
The angels sang with all their might.

4 *Three kings there came with their presénts
Of myrrh and gold and frankincense,
As clerkès sing in their sequence.

5. Now sit we down upon our knee,
And pray we to the Trinity,
Our help, and succour for to be.

Ashmolean MS. 1393. Printed *Early Bodleian Music,* 1901, and Chambers and Sidgwick; here collated with Richard Hill's MS. The proper tune is, however, unknown: we have therefore used the melody of a similar carol, 'Susanni, Susanni' (Vom Himmel hoch); the refrain is that of this German carol, which is given in Hölscher's *Niederdeutsche geistliche Lieder* (Berlin, 1854) from a source of 1588, but is of earlier origin.

119 ANGELS, FROM THE REALMS

(CHRISTMAS : EPIPHANY)

(M. S.)

p
Come and wor - ship
Come and wor - ship
Christ the new-born King
f
Come
Christ the new-born King
Come

.... and wor - ship, Wor-ship Christ the new - born King.
.... and wor - ship, Worship Christ the new - born King.

French tune. *J. Montgomery,* 1771–1854.

ANGELS, from the realms of glory,
Wing your flight o'er all the earth;
Ye who sang creation's story
Now proclaim Messiah's birth:
Come and worship,
Worship Christ the new-born King.

2 Shepherds in the field abiding,
Watching o'er your flocks by night,
God with man is now residing;
Yonder shines the infant Light:

3 Sages, leave your contemplations;
Brighter visions beam afar;
Seek the great Desire of Nations;
Ye have seen his natal star:

4 Saints before the altar bending,
Watching long in hope and fear,
Suddenly the Lord, descending,
In his temple shall appear:

5. Though an infant now we view him,
He shall fill his Father's throne,
Gather all the nations to him;
Every knee shall then bow down:

Montgomery's well-known hymn, first printed in his newspaper *Iris*, December, 24, 1816, and included among 'Three New Carols' in *The Christmas Box*, 1825 (the first complete book of the Religious Tract Society, and precursor of the popular 'Christmas Books'), reads almost like an early nineteenth-century translation of the opening verses of 'Les anges dans nos campagnes', the old French carol from which we take the tune. The fifth verse is taken from 'The Babe of Bethlehem', another carol in *The Christmas Box*.

120 IN BETHLEHEM, THAT FAIR CITY

(CHRISTMAS : INNOCENTS' DAY)

To bliss God bring us, all and some,
Christe redemptor omnium.

(G. S.)

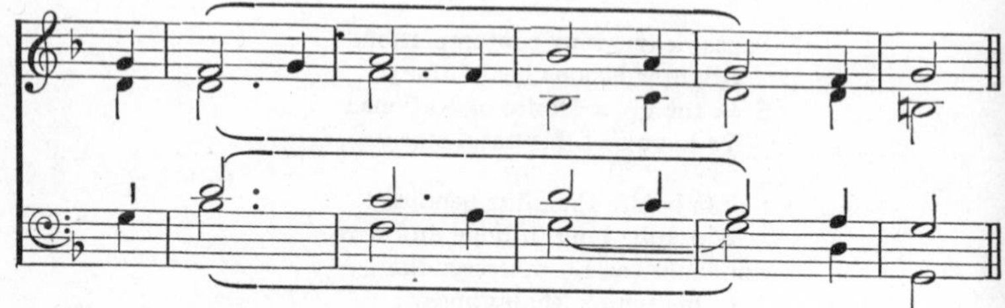

ALTERNATIVE VERSION (MELODY IN TENOR).

14th century. *15th century.*

IN Bethlehem, that fair city, *Alleluya,*
Was born a child that was so free, *Alleluya.*

2 Lord and prince of high degree,
Jam lucis orto sidere.

3 Jesu, for the love of thee,
Children were slain in great plenty,

4 In Bethlehem, that fair city,
A solis ortus cardine.

5 As the sun shineth through the glass,
So Jesu in her body was.

6 Then him to serve God give us grace,
O lux beata Trinitas.

7 Now is he born our Lord Jesus,
He that made merry all of us:

8. Then be all merry in this house,
Exultet coelum laudibus.

Christe, &c.] Christ, redeemer of all (Christmas Mattins hymn, *E.H.* 17). 2. *Jam lucis,* &c.] 'Now that the daylight fills the sky' (Prime, *E.H.* 254). 4. *A solis,* &c. and 6. *O lux,* &c.] See No. 23. 8. *Exultet,* &c.] Let heaven exult with praises, *E.H.* 176.

There are different versions of this carol in the fifteenth-century Cambridge T.C.C. (O 3. 58) MS., in Richard Hill's MS., &c. These different versions are printed in Fuller Maitland, Wright, &c., and in Chambers and Sidgwick. The refrain belongs to the fourteenth-century melody of 'Puer natus in Bethlehem', of which there are very many variants, the earliest (fifteenth century) MSS. being at Strasburg and Munich. Our version of the tune appears in *Piae Cantiones,* and was harmonized by Bach (1685–1750).

121 FALAN-TIDING

(EPIPHANY : CHRISTMAS)

Tyrolese tune. c. 1610.

OUT of the orient crystal skies
  A blazing star did shine,
Showing the place where poorly lies
  A blessèd babe divine,

2 Born of a maid of royal blood
  Who Mary hight by name,
A sacred rose which once did bud
  By grace of heavenly flame.

3 This shining star three kings did guide
  Even from the furthest East,
To Bethlehem where it betide
  This blessèd babe did rest,

4 Laid in a silly manger poor,
  Betwixt an ox and ass,
Whom these three kings did all adore
  As God's high pleasure was.

5 And for the joy of his great birth
  A thousand angels sing:
'Glory and peace unto the earth
  Where born is this new King!'

6. The shepherds dwelling there about,
  When they this news did know,
Came singing all even in a rout,
  'Falan-tiding-dido!'

4. silly] simple.
In the B.M. Add. MS. 29401, with a contemporary five-part setting; as this is a motet we are not including it, but have used the tune of a Tyrolese carol, 'Ihr Hirten, stehet alle auf'.

122 HERRICK'S CAROL

(CHRISTMAS)

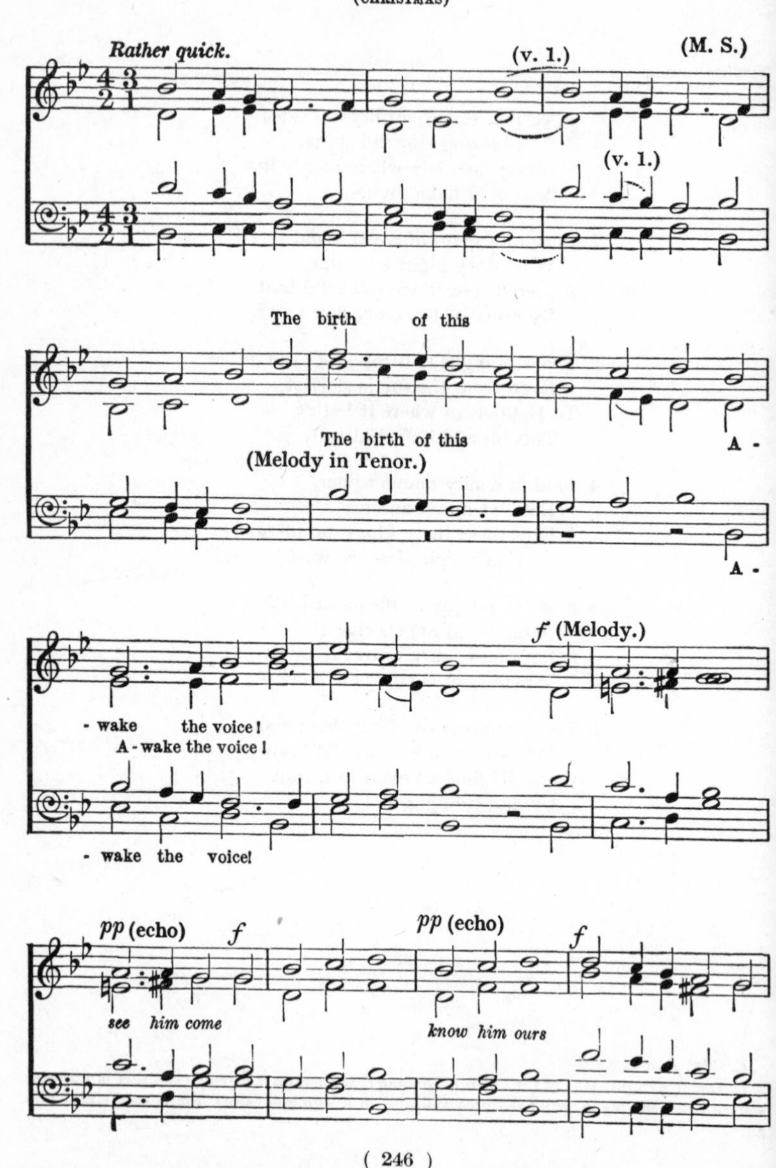

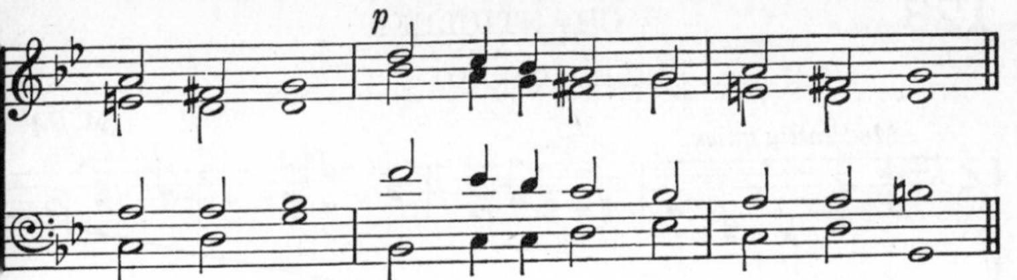

German tune. *Robert Herrick* (1647).

WHAT sweeter music can we bring
Than a carol, for to sing
The birth of this our heavenly King?
Awake the voice! Awake the string:

We see him come, and know him ours,
Who with his sunshine and his showers
Turns all the patient ground to flowers.

2 Dark and dull night, fly hence away,
And give the honour to this day,
That sees December turned to May,
If we may ask the reason, say:

3 The darling of the world is come,
And fit it is we find a room
To welcome him. The nobler part
Of all the house here is the heart:

4. Which we will give him, and bequeath
This holly and this ivy wreath,
To do him honour who's our King,
And Lord of all this revelling:

Herrick's *Hesperides*, from which these words are taken, was performed before Charles I, 'in the Presence, at Whitehall'. The words are here arranged for 'Als ich bei meinen Schafen wacht', a Christmas-play carol in the *Cölner Gesangbuch* (1623), and elsewhere, reprinted in Böhme.

123 CHANTICLEER

(NATIVITY)

(M. S.)

English Traditional.

W. Austin, 1587-1633.

ALL this night shrill chanticleer,
Day's proclaiming trumpeter,
Claps her wings and loudly cries,
Mortals, mortals, wake and rise!
See a wonder
Heaven is under;
From the earth is risen a Sun
Shines all night, though day be done.

2 Wake, O earth, wake everything!
Wake and hear the joy I bring;
Wake and joy; for all this night
Heaven and every twinkling light,
All amazing,
Still stand gazing.
Angels, Powers, and all that be,
Wake, and joy this Sun to see.

3. Hail, O Sun, O blessèd Light,
Sent into the world by night!
Let thy rays and heavenly powers
Shine in these dark souls of ours;
For most duly
Thou art truly
God and man, we do confess:
Hail, O Sun of Righteousness!

From '*Devotionis Augustinianae Flamma* by William Austin, of Lincolnes Inne Esquier', who died 16 January 1633 (published, 1635). There is a monument to him in St. Saviour's, Southwark. The tune is adapted from an English traditional melody.

124

SUMMER IN WINTER

(NATIVITY)

Alsatian tune. *R. Crashaw, c.* 1613–49.

GLOOMY night embraced the place
  Where the noble infant lay;
The babe looked up and shewed his face,
  In spite of darkness it was day!
It was thy day, Sweet, and did rise,
Not from the East, but from thine eyes.

2 Winter chid aloud, and sent
  The angry North to wage his wars.
The North forgot his fierce intent,
  And left perfumes, instead of scars.
By those sweet eyes' persuasive powers
Where he meant frost, he scattered flowers.

3 We saw thee in thy balmy nest,
  Bright dawn of our eternal day!
We saw thine eyes break from their east
  And chase the trembling shades away;
We saw thee, and we blessed the sight,
We saw thee by thine own sweet light.

4. Welcome, all wonder in one sight,
  Eternity shut in a span,
Summer in winter, day in night,
  Heaven in earth, and God in man!
Great little one! whose all-embracing birth
Lifts earth to heaven, stoops heaven to earth.

From the eighteen stanzas of Crashaw's 'Hymn in the Holy Nativity', 1648. The melody is from *Cantiques de Strasbourg*, 1697.

125

RORATE

(NATIVITY)

Scottish Traditional. *William Dunbar, c.* **1465–1530.**

RORATE coeli desuper!
Heavens, distil your balmy showers;
For now is risen the bright Daystar,
From the rose Mary, flower of flowers:
The clear Sun, whom no cloud devours,
Surmounting Phoebus in the east,
Is comen of his heavenly towers,
Et nobis puer natus est.

2 Sinners be glad, and penance do,
And thank your Maker heartfully;
For he that ye might not come to,
To you is comen full humbly,
Your soulès with his blood to buy,
And loose you of the fiend's arrest,
And only of his own mercy;
Pro nobis puer natus est.

3 Celestial fowlès in the air,
Sing with your notès upon height,
In firthès and in forests fair
Be mirthful now at all your might;
For passèd is your dully night;
Aurora has the cloudès pierced,
The sun is risen with gladsome light,
Et nobis puer natus est.

4. Sing heaven imperial, most of height,
Regions of air make harmony,
All fish in flood and fowl of flight
Be mirthful and make melody:
All *Gloria in excelsis* cry,
Heaven, earth, sea, man, bird, and beast;
He that is crowned above the sky
Pro nobis puer natus est.

1. *Rorate,* &c.] Drop down, ye heavens, from above (Is. 45, 8). *Et nobis,* &c.] And for us a boy is born.

On the eve of the Reformation, Dunbar, the Scottish diplomat, ex-Franciscan, and poet, still uses the sounded 'e' when he thinks fit; he is, as Palgrave says, 'the fine flower of expiring medievalism'. The verses are here set to a little-known Scottish melody.

126 CANDLEMAS EVE

(FEB. 1ST, AND SPRING)

(M. S.)

(v. 6) Thus times do shift, thus times do shift; each
thing his turn does hold; New things succeed, new things succeed, as former things grow old.

Church-gallery book. *R. Herrick*, 1591–1674.

DOWN with the rosemary and bays,
Down with the mistletoe;
Instead of holly, now upraise
The greener box, for show.

2 The holly hitherto did sway:
Let box now domineer
Until the dancing Easter day,
Or Easter's eve appear.

3 Then youthful box, which now hath grace
Your houses to renew,
Grown old, surrender must his place
Unto the crispèd yew.

4 When yew is out, then birch comes in,
And many flowers beside,
Both of a fresh and fragrant kin,
To honour Whitsuntide.

5 Green rushes then, and sweetest bents,
With cooler oaken boughs,
Come in for comely ornaments,
To readorn the house.

6. Thus times do shift; each thing his turn does hold;
New things succeed, as former things grow old.

The tune is from an old church-gallery book, discovered by the Rev. L. J. T. Darwall.

127 GOD IS ASCENDED

(ASCENSION)

(M. S.)

Al - le - lu-
- ya,............... Al - le - lu - ya.
Al - le - lu - ya,............ Al - le - lu - ya.

German, 16th century. *Henry More,* 1614–87.

GOD is ascended up on high, *Alleluya.*
With merry noise of trumpet's sound, *Alleluya.*
And princely seated in the sky, *Alleluya.*
Rules over all the world around, *Alleluya.*

2 In human flesh and shape he went,
Adornèd with his passion's scars,
Which in heaven's sight he did present
More glorious than the glittering stars.

3. Lord, raise our sinking minds therefore
Up to our proper country dear,
And purify us evermore,
To fit us for those regions clear.

The German text and melody of 'Gen Himmel aufgefahren ist' are in David Corner, 1631, as 'Ein altes Lobgesang von Christi Himmelfahrt'. More's first stanza almost exactly reproduces the short text of the original as reprinted in Riemann. Henry More, the saintly Cambridge Platonist, became Fellow of Christ's College in 1639.

WELCOME, SUMMER

Irish Traditional. *Geoffrey Chaucer, c.* 1340–1400.

Moderately quick.

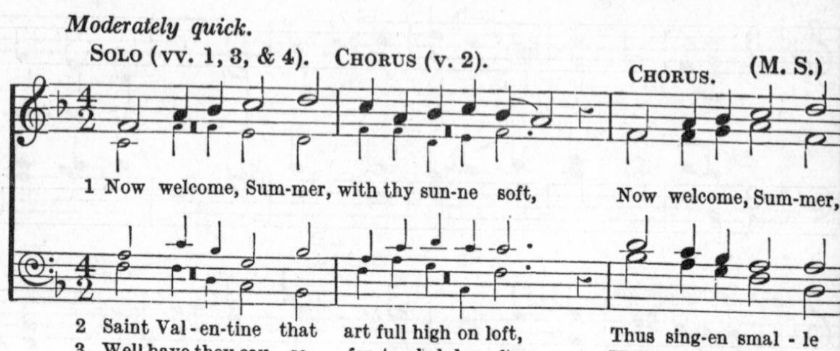
SOLO (vv. 1, 3, & 4). CHORUS (v. 2).
CHORUS. (M. S.)
1 Now welcome, Sum-mer, with thy sun-ne soft,
Now welcome, Sum-mer,
2 Saint Val-en-tine that art full high on loft,
3 Well have they cau - se for to glad-den oft,
4. 'Now welcome, Sum-mer, with thy sun-ne soft,
Thus sing-en smal - le
Well have they cau - se
Now welcome, Sum-mer,

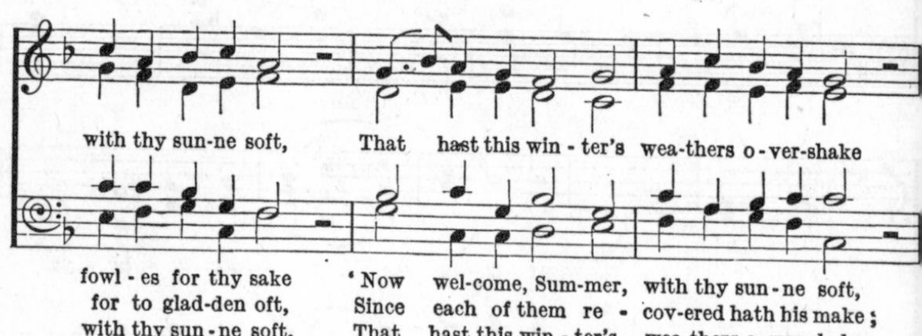
with thy sun-ne soft, That hast this win - ter's wea-thers o-ver-shake
fowl - es for thy sake 'Now wel-come, Sum-mer, with thy sun-ne soft,
for to glad-den oft, Since each of them re - cov-ered hath his make;
with thy sun - ne soft, That hast this win - ter's wea-thers o-ver-shake

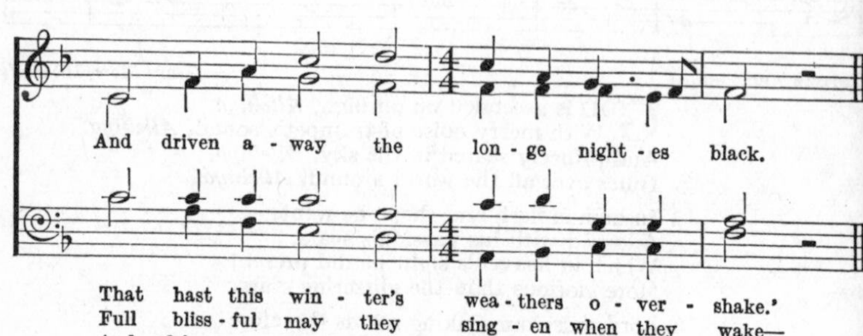
And driven a - way the lon - ge night - es black.
That hast this win - ter's wea - thers o - ver - shake.'
Full bliss - ful may they sing - en when they wake—
And driven a - way the lon - ge night - es black.'

1. overshake] shaken off. 2. on loft] in the air. fowlès (foules)] birds.
3. gladden] rejoice. make] mate.

This roundel comes at the end of *The Parlement of Foules.* We have set it to an old Irish carol tune, slightly adapted.

129 PLEASURE IT IS

(SUMMER AND HARVEST)

(M. S.)

In moderate time.

B. Waldis, 1553. *William Cornish, d.* 1523.

PLEASURE it is
 To hear, I wis,
 The birdès sing.
The deer in the dale,
The sheep in the vale,
 The corn springing;

God's purveyance
For sustenance
 It is for man.
Then we always
To him give praise,
 And thank him then.

William Cornish, or Cornysshe, was Master of the Chapel Royal under Henry VII and Henry VIII, for whom he composed music and acted in court pageants; in 1518 he forced Wolsey to give up one of his choristers to the Chapel Royal. The words occur in a book of which only one copy is known to exist (B.M., K. 1, e. 1), '*Bassus.* In this boke ar cōteynyd XX sōgs, IX of IIII partes and XI of thre partes', printed by Wynkyn de Worde, 1530. The melody is lost, only the bass part being given in *Bassus*: the words are here set to B. Waldis's tune for Ps. 124 (1553), printed by Zahn, no. 5571.

130 WATTS'S CRADLE SONG

(GENERAL)

Verses 1 & 2 (Verse 1 sung as a Soprano Solo unaccompanied. Verse 2, the words sung by Sopranos, other parts hum accompaniment.)

Rather slowly, but with flowing movement. (Freely arr. M. S.)

Verse 3 (all sing words).
1st time.
Verse 4.
Hush! my dear, lie still and slum - ber;
Soft and ea-sy is thy cra - dle; etc.
Hush! my dear, lie still and slum - ber;
Verse 5.
rit. e dim.

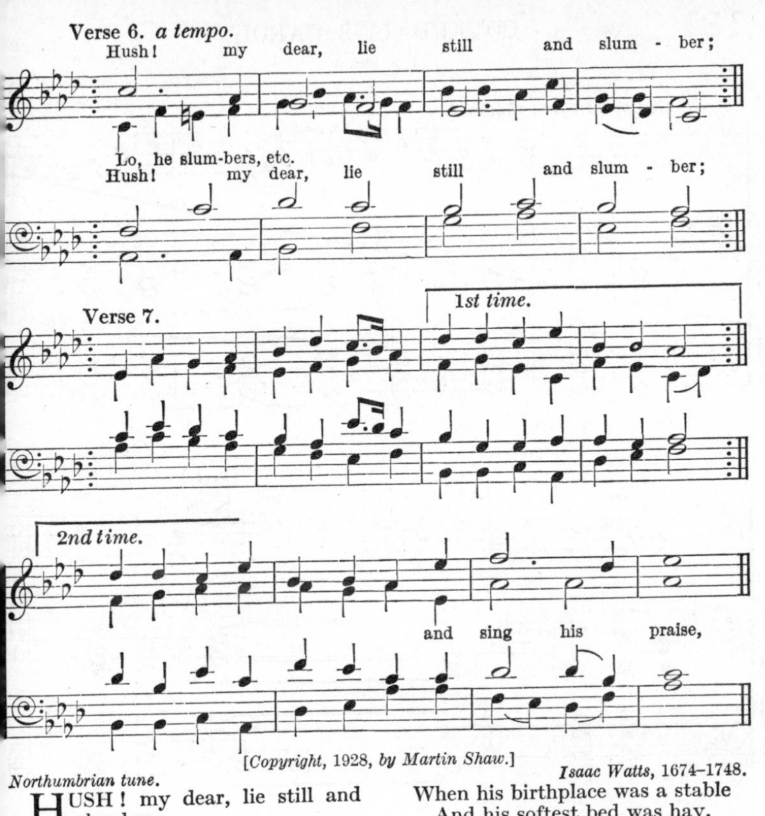
Verse 6. a tempo.
Hush! my dear, lie still and slum - ber;
Lo, he slum-bers, etc.
Hush! my dear, lie still and slum - ber;
Verse 7.
1st time.
2nd time.
and sing his praise,

Northumbrian tune.

Isaac Watts, 1674–1748.

HUSH! my dear, lie still and slumber;
Holy Angels guard thy bed!
Heavenly blessings without number
Gently falling on thy head.

2 Sleep, my babe; thy food and raiment,
House and home, thy friends provide;
All without thy care and payment,
All thy wants are well supplied.

3 How much better thou'rt attended
Than the Son of God could be
When from Heaven he descended
And became a child like thee.

4 Soft and easy is thy cradle;
Coarse and hard thy Saviour lay,
When his birthplace was a stable
And his softest bed was hay.

5 See the lovely Babe adressing;
Lovely Infant, how he smiled!
When he wept, the mother's blessing
Soothed and hushed the holy Child.

6 Lo, he slumbers in his manger,
Where the hornèd oxen fed;
—Peace, my darling! here's no danger;
Here's no ox a-near thy bed.

7. Mayst thou live to know and fear him,
Trust and love him all thy days:
Then go dwell for ever near him,
See his face and sing his praise.

Watts's words are here set to a traditional carol tune, sung to these words, and noted in Northumberland by R. Vaughan Williams.

131

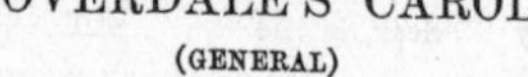

COVERDALE'S CAROL

(GENERAL)

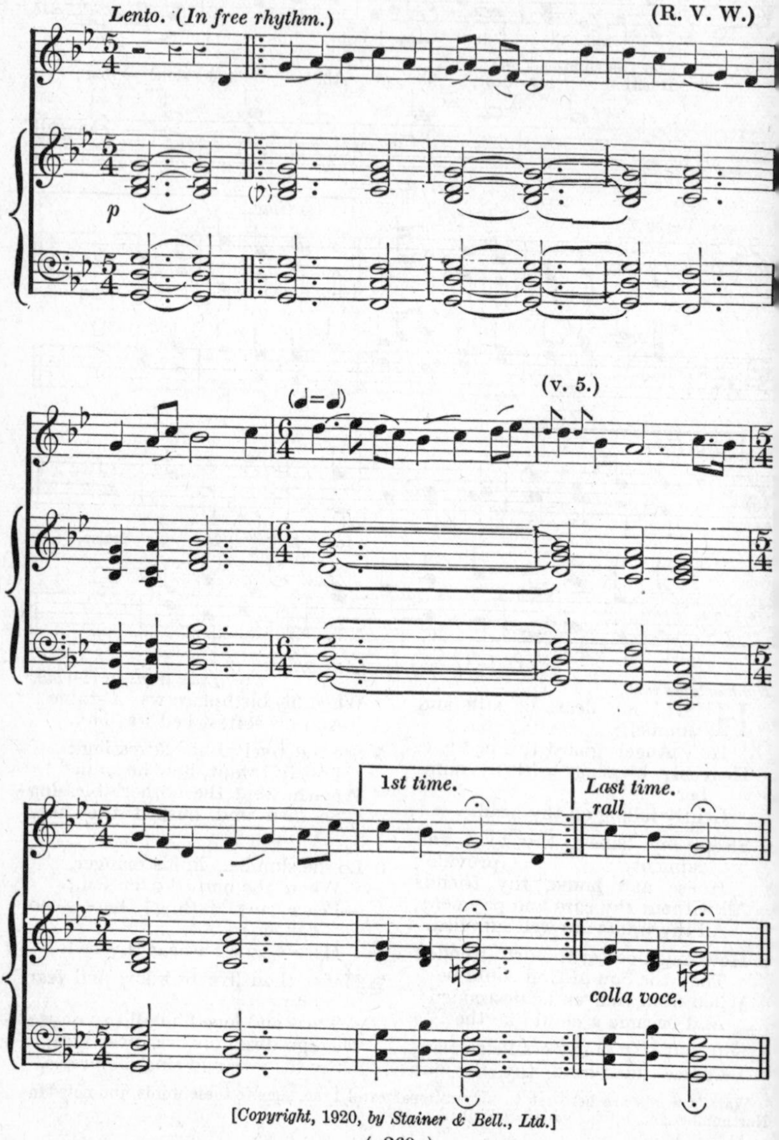

Lento. (In free rhythm.) (R. V. W.)

p

(♭)

(𝅗𝅥 = 𝅗𝅥)

(v. 5.)

1st time. *Last time.*

rall

colla voce.

ARRANGEMENT FOR UNACCOMPANIED VOICES.

(The words to be sung by the Treble only; the other parts to vocalize.)

English Traditional.

Miles Coverdale ‡, 1487–1568.

NOW blessèd be thou, Christ Jesu,
Thou art man born, and this is true:
With our poor flesh and our poor blood,
Was clothed that everlasting Good.

2 Eternal light doth now appear
Unto the world both far and near;
It shineth clear even at midnight,
Making us children of his light.

3 The Lord Christ Jesus, God's Son dear,
Was once a guest and stranger here,
Us for to bring from misery,
That we might live eternally.

4 Into this world right poor came he,
To make us rich in his mercy;
Therefore would he our sins forgive,
That we with him in heaven might live.

5. All this did he for us freely,
For to declare his great mercy.
All Christendom be merry therefore,
And give him thanks for evermore!

The melody was noted from Mrs. Esther Smith, Dilwyn, sung by her to the strange carol or song about the farmer who ploughed on Christmas Day—see *Twelve Traditional Carols from Herefordshire*, E. M. Leather and R. Vaughan Williams (Stainer & Bell). The words are a translation of 'Gelobet seist du Jesu Christ' from Coverdale's *Goostly Psalmes and Spiritualle Songes*, 1546: the unique copy is at Queen's College, Oxford, reprinted by the Parker Society.

132 PSALM OF SION

(GENERAL)

In moderate time. (R. V. W.)

English Traditional. *W. Prid* (1585).

O MOTHER dear, Jerusalem,
Jehovah's throne on high,
O sacred city, queen, and wife
Of Christ eternally!

2 O comely queen, in glory clad,
In honour and degree;
All fair thou art, exceeding bright,
No spot there is in thee.

3 Thy part, thy shape, thy stately grace,
Thy favour fair in deed,
Thy pleasant hue and countenance,
All others doth exceed.

4 O then thrice happy, should my state
In happiness remain,
If I might once thy glorious seat
And princely place attain,

5 And view thy gallant gates, thy walls,
Thy streets and dwellings wide,
Thy noble troop of citizens
And mighty King beside.

6 He is the King of kings, beset
Amidst his servants' right;
And they his happy household all
Do serve him day and night.

7. O mother dear, Jerusalem,
The comfort of us all,
How sweet thou art and delicate;
No thing shall thee befall!

Versions of the New Jerusalem Hymn formed part of English folk-carol singing from the end of the sixteenth century onwards, and sometimes fragments strayed into other carols (as in No. 46). There are two originals, that by Prid in *The Glasse of vaine-glorie: Faithfully translated* (*out of S. Augustine his booke intituled Speculum peccatoris*), by W. Prid, Doctor of the Laws, printed by J. Windel, London, 1585; and the less close paraphrase of Augustine in the British Museum MS., by 'F. B. P.', beginning 'Jerusalem, my happy home', about the same date. Versions appeared in the broadsides: Julian describes an English one of *c.* 1660, and a Scottish one of the eighteenth century, which latter combines Prid with 'F. B. P.' The version of 1801 attributed to Montgomery in the *Oxford Hymn Book* is probably by Joseph Bromehead.

'F. B. P.'s' version was sung to the tune 'Diana', of which one part only has been discovered. The *c.* 1660 version was sung to 'O man in desperation'. We have used the old carol tune, 'Saint Austin' ('In Pescod time', Chappell), which is set in the *English Hymnal* and *Songs of Praise* to the 'F. B. P.' version.

PART III

MODERN CAROLS

WRITTEN FOR OR ADAPTED TO TRADITIONAL TUNES

133 CAROL OF THE ADVENT

(NOVEMBER AND DECEMBER)

SOLO OR SEMI-CHORUS.
(M. S.)
CHORUS.
Love the Guest
Peo - ple, look East,...........
Peo - ple, look East,
Love is on his way.
Peo - ple, look East, Love the Guest

A Besançon tune. *Eleanor Farjeon*

PEOPLE, look East. The time is near
Of the crowning of the year.
Make your house fair as you are able,
Trim the hearth, and set the table.
People, look East, and sing to-day:
Love the Guest is on the way.

2 Furrows, be glad. Though earth is bare,
One more seed is planted there:
Give up your strength the seed to nourish,
That in course the flower may flourish.
People, look East, and sing to-day:
Love the Rose is on the way.

3 Birds, though ye long have ceased to build,
Guard the nest that must be filled.
Even the hour when wings are frozen
He for fledging-time has chosen.
People, look East, and sing to-day:
Love the Bird is on the way.

4 Stars, keep the watch. When night is dim
One more light the bowl shall brim,
Shining beyond the frosty weather,
Bright as sun and moon together.
People, look East, and sing to-day:
Love the Star is on the way.

5. Angels, announce to man and beast
Him who cometh from the East.
Set every peak and valley humming
With the Word, the Lord is coming.
People, look East, and sing to-day:
Love the Lord is on the way.

The tune is an old Besancon carol tune. Cf. No. 106.

134 IF YE WOULD HEAR

(ADVENT: CHRISTMAS EVE)

Verses 1, 2, 4, & 6. With movement.
(Adapted, R. V. W. and M. S.)
Verses 3, 5, & 7.
Rise, and bake your Christ - mas bread: Chris - tians, rise! the
Rise, and bake your Christ - mas bread: the
Rise, and bake your Christ - mas bread: Chris - tians, rise! the
world is bare, And blank, and dark with

want and care, Yet Christ - mas comes in the morn - ing.

Dutch iune. *Dora Greenwell,* 1821–82.

IF ye would hear the angels sing
'Peace on earth and mercy mild',
Think of him who was once a child,
On Christmas Day in the morning.

2 If ye would hear the angels sing,
Rise, and spread your Christmas fare;
'Tis merrier still the more that share,
On Christmas Day in the morning.

3 *Rise, and bake your Christmas bread:*
Christians, rise! the world is bare,
And blank, and dark with want and care,
Yet Christmas comes in the morning.

4 If ye would hear the angels sing,
Rise, and light your Christmas fire;
And see that ye pile the logs still higher
On Christmas Day in the morning.

5 *Rise, and light your Christmas fire;*
Christians, rise! the world is old,
And Time is weary, and worn, and cold,
Yet Christmas comes in the morning.

6 If ye would hear the angels sing,
Christians! see ye let each door
Stand wider than it e'er stood before,
On Christmas Day in the morning.

7. *Rise, and open wide the door;*
Christians, rise! the world is wide,
And many there be that stand outside,
Yet Christmas comes in the morning.

A Dutch melody, from *Souter Liedekens Ghemaect ter Eeren Gods*, Antwerp, 1539, has been adapted to these words.

135 EARTHLY FRIENDS

(CHRISTMAS)

(GEOFFREY SHAW.)

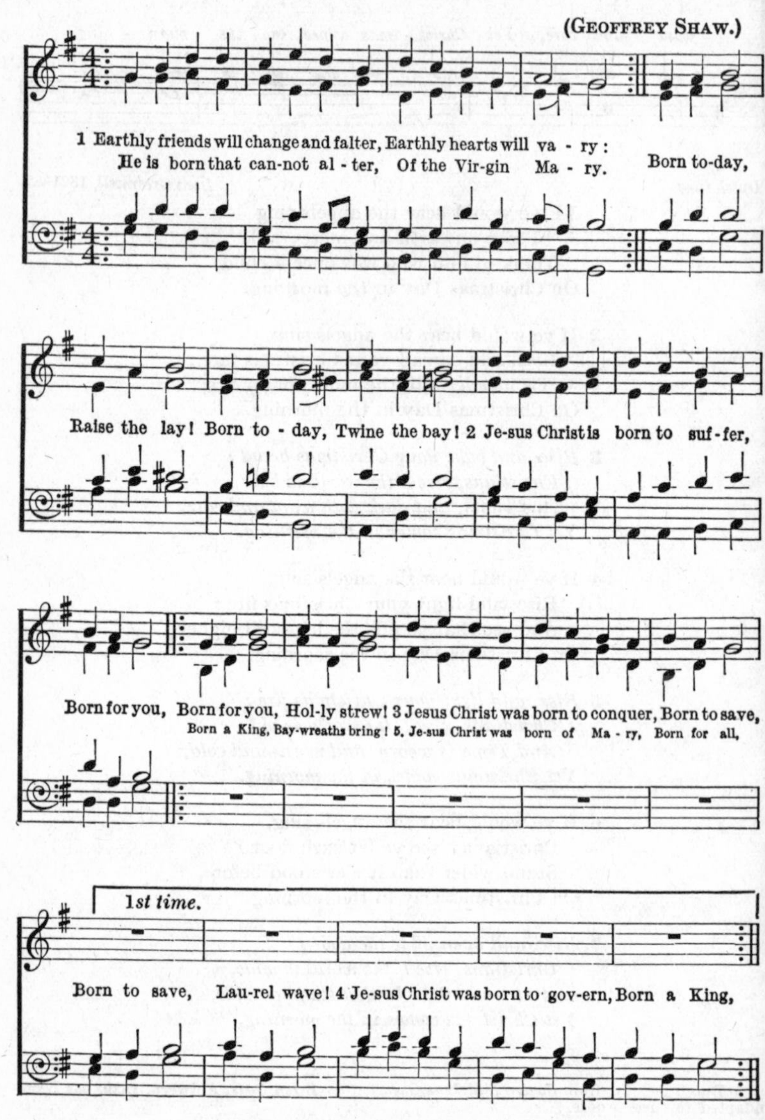

1 Earthly friends will change and falter, Earthly hearts will va - ry:
He is born that can-not al - ter, Of the Vir-gin Ma - ry. Born to-day,
Raise the lay! Born to - day, Twine the bay! 2 Je-sus Christ is born to suf-fer,
Born for you, Born for you, Hol-ly strew! 3 Jesus Christ was born to conquer, Born to save,
Born a King, Bay-wreaths bring! 5. Je-sus Christ was born of Ma - ry, Born for all,
1st time.
Born to save, Lau-rel wave! 4 Je-sus Christ was born to gov-ern, Born a King,

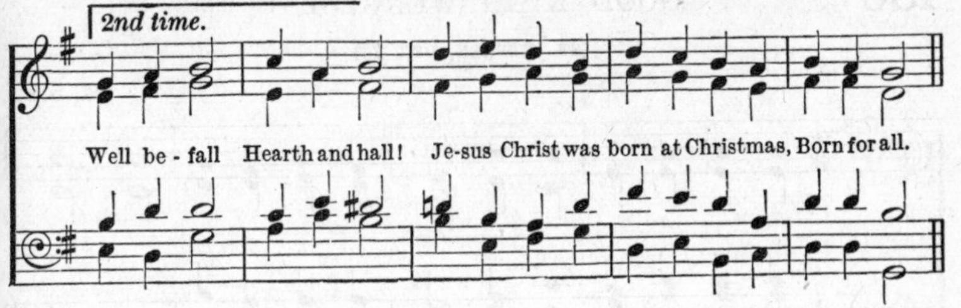
2nd time.
Well be - fall Hearth and hall! Je-sus Christ was born at Christmas, Born for all.

German, 16th century. *J. M. Neale*, 1818–66.

EARTHLY friends will change and falter,
Earthly hearts will vary :
He is born that cannot alter,
Of the Virgin Mary.
Born to-day,
Raise the lay !
Born to-day,
Twine the bay !

2 Jesus Christ is born to suffer,
Born for you,
Born for you,
Holly strew !

3 Jesus Christ was born to conquer,
Born to save,
Born to save,
Laurel wave !

4 Jesus Christ was born to govern,
Born a King,
Born a King,
Bay-wreaths bring !

5. Jesus Christ was born of Mary,
Born for all.
Well befall
Hearth and hall !
Jesus Christ was born at Christmas,
Born for all.

Words written in 1853 by Dr. Neale for the melody in *Piae Cantiones* (cf. No. 141) of 'Omnis mundus jucundetur'. The tune is printed in Quentel, *Alte Catholische Geistliche Kirchengeseng*, 1599, the *Constanzer Gesangbuch*, 1600, and in many German books of the seventeenth century.

136

GOOD KING WENCESLAS

(ST. STEPHEN, DEC. 26)

(M. S.)

Piae Cantiones. **J. M. Neale, 1818-66.**

GOOD King Wenceslas looked out,
On the Feast of Stephen,
When the snow lay round about,
Deep, and crisp, and even :
Brightly shone the moon that night,
Though the frost was cruel,
When a poor man came in sight,
Gathering winter fuel.

2 'Hither, page, and stand by me,
If thou know'st it, telling,
Yonder peasant, who is he ?
Where and what his dwelling ?'
'Sire, he lives a good league hence,
Underneath the mountain,
Right against the forest fence,
By Saint Agnes' fountain.'

3 'Bring me flesh, and bring me wine,
Bring me pine-logs hither :
Thou and I will see him dine,
When we bear them thither.'
Page and monarch, forth they went,
Forth they went together ;
Through the rude wind's wild lament
And the bitter weather.

4 'Sire, the night is darker now,
And the wind blows stronger ;
Fails my heart, I know not how ;
I can go no longer.'
'Mark my footsteps, good my page ;
Tread thou in them boldly :
Thou shalt find the winter's rage
Freeze thy blood less coldly.'

5. In his master's steps he trod,
Where the snow lay dinted ;
Heat was in the very sod
Which the Saint had printed.
Therefore, Christian men, be sure,
Wealth or rank possessing,
Ye who now will bless the poor,
Shall yourselves find blessing.

This rather confused narrative owes its popularity to the delightful tune, which is that of a Spring carol, 'Tempus adest floridum', No. 99. Unfortunately Neale in 1853 substituted for the Spring carol this 'Good King Wenceslas', one of his less happy pieces, which E. Duncan goes so far as to call 'doggerel', and Bullen condemns as 'poor and commonplace to the last degree'. The time has not yet come for a comprehensive book to discard it; but we reprint the tune in its proper setting ('Spring has now unwrapped the flowers'), not without hope that, with the present wealth of carols for Christmas, 'Good King Wenceslas' may gradually pass into disuse, and the tune be restored to spring-time. Neale did the same kind of thing to another Spring carol, 'In vernali tempore' (No. 98; cf. No. 102); but this was not popularized by Bramley & Stainer.

137 MASTERS IN THIS HALL

(CHRISTMAS)

(arr. GUSTAV HOLST.)

Allegro moderato.
First verse Full.
Subsequent verses women's voices only.
1 Mas - ters in this Hall, ...
f
p
Hear ye news to-day . . . . Brought from o - ver sea, ... And
cres.
ev - er I you pray :
Now - ell! Now - ell! Now - ell!
cres.

Now - ell sing we clear ! Holp - en are all folk on earth, Born
in God's son so dear :
Tutti.
Now - ell ! Now - ell ! Now - ell !
f
ff
Now - ell sing we loud ! God to - day hath poor folk raised And
ff

cast a-down the proud.
(Men's voices only until last verse. Last verse Tutti.)
p
2 *Go - ing o'er the hills, Through the milk-white snow,......
cres.
Heard I ewes bleat While the wind did blow:
cres.

f
Now-ell! Now-ell! Now-ell! Now-ell sing we clear! Holp-en
f
are all folk on earth, Born is God's son so dear:
ff Tutti.
Now-ell! Now-ell! Now-ell! Now-ell sing we loud! God to-
ff

French tune. *William Morris*, 1834–96.

MASTERS in this Hall,
Hear ye news to-day
Brought from over sea,
And ever I you pray:

Nowell! Nowell! Nowell!
Nowell sing we clear!
Holpen are all folk on earth,
Born is God's son so dear:
Nowell! Nowell! Nowell!
Nowell sing we loud!
God to-day hath poor folk raised
And cast a-down the proud.

2 *Going o'er the hills,
Through the milk-white snow,
Heard I ewes bleat
While the wind did blow:

3 *Shepherds many an one
Sat among the sheep,
No man spake more word
Than they had been asleep:

4 *Quoth I, 'Fellows mine,
Why this guise sit ye?
Making but dull cheer,
Shepherds though ye be?'

5 *‘ Shepherds should of right
Leap and dance and sing,
Thus to see ye sit,
Is a right strange thing ’ :

6 *Quoth these fellows then,
‘ To Bethlem town we go,
To see a mighty lord
Lie in manger low ’ :

7 *‘ How name ye this lord,
Shepherds ? ’ then said I,
‘ Very God,’ they said,
‘ Come from Heaven high ’ :

8 Then to Bethlem town
We went two and two,
And in a sorry place
Heard the oxen low :

9 Therein did we see
A sweet and goodly may
And a fair old man,
Upon the straw she lay :

10 And a little child
On her arm had she,
‘ Wot ye who this is ? ’
Said the hinds to me :

11 *Ox and ass him know,
Kneeling on their knee,
Wondrous joy had I
This little babe to see :

12. *This is Christ the Lord,
Masters be ye glad !
Christmas is come in,
And no folk should be sad :

The words were written for the old French carol tune shortly before 1860 by Morris, who was in Street's office with Edmund Sedding (architect and compiler of carols, brother of the more famous J. D. Sedding ; he died early, in 1868). Sedding had obtained the tune from the organist at Chartres Cathedral, and he published the words and tune in his *Antient Christmas Carols*, 1860. The melody is here reharmonized. The starred verses can be omitted (the chorus gives the answer to v. 10) ; but a long carol is useful sometimes for processions, both in and out of church. This one should be popular with children. The characters can be distinguished in the singing, and the chorus sung by all.

138

O LITTLE TOWN

(CHRISTMAS EVE: CHRISTMAS)

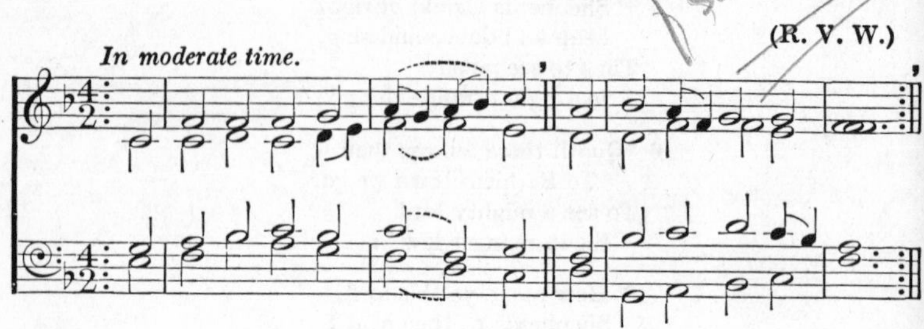

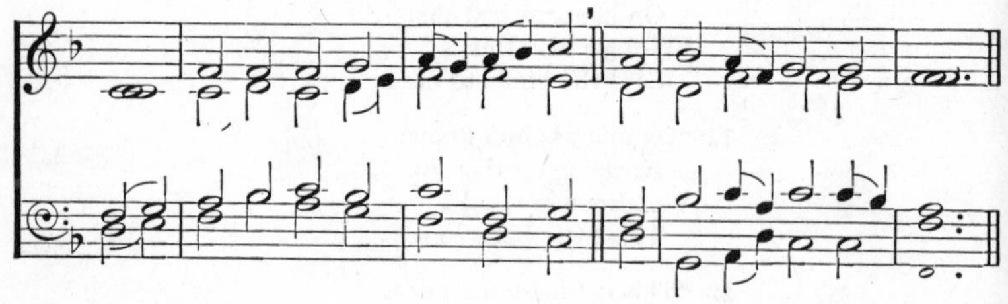

English Traditional. *Bishop Phillips Brooks,* 1835–93.

O LITTLE town of Bethlehem,
How still we see thee lie!
Above thy deep and dreamless sleep
The silent stars go by.
Yet in thy dark streets shineth
The everlasting light;
The hopes and fears of all the years
Are met in thee to-night.

2 O morning stars, together
Proclaim the holy birth,
And praises sing to God the King,
And peace to men on earth;
For Christ is born of Mary;
And, gathered all above,
While mortals sleep, the angels keep
Their watch of wondering love.

3 How silently, how silently,
The wondrous gift is given!
So God imparts to human hearts
The blessings of his heaven.
No ear may hear his coming;
But in this world of sin,
Where meek souls will receive him, still
The dear Christ enters in.

4 Where children pure and happy
Pray to the blessèd Child,
Where misery cries out to thee,
Son of the mother mild;
Where charity stands watching
And faith holds wide the door,
The dark night wakes, the glory breaks,
And Christmas comes once more.

5. O holy Child of Bethlehem,
Descend to us, we pray;
Cast out our sin, and enter in,
Be born in us to-day.
We hear the Christmas Angels
The great glad tidings tell:
O come to us, abide with us,
Our Lord Emmanuel.

This hymn, with its tune ('The Ploughboy's Dream') from the *English Hymnal* and *Songs of Praise*, is so much a carol that we feel bound to include it in this book also.

139 INFINITE LIGHT

(EPIPHANY: LENT: GENERAL: MISSIONARY)

English Traditional. *B. M. G.*

THE greatness of God in his love has been shown,
The light of his life on the Nations is thrown;
And that which the Jews and the Greeks did divine
Is come in the fullness of Jesus to shine:

The Light of the World in the darkness has shone,
And grows in our sight as the ages flow on.

2 He rolls the grim darkness and sorrow away
And brings all our fears to the light of the day;
The idols are fallen of anger and blood,
And God is revealed as the loving and good:

3 And, though we have sinned like the Prodigal Son,
His love to our succour and welcome will run.
His gospel of pardon, of love and accord,
Will master oppression and shatter the sword:

4. The Light of the World is more clear to our sight
As errors disperse and men see him aright:
In lands long in shadow, his Churches arise
And blaze for their neighbours the Way of the Wise:

This carol has been written to carry another traditional 'Virgin unspotted' tune, which has been familiar for many years. Cf. Nos. 4 and 114.

140 THE BAND OF CHILDREN

(INNOCENTS' DAY: EPIPHANY TO LENT)

Moderately quick. M. S.

French tune. *Frank Kendon.*

THE stars shall light your journey ;
Your mother holds you close and warm ;
The donkey's pace shall rock you :
Sleep, baby ; dream no harm.

What songs are these, faint heard and far ?
The wind, maybe, in palm trees tall,
Or running stream, or night-bird's call ;
The dark lies deep on desert,
Where Joseph walked and Mary rode,
The dark lies deep on desert—
Sleep well, thou Child of God :

2 What songs are these, faint heard and far ?
'Tis neither wind in palm trees tall,
Nor water-brook, nor night-bird's call,
It is the voice of children
Where Joseph walked and Mary rode,
The fierce wild beasts are friendly—
Sleep well, thou Child of God :

3 What forms are these, clear on the dark,
That shine, and yet are flesh and blood,
That laugh and sing along the road ?
It is a crowd of children
Where Joseph walked and Mary rode,
A singing crowd of children—
Sleep well, thou Child of God :

4. Never was seen so strange a guard :
About the footsore travellers they
In lovely circles moved, till day,
Until the baby wakened,
While Joseph trudged and Mary rode !
Such lullaby be all men's,
Sleep well, thou Child of God :

The words have been written for this tune, which is given as a 'noël ancien' by the Abbé Pellegrin (1663–1745) early in the eighteenth century, and is reprinted in the *Grand Bible des Noëls angevins* in 1766. The tune is still sung in the west of France to 'Laissez paître vos bêtes'; another and earlier carol, 'Laisse-qu'y tes affaires', is also associated with it. The refrain may be sung at the end of each verse, as well as at the beginning.

141 JANUARY CAROL

(JANUARY AND FEBRUARY)

Piae Cantiones. *J. M Neale*, 1818–66.

EARTH to-day rejoices,
Alleluya, Alleluya, Alleluya,
Death can hurt no more;
And celestial voices,
Alleluya, Alleluya, Alleluya,
Tell that sin is o'er.
David's sling destroys the foe:
Samson lays the temple low:

War and strife are done;
God and man are one.

2 Reconciliation,
Alleluya, Alleluya, Alleluya,
Peace that lasts for ay,
Gladness and salvation,
Alleluya, Alleluya, Alleluya,
Came on Christmas Day.
Gideon's fleece is wet with dew:
Solomon is crowned anew:

3. Though the cold grows stronger,
Alleluya, Alleluya, Alleluya,
Though the world loves night;
Yet the days grow longer,
Alleluya, Alleluya, Alleluya,
Christ is born our Light.
Now the dial's type is learnt:
Burns the bush that is not burnt:

Written by Dr. Neale in 1853 for the tune 'Ave maris stella lucens' in *Piae Cantiones* (1582).

The now famous *Piae Cantiones* was compiled by Theodoricus Petrus of Nyland in Finland, in 1582, when he was a student at Rostock near Lübeck: he was still alive in 1625. The songs spread in the reformed Church of Sweden and Finland, and were still sung in Swedish schools in 1700, and in Finland late in the nineteenth century. Peter of Nyland's *Piae Cantiones* (perhaps the unique copy) was brought over by the British Minister at Stockholm, who gave it to Dr. Neale, *c.* 1852. Neale gave it to Helmore; and together they published from it *Carols for Christmastide* (1853) and *Carols for Eastertide* (1854), from which collections Neale's carols are taken. An edition of *Piae Cantiones* (altered) was published by Dr. G. R. Woodward in 1910. The original copy is now in the British Museum. See p. xvi.

CHILDREN'S SONG OF THE NATIVITY

In moderate time. Voices in Unison. (R. V. W.)

1 How far is it to Beth - le-hem? Not ve - ry far.
(Omit in v. 5.)

Shall we find the sta - ble-room Lit by a star?

2 Can we see the lit - tle child, Is he with - in?
(Omit in v. 7.)
(Omit in v. 7.)

If we lift the wood - en latch May we go in?
(Omit in vv. 6 & 7.)
vv. 5 & 6.
5 Great kings have pre - cious gifts, And we have naught,
Little smiles and lit-tle tears Are all........ we brought. 6 For
all wea - ry chil - dren Ma - ry must weep.
Here, on his bed of straw Sleep, chil-dren, sleep.

For v. 7 repeat music of v. 2.

English Traditional. *Frances Chesterton.*

HOW far is it to Bethlehem?
  Not very far.
Shall we find the stable-room
  Lit by a star?

2 Can we see the little child,
  Is he within?
If we lift the wooden latch
  May we go in?

3 May we stroke the creatures there,
  Ox, ass, or sheep?
May we peep like them and see
  Jesus asleep?

4 If we touch his tiny hand
  Will he awake?
Will he know we've come so far
  Just for his sake?

5 Great kings have precious gifts,
  And we have naught,
Little smiles and little tears
  Are all we brought.

6 For all weary children
  Mary must weep.
Here, on his bed of straw
  Sleep, children, sleep.

7. God in his mother's arms,
  Babes in the byre,
Sleep, as they sleep who find
  Their heart's desire.

This appears in the children's section of *Songs of Praise* (426). We reprint it here, because with its folk-tune 'Stowey' it is too much of a carol to be omitted.

143 THE WORLD'S DESIRE

(NATIVITY)

Traditional. *G. K. Chesterton*

THE Christ-child lay on Mary's lap,
His hair was like a light.
(O weary, weary were the world,
But here is all aright.)

2 The Christ-child lay on Mary's breast,
His hair was like a star.
(O stern and cunning are the Kings,
But here the true hearts are.)

3 The Christ-child lay on Mary's heart,
His hair was like a fire.
(O weary, weary is the world,
But here the world's desire.)

4. The Christ-child stood at Mary's knee,
His hair was like a crown,
And all the flowers looked up at him,
And all the stars looked down.

Set to a tune kindly communicated by the Rev. J. R. Van Pelt, Theological Seminary, Atlanta, Georgia, U.S.A.

144 WHITE LENT

(ASH WEDNESDAY TO THE EVE OF PASSION SUNDAY)

Verse 1 and any other selected verses (except the last).

The Soprano and Alto sing the words. The Tenor and Bass hum the accompaniment.

In moderate time. **M. S.**

'Come buy, come buy, Come buy with love the love most

high, Come buy, come buy, Come buy with love the love most high!'

The last verse and any other selected verses. (All sing the words.)

Rather quick.

A - rise ! and make a par - a -
A - rise, a - rise, a -

A - rise !
A - rise !
A - rise ! and make a par - a -
- dise !
- rise, a-rise !
A - rise !
A - rise ! A - rise ! and make a par - a - dise !
- dise !

Angevin tune. L. M

Now quit your care
And anxious fear and worry;
For schemes are vain
And fretting brings no gain.
To prayer, to prayer!
Bells call and clash and hurry,
In Lent the bells do cry,
'Come buy, come buy,
Come buy with love the love most high!'

2 Lent comes in the spring,
And spring is pied with brightness;
The sweetest flowers,
Keen winds, and sun, and showers,
Their health do bring
To make Lent's chastened whiteness;
For life to men brings light
And might, and might,
And might to those whose hearts are right.

3 To bow the head
In sackcloth and in ashes,
Or rend the soul,
Such grief is not Lent's goal;
But to be led
To where God's glory flashes,
His beauty to come nigh,
To fly, to fly,
To fly where truth and light do lie.

4 For is not this
The fast that I have chosen?—
The prophet spoke—
To shatter every yoke,
Of wickedness
The grievous bands to loosen,
Oppression put to flight,
To fight, to fight,
To fight till every wrong's set right.

5 For righteousness
And peace will show their faces
To those who feed
The hungry in their need,
And wrongs redress,
Who build the old waste places,
And in the darkness shine.
Divine, divine,
Divine it is when all combine!

6. Then shall your light
Break forth as doth the morning;
Your health shall spring,
The friends you make shall bring
God's glory bright,
Your way through life adorning;
And love shall be the prize.
Arise, arise,
Arise! and make a paradise!

The words, based on the carol 'Quittez, Pasteurs', are in part a paraphrase of the Lent Lesson, Isaiah lviii. The tune is printed in L. Roques, *Noëls Anciens* (nineteenth century, undated); there is a slightly different version in L. Eugène Grimault, *Noëls Angevins,* 1878.

145 MOTHERING SUNDAY

(MID-LENT)

'He who goes a-mothering finds violets in the lane.'

German, 14th century. *George Hare Leonard.*

IT is the day of all the year,
Of all the year the one day,
When I shall see my Mother dear
And bring her cheer,
A-mothering on Sunday.

2 So I'll put on my Sunday coat,
And in my hat a feather,
And get the lines I writ by rote,
With many a note,
That I've a-strung together.

3 And now to fetch my wheaten cake,
To fetch it from the baker,
He promised me, for Mother's sake,
The best he'd bake
For me to fetch and take her.

4 Well have I known, as I went by
One hollow lane, that none day
I'd fail to find—for all they're shy—
Where violets lie,
As I went home on Sunday.

5 *My sister Jane is waiting-maid
Along with Squire's lady;
And year by year her part she's played,
And home she stayed,
To get the dinner ready.

6 *For Mother'll come to Church, you'll see—
Of all the year it's the day—
'The one,' she'll say, 'that's made for me.'
And so it be:
It's every Mother's free day.

7 *The boys will all come home from town,
Not one will miss that one day;
And every maid will bustle down
To show her gown,
A-Mothering on Sunday.

8\. It is the day of all the year,
Of all the year the one day;
And here come I, my Mother dear,
To bring you cheer,
A-Mothering on Sunday.

'He who goes a-mothering finds violets in the lane.' In many parts of the country it was the custom for the children of the family who had left the old home to come back to visit their Mother on the 4th Sunday in Lent (Mid-Lent Sunday). The eldest son would bring a wheaten cake—in modern times a plum cake with an icing of sugar, or a simnel-cake. Sometimes cinnamon comfits ('lambs'-tails'), or little white sugar-plums with a carraway seed, or some morsel of spice, within—such as may still be found at country fairs—were brought for an offering. One of the children home for the day would stay in and mind the house, so that the mother should be free for once to attend morning service at the church.

A folk-tune of the fourteenth-century, made into a carol ('Ich weiss ein lieblich Engelspiel'), c. 1450. In a fifteenth-century Strasburg MS. (which was burnt in the war of 1870), printed by Wackernagel and others.

The artless German words may be thus translated (and sung when a carol of more general character is wanted):—

I know a lovely angel-game,
Where sorrow has its ending;
And heaven is there with joy aflame,
And endless fame:
'Tis there we would be wending.

2 May God through his abounding grace
Us there in love be leading!
Now stand up, noble soul, and face
That happy place
To which thou would'st be speeding!

3\. Then God a ring from off his hand
Will place upon thy finger,
And pledge thee,—''Mid this happy band
Within this land
For ever shalt thou linger.'

146 THE MERCHANTS' CAROL

(PALM SUNDAY: HOLY WEEK)

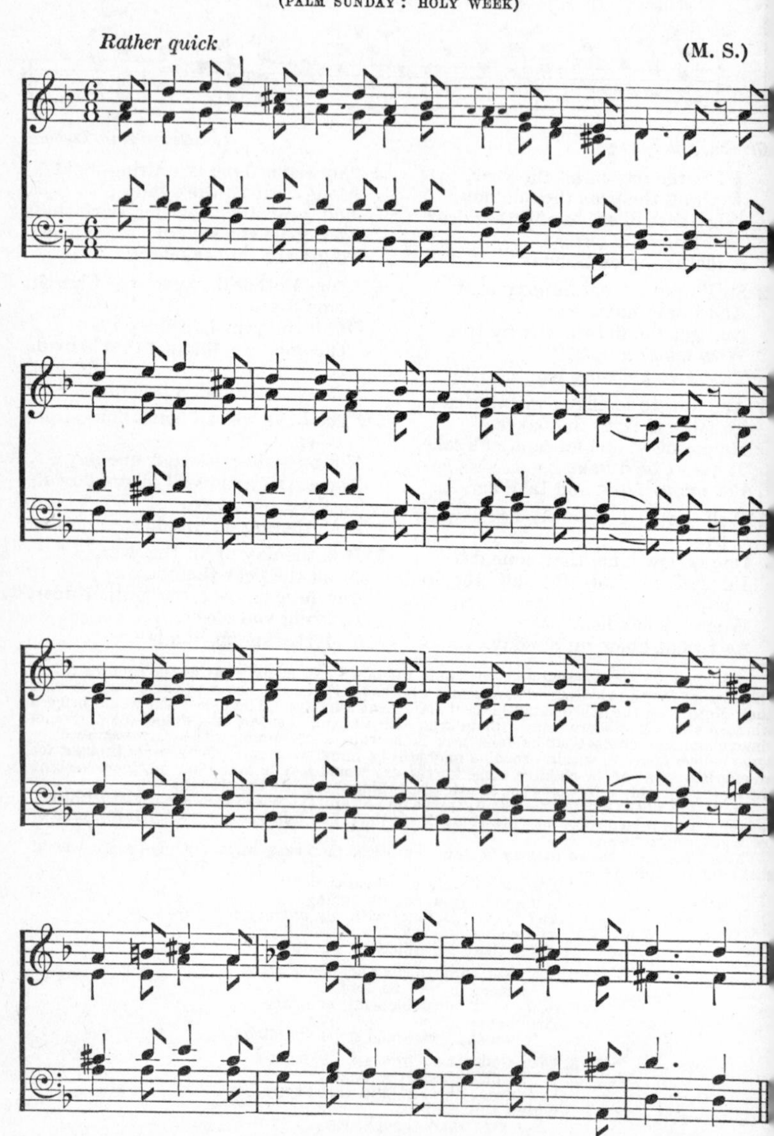

English Traditional. *Frank Kendon.*

AS we rode down the steep hillside,
Twelve merchants with our fairing,
A shout across the hollow land
Came loud upon our hearing,
A shout, a song, a thousand strong,
A thousand lusty voices:
'Make haste,' said I, I knew not why,
'Jerusalem rejoices!'

2 Beneath the olives fast we rode,
And louder came the shouting:
'So great a noise must mean,' said we,
'A king, beyond all doubting!'
Spurred on, did we, this king to see,
And left the mules to follow;
And nearer, clearer rang the noise
Along the Kidron hollow.

3 Behold, a many-coloured crowd
About the gate we found there;
But one among them all, we marked,
One man who made no sound there;
Still louder ever rose the crowd's
'Hosanna in the highest!'
'O King,' thought I, 'I know not why
In all this joy thou sighest.'

A Merchant:

4 'Then he looked up, he looked at me
But whether he spoke I doubted:
How could I hear so calm a speech
While all the rabble shouted?
And yet these words, it seems, I heard:
"I shall be crowned to-morrow."
They struck my heart with sudden smart,
And filled my bones with sorrow.'

5. We followed far, we traded not,
But long we could not find him.
The very folk that called him king
Let robbers go and bind him.
We found him then, the sport of men,
Still calm among their crying;
And well we knew his words were true—
He was most kingly dying.

The words written for the traditional tune, which we have distinguished by the name of Golden'; cf. Nos. 165 and 173.

147 EASTER CAROL

French tune. **N. S. T.**

CHEER up, friends and neighbours,
  Now it's Easter tide;
Stop from endless labours,
  Worries put aside:
Men should rise from sadness,
  Evil, folly, strife,
When God's mighty gladness
  Brings the earth to life.

2 Out from snowdrifts chilly,
  Roused from drowsy hours,
Bluebell wakes, and lily;
  God calls up the flowers!
Into life he raises
  All the sleeping buds;
Meadows weave his praises,
  And the spangled woods.

3 All his truth and beauty,
  All his righteousness,
Are our joy and duty,
  Bearing his impress:
Look! the earth waits breathless
  After Winter's strife:
Easter shows man deathless,
  Spring leads death to life.

4. Ours the more and less is;
  But, changeless all the days,
God revives and blesses,
  Like the sunlight rays.
'All mankind is risen,'
  The Easter bells do ring,
While from out their prison
  Creep the flowers of Spring!

Words written for the French carol tune, 'Nous allons, ma mie', printed by Grimault, Roques, and others.

148 CHRIST THE LORD IS RISEN

(EASTER)

(arr. GEOFFREY SHAW.)

German tune. *I. Watts* (1709).

CHRIST *the Lord is risen!*
Now is the hour of darkness past;
Christ hath assumed his reigning power.
Behold the great accuser cast
Down from the skies, to rise no more:
Alleluya, Alleluya.

2 *Christ the Lord is risen!*
'Twas by thy blood, immortal Lamb,
Thine armies trod the tempter down;
'Twas by thy word and powerful name
They gained the battle and renown:
Alleluya, Alleluya.

3. *Christ the Lord is risen!*
Rejoice, ye heavens! let every star
Shine with new glories round the sky!
Saints, while ye sing the heavenly war,
Raise your Redeemer's name on high!
Alleluya, Alleluya.

Verses by Isaac Watts (1674–1748), with refrains added, to fit an old German melody reprinted in the *Gesang- und Gebetbuch für die Diöcese Trier*, 1871.

149 LOVE IS COME AGAIN

(EASTER)

In moderate time.

(M. S.)

French tune. *J. M. C. Crum.*

NOW the green blade riseth from the buried grain,
Wheat that in dark earth many days has lain;
Love lives again, that with the dead has been:

Love is come again,
Like wheat that springeth green.

2 In the grave they laid him, Love whom men had slain,
Thinking that never he would wake again,
Laid in the earth like grain that sleeps unseen:

3 Forth he came at Easter, like the risen grain,
He that for three days in the grave had lain,
Quick from the dead my risen Lord is seen:

4. When our hearts are wintry, grieving, or in pain,
Thy touch can call us back to life again,
Fields of our hearts that dead and bare have been:

Words written for the old French tune associated with 'Noël nouvelet'.

150 THE WORLD ITSELF

(EASTER)

(G. S.)

Piae Cantiones. *J. M. Neale* †, 1818–66.

THE world itself keeps Easter Day,
And Easter larks are singing;
And Easter flowers are blooming gay,
And Easter buds are springing:
Alleluya, Alleluya:
The Lord of all things lives anew,
And all his works are rising too:
Hosanna in excelsis.

2 There stood three Maries by the tomb,
On Easter morning early;
When day had scarcely chased the gloom,
And dew was white and pearly:
Alleluya, Alleluya:
With loving but with erring mind,
They came the Prince of life to find:

3 But earlier still the angel sped,
His news of comfort giving;
And 'Why,' he said, 'among the dead
Thus seek ye for the Living?'
Alleluya, Alleluya:
'Go, tell them all, and make them blest;
Tell Peter first, and then the rest':

4 But one, and one alone remained,
With love that could not vary;
And thus a joy past joy she gained,
That sometime sinner, Mary,
Alleluya, Alleluya:
The first the dear, dear form to see
Of him that hung upon the tree:

5. The world itself keeps Easter Day,
Saint Joseph's star is beaming;
Saint Alice has her primrose gay,
Saint George's bells are gleaming:
Alleluya, Alleluya:
The Lord hath risen, as all things tell:
Good Christians, see ye rise as well!

The words were written by Neale (*Carols for Eastertide*, 1854) for the tune 'O Christe, rex piissime' in *Piae Cantiones* (cf. No. 141) with the Alleluyas repeated for the concluding refrain. As this does not fit the melody, 'Hosanna in excelsis' has been substituted.

151 ATHENS

(EASTER)

(Geoffrey Shaw.)

Piae Cantiones. J. M. Neale, 1818–66.

'TWAS about the dead of night,
And Athens lay in slumber;
Moonlight on the temples slept,
And touched the rocks with umber;
And the Court of Mars were met
In grave and reverend number:
Evermore and evermore,
Christians, sing Alleluya.

2 Met were they to hear and judge
The teaching of a stranger;
O'er the ocean he had come,
Through want, and toil, and danger;
And he worshipped for his God
One cradled in a manger:

3 While he spake against their gods,
And temples' vain erection,
Patiently they gave him ear,
And granted him protection;
Till with bolder voice and mien
He preached the Resurrection:

4 Some they scoffed, and some they spake
Of blasphemy and treason;
Some replied with laughter loud,
And some replied with reason;
Others put it off until
A more convenient season:

5. Athens heard and scorned it then,
Now Europe hath received it,
Wise men mocked and jeered it once,
Now children have believed it;
This, good Christians, was the day
That gloriously achieved it:

Also written by Neale in 1853 for a tune (' Scribere proposui ') in *Piae Cantiones* (cf. No. 141).

152 FESTIVAL CAROL

(EASTER TO TRINITY SUNDAY, ETC.)

(GEOFFREY SHAW.)

Dutch tune. **S. P.**

HOW great the harvest is
Of him who came to save us!
The hearts of men are his,
Our law the love he gave us.
The world lay cruel, blind,
Nought holding, nought divining;
He came to human kind,
And now the light is shining, is shining.

2 And though the news did seem
Too good for man's believing,
'Tis not an empty dream
Too high for our achieving.
He triumphed in the strife,
O'er all his foes he towered;
They killed the Prince of life,
But he hath death o'erpowered, o'erpowered.

3 Then came the Father's call;
His work on earth was ended;
That he might light on all,
To heaven the Lord ascended.
To heaven so near to earth,
Our hearts we do surrender:
There all things find their worth
And human life its splendour, its splendour.

4 The power by which there came
The Word of God among us
Was Love's eternal flame,
Whose light and heat are flung us;
That Spirit sent from God,
Within our hearts abiding,
Hath brought us on our road
And still the world is guiding, is guiding.

5. In Three made manifest,
Thou source of all our being,
Thou loveliest, truest, best,
Beyond our power of seeing;
Thou power of light and love,
Thou life that never diest—
To thee in whom all move
Be glory in the highest, the highest!

Words written for the Dutch tune, 'De Liefde Voortgebracht', a very popular song in the seventeenth century, which was set to 'Hoe groot de Vruechten zijn' in the Amsterdam Psalter of J. Oudaen.

153 SONG OF THE SPIRIT

(WHITSUNTIDE, ETC.)

SOLO.
(M. S.)
Now sing we of the Par - a-clete, The Light, the Beam of God, to greet.

CHORUS.
Let not your

heart be
TENOR. { When
Then
The
He

he is come,
came the age,
power of fraud,
sci - ence finds,
To all the truth, tho' now
Could serve, and so, a third
Vain forms, and fear, love's crown
And he the light, and his

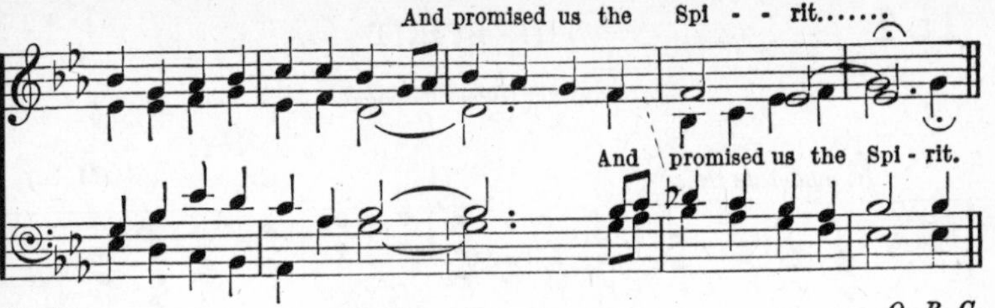
And promised us the Spi - - rit.......
And promised us the Spi - rit.

Dutch tune. O. B. C.

Now sing we of the Paraclete,
The Light, the Beam of God, to greet.

WHEN Christ blessed his disciples,
'Ye are my friends,' he said,
'Let not your heart be troubled,
And be ye not afraid;
When he the Breath of Truth is come,
To all the truth he'll bring you home,
Though now ye cannot bear it.'
So spoke he unto Christendom,
And promised us the Spirit.

2 Long after, rose a prophet
Who hailed the Spirit's day,
And said, 'Men first in terror
As slaves did God obey.
Then came the age when man as son
Could serve, and so God's grace be won:
A third—and we are near it—
Will be of love, all blindness gone,
The freedom of the Spirit.'

3 From slavery and childhood
Man grows to noble youth,
And free the Spirit makes us
To follow after truth:
The power of fraud, and dull pretence,
Vain forms, and fear, is banished hence;
Love's crown is ours to wear it;
Through all our faithless impotence
The light shines from the Spirit.

4. Brave thinkers saw the vision,
The story poets wove,
Of truth and grace unhindered,
The eternal Spirit's love:
For he the knowledge science finds,
And he the light in artists' minds,
And his the hero's merit;
All lovely things of all the kinds
Are planets of the Spirit.

The words have been written for an old Dutch carol tune, given by J. A. Thijm to E. Sedding, who published it in England in 1864. The reference in v. 2 is to the twelfth-century mystic, Joachim of Floris, Dante's—

Il Calavrese abate Giovacchino
Di spirito profetico dotato,

(*Paradiso*, xii) who was the precursor of Francis of Assisi.

154

THE SPIRIT

(WHITSUNTIDE : GENERAL)

In moderate time. (M. S.)

(Soprano and Alto sing all the words.)
Seek-ers we, seek-ers we, Doubt we

not, doubt we not.

Angevin tune.

Geoffrey Dearmer.

WINDS of God unfailing fill the sunlit sails
Of a great ship sailing where conjecture fails:
Seekers we, and we must discover,
Doubt we not though the chart is hid—
Chart we may not see,
Plotted by the world's great Lover
Down in Galilee;
Captain, prince, and pilot he.

2 If ye then perceive and if the heart desire,
Shall the mind achieve, and spirit shall aspire;
Then shall man see him, and shall praise him
In the fern, in the sea and cloud;
Every flower and tree
In the sap of life must raise him,
As in Galilee
In the form of man rose he.

3 His is each profession, every man his priest
Who in work's expression finds his joy increased:
In his Church are the ploughman, sailor,
Merchant, prince, artizan, and clerk,
All whoe'er they be,
Craftsman, thinker, tinker, tailor,
Come to Galilee,
Find a plan, and that is he.

4. Those who love him wholly need not him confess,
Since their lives must solely him in them express;
He's the goal that man ever searches,
How should man see that goal afar?
Each in his degree
That doth love him, of his Church is.
Down in Galilee
Founder of our Church was he.

Words written for the melody 'Courons à la fête', in the *Grande Bible des Noëls Angevins*, 1766, republished by Grimault in 1878. Cf. Legeay, *Noëls Anciens*, 1875.

155 APRIL

Welsh tune. *Geoffrey Dearmer.*

NOW April has come,
The country grows sweet here,
The chiff-chaff and wheatear,
Behold, from the land of ripe oranges come!
And cherry and plum,
With white blossom gleaming,
The hill-sides are seaming.
Too long have been dumb
The woods and the wold:
With buttercups blest,
The lark builds her nest
In green and in gold.
There 's cover for all birds,
For large birds and small birds,
Where furled leaves unfold.
She comes like a bride
In front of the tide
Of emerald mist.
No keen weather stays her;
No bird disobeys her;
No bud can resist.

2. A touch of her wand—
The buds rise to meet her,
And birds' eyes all greet her—
Why even the garrulous ducks on the pond
See signs of her wand!
As if the Magician
Sent ducks on a mission
With news from Beyond,
With tidings which they
Through natural art
Feel bound to impart!
But April and May
Themselves are their voices,
And no bird rejoices
Superbly as they.
They come like a bride
In front of the tide
Of emerald mist.
No keen weather stays them;
No bird disobeys them;
No bud can resist.

Words written for the Welsh traditional carol tune, 'Hir Oes f Fair'.

SUMMER TIME

Moderately quick.
(M. S.)
Al-le-lu-ya, Al-le-lu-
-ya, Praise the Lord with thanks-giv-ing: praises sing to God.

French tune. *Rose Fyleman.*

LIFT your hidden faces
Ye who wept and prayed;
Leave your covert places
Ye who were afraid.
Here 's a golden story,
Here is silver news,
Here be gifts of glory
For all men to choose:
Alleluya, Alleluya, Praise the Lord with
thanksgiving: praises sing to God.

2 Now from mead and spinney
Now from flood and foam,
Feathered, furred and finny,
All ye creatures come.
Here ye shall discover
That for which ye wait;
Winter days are over,—
Sing and celebrate!

3. Fathers, leave your labours,
Sons, be glad and gay;
Tell your friends and neighbours
Of our Holy-day.
Joyfully foregather,
Sorrow now is done:
We have found a Father,
We have found a Son:

Based on the French carol, 'Une vaine crainte', with last part of the refrain from Ps. 147. Roques prints the melody, and also Grimault (to the words 'Grace soit rendue') who says there are many variants in Champagne, Burgundy, and Anjou.

Summer carols seem to have been more common in Wales than in England. Hone, analysing the *Blodeugerdd Cymru*, an Anthology for Wales, in his *Ancient Mysteries*, at the beginning of the nineteenth century, says that it contains '48 Christmas carols, 9 summer carols, 3 May carols, one winter carol, one nightingale carol, and a carol to Cupid'.

157 SUMMER CAROL

In moderate time. M. S.

Béarnais tune. *Geoffrey Dearmer.*

THE dawn-wind now is waking,
  Round go the windmill's arms,
And sun on shadow breaking
  Lights up the sheltered farms.
Under cows the milkmaids crouching
  In the mists of morning grow;
Boys with heavy horses slouching
  Down to water lumber slow;
Grey as rocks the straggling shadowy flocks
      With silent shepherds go.

2 Now quickly goes the grey light;
  Aslant, the sun redeems
A whole long day of daylight;
  Gold crowd a wealth of beams.
Chickens flutter, strut and babble;
  Running ducks the duck-ponds fill;
Early breezes bear the gabble,
  And the light increases till
Soon it finds beyond the rabble
      The blackbird's yellow bill.

3. Bright flowers the woods adorning
  Show earth 's no longer blind,
As once on Christmas morning;
  When snow the world did bind,
When the shepherds and the sages
  And the kings first met their King,
Brought him wisdom, wealth, and wages,
  Though he was the littlest thing;
Suddenly the iron ages
      Had yielded to the Spring.

Written for the Béarnais carol-tune, 'Haut! haut! Pierrot', printed by P. Darricades, in *Noëls Béarnais*, 1877.

158 THANKSGIVING CAROL

(HARVEST: AUTUMN)

GEOFFREY SHAW.

German, 15th century. *Eleanor Farjeon.*

FIELDS of corn, give up your ears,
  Now your ears are heavy,
Wheat and oats and barley-spears,
  All your harvest-levy.
Where your sheaves of plenty lean,
Men once more the grain shall glean
  Of the Ever-Living,
God the Lord will bless the field,
Bringing in its Autumn yield
  Gladly to Thanksgiving.

2 Vines, send in your bunch of grapes,
  Now the bunch is clustered,
Be your gold and purple shapes
  Round the altar mustered.
Where the hanging bunches shine
Men once more shall taste the wine
  Of the Ever-Living,
God the Lord will bless the root,
Bringing in its Autumn fruit
  Gladly to Thanksgiving.

3. Garden, give your gayest flowers,
  Hedge, your wildest bring in,
Turn the churches into bowers
  Little birds shall sing in.
Where the children sing their glee
Men once more the Flower shall see
  Of the Ever-Living,
God the Lord will bless the throng,
Lifting up its Autumn song
  Gladly in Thanksgiving.

Words based upon 'Der Tag der ist so freudenreich'; with melody in M. Vehe's *Gesangbuch*, 1537, Strasburg, *Gros-Kirchengesangbuch*, 1560, Corner, 1631, &c. A melody, says Riemann, at latest of the fifteenth century; set by J. S. Bach in the seventeenth century. Mone gives the Latin words (' Dies est laetitiae) from a fifteenth-century MS.: but there are many versions of the German words, and several melodies are given by Baümker.

159 GOLDEN SHEAVES

(HARVEST)

Moderately quick. (M. S.)

Sing to the Lord, Sing songs of love and praise;
Sing to the Lord..

C♯ for last verse.

Basque tune. *J. S. B. Monsell*, 1811-75.

SING to the Lord of harvest,
Sing songs of love and praise :
With joyful hearts and voices
Your alleluyas raise :
By him the rolling seasons
In fruitful order move,
Sing to the Lord of harvest
A song of happy love.

2 By him the clouds drop fatness,
The deserts bloom and spring,
The hills leap up in gladness,
The valleys laugh and sing :
He filleth with his fullness
All things with large increase,
He crowns the year with goodness,
With plenty and with peace.

3. Heap on his sacred altar
The gifts his goodness gave,
The golden sheaves of harvest,
The souls he died to save :
Your hearts lay down before him
When at his feet ye fall,
And with your lives adore him,
Who gave his life for all.

In verses 2 & 3 the three under parts sing the words 'Sing to the Lord' instead of the first line.

Monsell's words set to 'Khanta zagun', as given in C. Bordes, *Archives de la Tradition Basque*, and *Noëls Basques Anciens*, 1897.

ANGELS HOLY

(GENERAL: PRAISE)

In moderate time. (M. S.)

Flemish tune. *John Stuart Blackie,* 1809-95.

ANGELS holy, high and lowly,
Sing the praises of the Lord;
Earth and sky, all living nature,
Starry temples azure-floored,
Man, the stamp of thy Creator,
Praise ye, praise ye, God the Lord:
Praise ye, praise ye, God the Lord,
Praise ye, praise ye, God the Lord.

2 Ocean hoary, tell his glory,
Cliffs, where tumbling seas have roared,
Mighty mountains, purple breasted,
Crag where eagle's pride hath soared,
Peaks cloud-cleaving, snowy-crested,
Praise ye, praise ye, God the Lord:

3 Rolling river, praise him ever,
From the mountain's deep vein poured,
Silver fountain, clearly gushing,
Sing the praises of the Lord,
Troubled torrent, madly rushing,
Praise ye, praise ye, God the Lord:

4. Youth, whose morning smiles at warning,
Age, in counsel deeply stored,
Each glad soul its free course winging,
Praise him, Father, Friend, and Lord,
Each glad voice its free song singing,
Praise the great and mighty Lord:

Professor Blackie published this rendering of the *Benedicite* in the London *Inquirer* in 1840. By the omission of some lines we have adapted it to the fine Flemish melody, 'De Dryvoudige Geboorte'.

161 THE SHEPHERD

(GENERAL)

In moderate time. (M. S.)

(Two upper parts only sing the words.) (All sing words.)

Austrian tune. *Laurence Binyon.*

DOWN in the valley where summer's laughing beam
Under the willow-tree lights along the stream,
Shepherds come driving their flocks and seek the pool,
Plunging their sheep in the sunny water cool.

2 Ah, how they struggle, and pant, the silly sheep,
Fearing the hands that dip, fearing water deep.
Tenderly lifted up, gladly, one by one,
White in the green of the meadow, lo, they run.

3. Evening is over the land, with peace and light,
Now sits the shepherd alone in evening bright,
Now has he joy within, where he pipeth low,
Seeing his flock gathered round him white as snow.

The words written for the Austrian dialect folk-carol *Hirtenlied*, 'Schteff'l, du Schlafhaub'n geh' heb' dich aus dai'm Nest', printed by F. Tschischka and J. M. Schottky in *Oesterreichische Volkslieder mit ihren Singweisen*, Buda-Pesth, 1844.

162 BELL CAROL

(GENERAL)

In moderate time. (M. S.)

French tune. *Steuart Wilson.*

IN every town and village
The bells do ring,
O'er woods and grass and tillage,
Hey ding a ding,
Ringing for joy to start the week
again,
And call all Christian men
To pray and praise and sing.

2 Then pull your ropes with vigour,
And watch your ways
To thread with strictest rigour
The noisy maze;
Keep in your heart the fire of youth
alight,
That he who rings aright
May ring in happy days.

3. And we who hear the bells ring
With all their might,
As they do say the angels sing
Both day and night,
Praise we the men who built our
belfries high
That music from the sky
Might sound for our delight.

Words written for the French carol, 'Je sais, Vierge Marie'.

163 THE THREE TRAITORS

(GENERAL)

In moderate time. (M. S.)

Alternative Version. (May be used for verses 3, 6, 9, & 11, or for any other selection of verses if desired.)

(Melody in Tenor.)

IT was about the deep of night,
And still was earth and sky,
When 'neath the moonlight dazzling bright,
Three ghosts came riding by.

2 Beyond the sea, beyond the sea,
Lie kingdoms for them all:
I wot their steeds trod wearily—
The journey was not small.

3 By rock and desert, sand and stream,
They footsore late did go:
Now like a sweet and blessèd dream
Their path was deep with snow.

4 Shining like hoar-frost, rode they on,
Three ghosts in earth's array:
It was about the hour when wan
Night turns at hint of day.

5 O, but their hearts with woe distraught
Hailed not the wane of night,
Only for Jesu still they sought
To wash them clean and white.

6 For bloody was each hand, and dark
With death each orbless eye;—
It was three Traitors mute and stark
Came riding silent by.

7 Silver their raiment and their spurs,
And silver-shod their feet,
And silver-pale each face that stares
Into the moonlight sweet.

8 And he upon the left that rode
Was Pilate, Prince of Rome,
Whose journey once lay far abroad,
And now was nearing home.

9 And he upon the right that rode
Herod of Salem sate,
Whose mantle dipped in children's blood
Shone clear as Heaven's gate.

10 And he these twain betwixt that rode
Was clad as white as wool,
Dyed in the Mercy of his God
White was he crown to sole.

11 Throned mid a myriad Saints in bliss
Rise shall the Babe of Heaven
To shine on these three ghosts, I wis,
Smit through with sorrows seven.

12. Babe of the Blessèd Trinity
Shall smile their steeds to see:
Herod and Pilate riding by,
And Judas one of three.

The tune from Gilbert, 1823, 'The Three Knights.'

164 CAROL OF BEAUTY

(GENERAL, PRAISE)

In moderate time. (M. S.)

French tune. *Steuart Wilson.*

PRAISE we the Lord, who made all beauty
For all our senses to enjoy ;
Owe we our humble thanks and duty
That simple pleasures never cloy ;
Praise we the Lord who made all beauty
For all our senses to enjoy.

2 Praise him who makes our life a pleasure,
Sending us things which glad our eyes ;
Thank him who gives us welcome leisure,
That in our heart sweet thoughts may rise ;
Praise him who makes our life a pleasure
Sending us things which glad our eyes.

3 Praise him who loves to see young lovers,
Fresh hearts that swell with youthful pride ;
Thank him who sends the sun above us,
As bridegroom fit to meet his bride ;
Praise him who loves to see young lovers,
Fresh hearts that swell with youthful pride.

4 Praise him who by a simple flower
Lifts up our hearts to things above ;
Thank him who gives to each one power
To find a friend to know and love ;
Praise him who by a simple flower
Lifts up our hearts to things above.

5. Praise we the Lord who made all beauty
For all our senses to enjoy ;
Give we our humble thanks and duty
That simple pleasures never cloy ;
Praise we the Lord who made all beauty
For all our senses to enjoy.

Words written for the French carol, 'Quelle est cette odeur agréable'. The tune found its way to England so long ago as to appear in Gay's *Beggar's Opera*, 1728.

165 GOLDEN MORNINGS

(GENERAL)

In moderate time. (M. S.)

English Traditional. *A. F. D.*

THEY saw the light shine out afar
  On Christmas in the morning;
And straight they knew it was the star,
  That came to give them warning:
Then did they fall on bended knee,
  The light their heads adorning,
And praised the Lord, who let them see
  His glory in the morning.

2 For three short years he went abroad
  And set men's hearts a-burning;
That mission turned the world to God
  And brought the night to morning:
He bore for man repulse and pain,
  Ingratitude, and scorning;
He suffered, died, he rose again
  At Easter in the morning.

3. O ever thought be of his grace,
  On each day in the morning;
And for his kingdom's loveliness
  Our souls be ever yearning:
So may we live, to Heaven our hearts
  In hope for ever turning;
Then may we die, as each departs,
  In joy at our new morning.

PART 2.

Paean.

LIFT up your heads, rejoice and dance,
  Forget the days of mourning!
The waves of light advance, advance,
  The fire of love is burning.
Farewell to hate and stupid fears,
  To ignorance and sorrow!
He who was with us through the years
  Shall bring us to the morrow!

There are two tunes (this, from Fyfe's *Carols*, 1860, and No 146) to which the name of 'Golden Carol' is found attached, with a pair of indifferent verses, in some publications of about sixty years ago. The name 'Golden Carol' was loosely used and was sometimes applied to 'The First Nowell'; but the real text of the Golden Carol is in a different metre, fifteenth century in its earlier form, and its tune is lost (see No. 173). The two tunes, which we are calling 'Golden Mornings' (No. 165) and 'Golden' (No. 146) are, however, fine and distinct traditional tunes; and the verses attached to them seem to contain phrases of an original which may have been sung to them. These phrases have therefore been retained in this new text, which may be sung equally well to No. 146.

Part 2 has been supplied for occasions when one concluding verse is needed for a carol recital or service (cf. No. 16); it can also be treated as a fourth verse to this carol.

166 CAROL OF SERVICE

(GENERAL)

Moderately quick. (M. S.)

French tune

Steuart Wilson.

UP, my neighbour, come away,
See the work for us to-day,
The hands to help, the mouths to feed,
The sights to see, the books to read:

Up and get us gone, to help the world along,
Up and get us gone, my neighbour.

2 Up, my neighbour, see the plough
For our hands lies waiting now;
Grasp well the stilt, yoke up the team,
Stride out to meet the morning beam:

3 Up, my neighbour, see the land
Ready for the sower's hand;
The plough has made an even tilth,
The furrows wait the golden spilth:

4 Up, my neighbour, now the corn
Ripens at the harvest morn;
Then let it to our sickle yield,
And pile with sheaves the golden field:

5. Up, my neighbour, let us pray,
Thank our Maker every day,
Who gave us work our strength to test
And made us proud to do our best:

'Promptement levez-vous, mon voisin', upon which these words are based, is an example of a carol made up for a familiar folk-tune, in this case an old ritournelle, 'C'est de nos moutons l'allure, mon cousin'. The carol is sung in many parts of France, and is printed by Grimault and by Legeay.

167 CAROL OF THE KINGDOM

(GENERAL)

(M. S.)

Manx tune *Steuart Wilson.*

WHEN Jesus was a baby
  And born of mortal men,
The first who asked to see him
  Came straight from their sheep-pen:
So let each one remember,
  When he his offering brings,
That Jesus loved the Shepherds
  As well as the three Kings.

2 When Jesus was a carpenter,
  He held the saw and adze,
And learned a trade to follow
  Like other simple lads:
So let us not be shamèd
  Of honest work and sweat,
Remembering that a better brow
  Than ours was often wet.

3 When Jesus was a-dying
  Upon the cruel tree,
Two thieves upon each hand of him
  He had for company:
So look not upon any man
  With vain or scornful eyes,
For one poor thief was called by him
  To dwell in Paradise.

4. Now Jesus has gone up on high,
  And truth and justice reign.
Let tenderness and kindliness
  Dwell in the hearts of men:
So, when we have to leave this earth,
  If only we can know
We leave it better than we found,
  We shall be glad to go.

The tune is a traditional Manx carol-tune 'Ny Drogh Vraane', noted by the late Dr. John Clague, apparently from T. Cowell, Marown.

PART IV

TRADITIONAL CAROLS

(together with some by old writers)

SET TO TUNES BY MODERN COMPOSERS

168 BEN JONSON'S CAROL

(CHRISTMAS EVE: CHRISTMAS)

RUTLAND BOUGHTON.

1 I sing the birth was born to-night, The Au-thor both of
life and light; The An - gels so did sound it, And,
like the ra-vished shepherds said, Who saw the light, and
were a - fraid, Yet searched, and true they found it.

Music by Rutland Boughton. *Ben Jonson,* 1573–1637.

I SING the birth was born to-night,
The author both of life and light;
The angels so did sound it,
And, like the ravished shepherds said,
Who saw the light, and were afraid,
Yet searched, and true they found it.

2 The Son of God, the eternal king,
That did us all salvation bring,
And freed our soul from danger,
He whom the whole world could not take,
The Word, which heaven and earth did make,
Was now laid in a manger.

3 The Father's wisdom willed it so,
The Son's obedience knew no No;
Both wills were in one stature,
And, as that wisdom had decreed,
The Word was now made flesh indeed,
And took on him our nature.

4. What comfort by him we do win,
Who made himself the price of sin,
To make us heirs of glory!
To see this babe, all innocence,
A martyr born in our defence,
Can man forget the story?

169 TYRLEY, TYRLOW

(CHRISTMAS)

 PETER WARLOCK.

Fast and gay.
TENORS.
1 A -
f Ob. & Fag.
Horns & Violas.
- bout the field they piped full right, So mer-ri - ly the shepherds be -
mp Strings.
- gan to blow; A - down from heaven they
Fl.
f Cl. & Horns.
mf Strings.

CHORUS. Lightly.
p
saw a light: * Tyr - ley, tyr - low, tyr - ley, tyr -
- low, tyr - ley, tyr - low!
Ob., Cl. & Fag.
f Strings sustain.

* Pronunciation nearer to *tyrol-y* than *turl-y*.

FEMALE VOICES in Unison.
2 Of an - gels there came a
mp Strings.
com - pa - ny, With mer - ry songs and mel - o - dy,
Fl. & Cl.
Ob.
cres.
f
Horns.
MALE VOICES in Unison.
The shep-herds a - non gan them a - spy:
Strings. mf

SOPRANOS.
Tyr - ley, tyr - low, tyr - ley, tyr - low, tyr - ley, tyr -
Cl.
p Fag.
+pizz.
- low!
Fl.
Clar.
Fl.
f Strings sustain.
Ped.
CHORUS. mf
3 The shep - herds hied them to Beth-l'em, To
Fl. & Clar.
mf W.-W. & Horns.

f
see that bless - ed sun - nes beam ; And
Strings.
p
there they found that glo - rious stream : .... Tyr -
Full, without Trombones.
p
Clar.

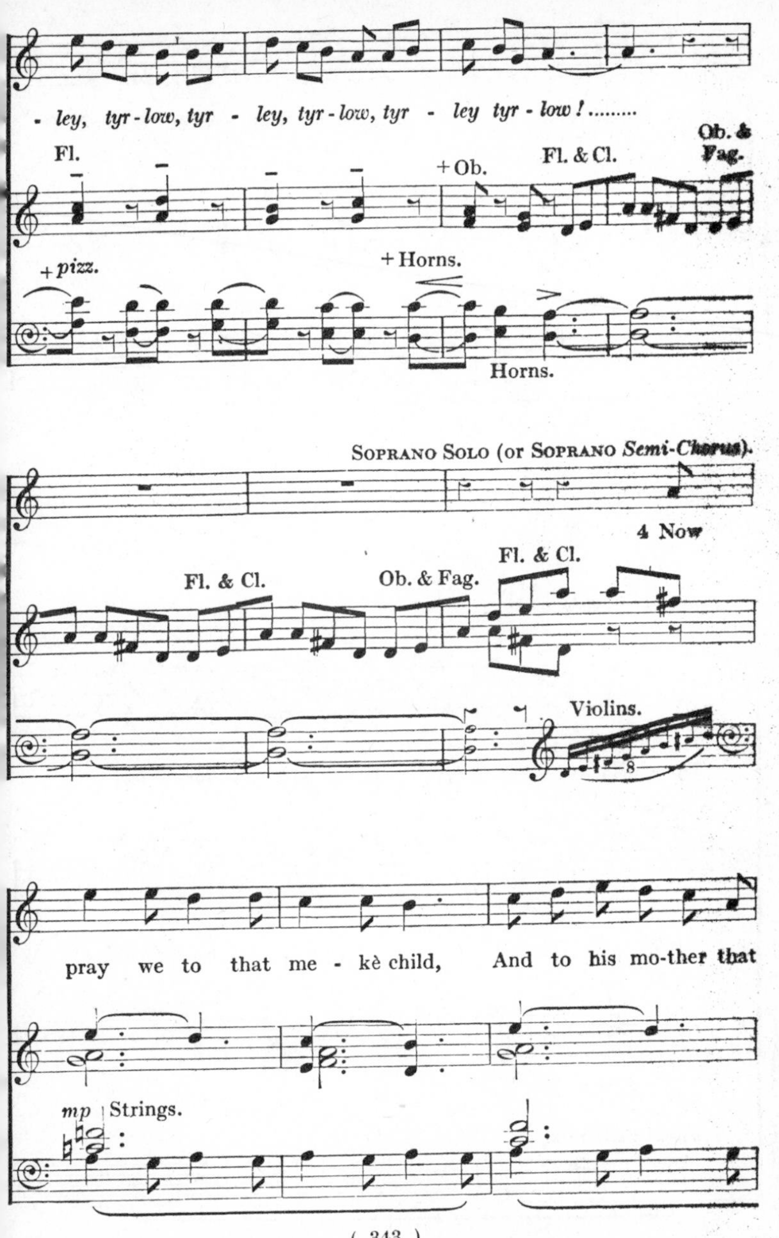
- ley, tyr - low, tyr - ley, tyr - low, tyr - ley tyr - low! ....
Fl.
+ Ob.
Fl. & Cl.
Ob. & Fag.
+ pizz.
+ Horns.
Horns.
Soprano Solo (or Soprano Semi-Chorus).
4 Now
Fl. & Cl.
Ob. & Fag.
Fl. & Cl.
Violins.
pray we to that me - kè child, And to his mo-ther that
mp Strings.

is so mild, The which was nev - er de-filed :
+ Horns.

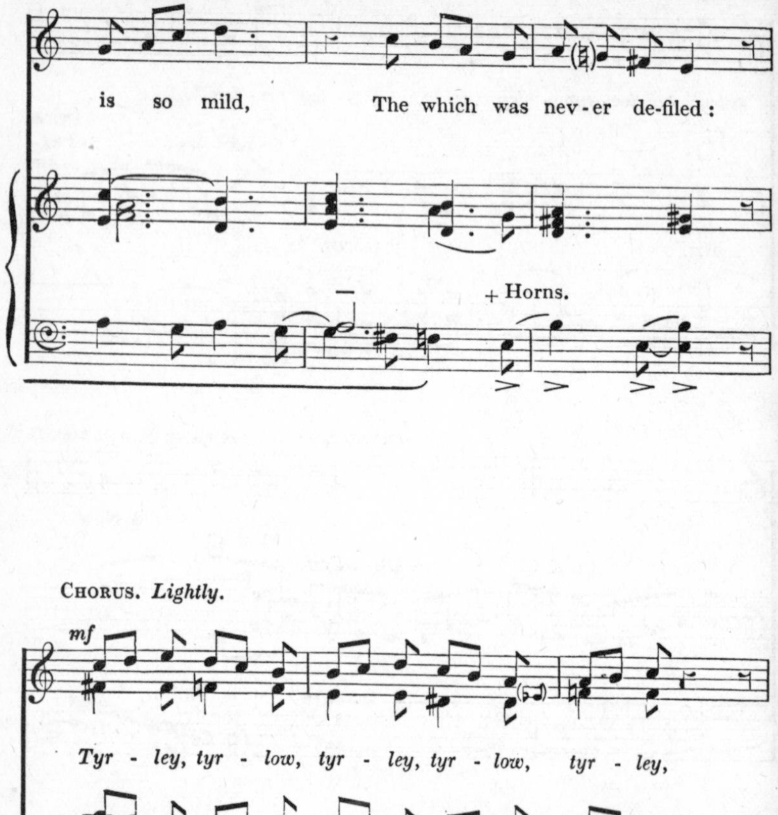

Chorus. *Lightly.*

mf

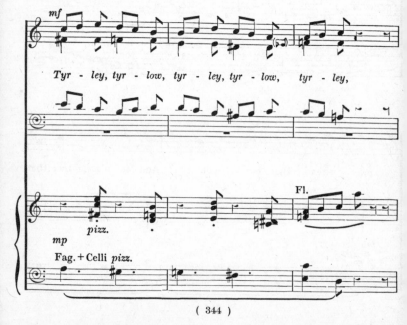

Tyr - ley, tyr - low, tyr - ley, tyr - low, tyr - ley,

Fl.

pizz.

mp

Fag. + Celli *pizz.*

tyr - low! 5 That

Fl.
Clar.
Ob.

Strings sustain.

Basses.
nev - er miss, Then may we sing in
W.-W. Horns,
f ff Trumpets, Glock.
mf Strings.
Sopranos. mf lightly.
Par - a - dise : Tyr -
Fl.
p Strings.
Clar.
+ Clar. & Fag.
mf legato.
- ley, tyr - low tyr - ley, tyr - low, tyr - ley, tyr - low!........
Ob., Cl. & Fag.
f Strings.
Ped.

6. I pray you all that be here,
Fl.
Brass alone.
+ Fag.
+ pizz

Allargando molto.

ff

For to sing and make good cheer, In the

W.-W. & Horns.

a tempo.

wor - ship of God this year :...............

ff Full orchestra.

Ob. + Fag.

Clar.

From the *Commonplace Book* of Richard Hill (cf. No. 36), *c.* 1500, and the Bodleian MS. (Engl. Poet. e. 1), 1460–90, the latter printed by Wright, *Songs and Carols* (Percy Society), 1847.

170 NEW PRINCE, NEW POMP

(CHRISTMAS)

JOHN IRELAND.

John Ireland. *Robert Southwell, c.* 1561–95.

Nowell, Nowell, Nowell, sing we with mirth!
Christ is come well, with us to dwell,
By his most noble birth.

BEHOLD a simple tender babe,
In freezing winter night,
In homely manger trembling lies:
Alas! a piteous sight.

2 The inns are full; no man will yield
This little pilgrim bed;
But forced he is with simple beasts
In crib to shroud his head.

3 Despise him not for lying there;
First what he is inquire:
An orient pearl is often found
In depth of dirty mire.

4 Weigh not his crib, his wooden dish,
Nor beasts that by him feed;
Weigh not his mother's poor attire,
Nor Joseph's simple weed.

5 This stable is a prince's court,
This crib his chair of state,
The beasts are parcel of his pomp,
The wooden dish his plate;

6 The persons in that poor attire
His royal liveries wear;
The Prince himself is come from heaven.
This pomp is prizèd there.

7. With joy approach, O Christian wight,
Do homage to thy King;
And highly praise this humble pomp,
Which he from heaven doth bring.

1 and 2. We have altered 'silly' to its modern equivalent 'simple'. 5. *Parcel* in the old sense of 'part' (from 'particella', 'parcelle').

The prelude 'Nowell', &c., is an old prelude, but not by Southwell.

Robert Southwell was the good Jesuit, executed for treason under Elizabeth.

171 SHAKESPEARE'S CAROL FIRST TUNE.

(CHRISTMAS, SECULAR)

Moderato.
mf
Dr. Arne [Arr. M. S.]
1 Blow, blow, thou win - ter
freeze, thou bit - ter
mf
wind, Thou art not so un - kind, Thou art not so un -
sky, That dost not bite so nigh As ben - e - fits for -
- kind As man's in - gra - ti - tude; Thy tooth is not so
- got, As ben - e - fits for - got: Though thou the wa - ters

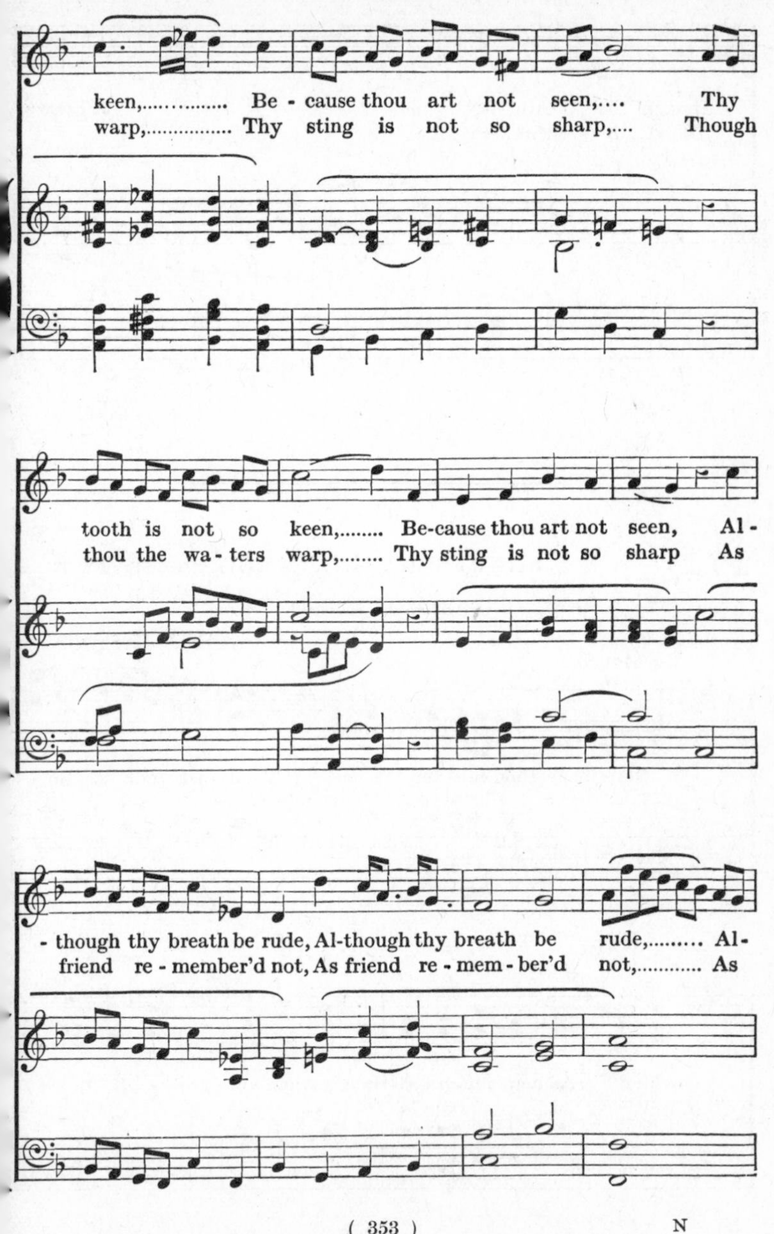
keen,.............. Be - cause thou art not seen,.... Thy
warp,................ Thy sting is not so sharp,.... Though
tooth is not so keen,........ Be-cause thou art not seen, Al -
thou the wa - ters warp,........ Thy sting is not so sharp As
- though thy breath be rude, Al-though thy breath be rude,......... Al-
friend re - member'd not, As friend re - mem - ber'd not,............ As

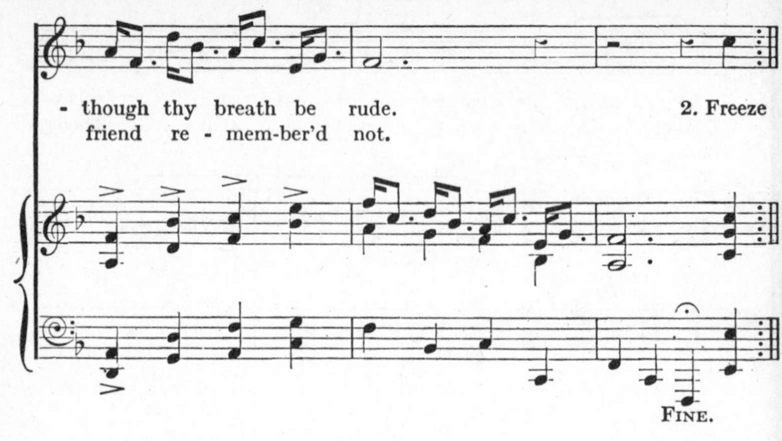
- though thy breath be rude. 2. Freeze
friend re - mem-ber'd not.
Fine.

171 SHAKESPEARE'S CAROL SECOND TUNE.

(CHRISTMAS, SECULAR)

R. J. S. Stevens.

Andante.
mf
Blow, blow, thou win - ter wind, Thou art not so un -

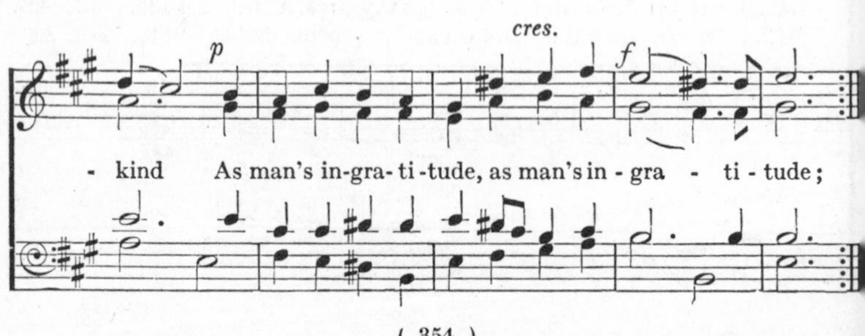
p
cres.
f
- kind As man's in-gra- ti -tude, as man's in - gra - ti - tude;

p
pp
Thy tooth is not so keen, Be-cause thou art not
cres.
f
seen, Al - though thy breath be rude, al -
Allegretto moderato.
p
- though thy breath be rude. Heigh - ho! Sing, heigh - ho! un -
cres.
- to the green hol-ly: Most friend - ship is feign ing, most

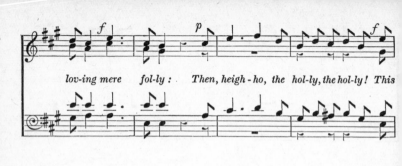

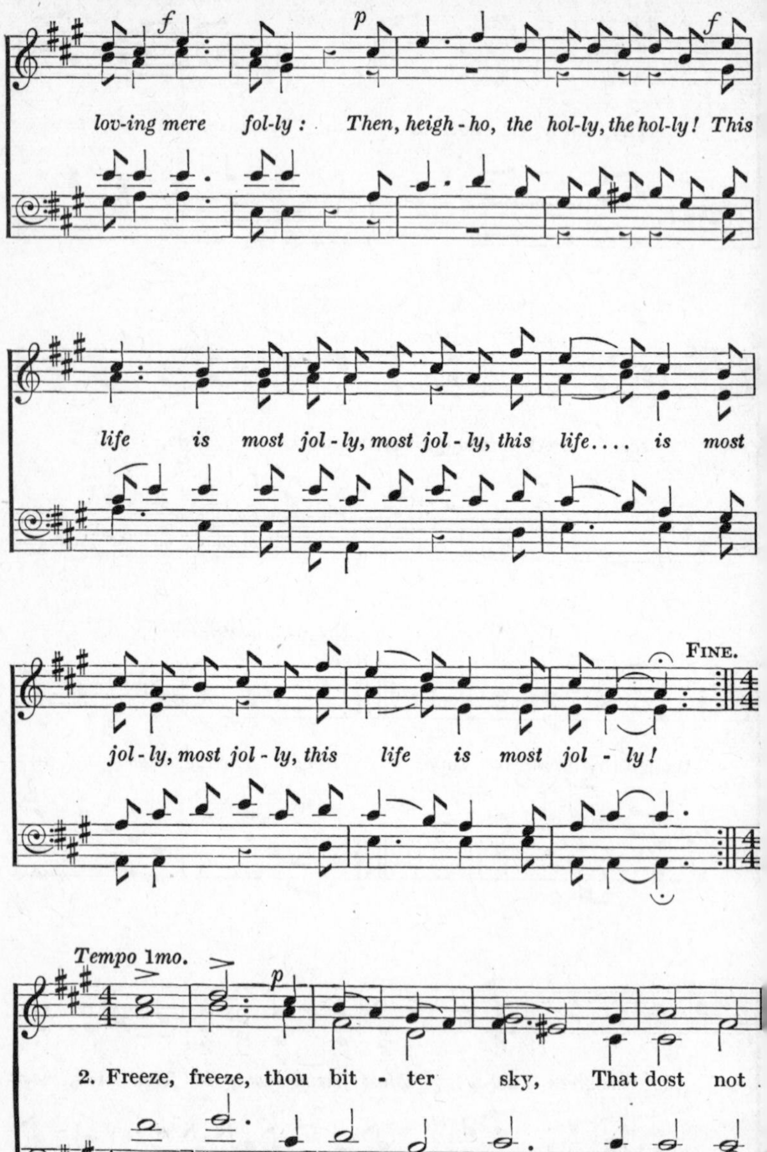

f
p
f
lov-ing mere fol-ly: Then, heigh-ho, the hol-ly, the hol-ly! This
life is most jol-ly, most jol-ly, this life.... is most
Fine.
jol-ly, most jol-ly, this life is most jol-ly!
Tempo 1mo.
p
2. Freeze, freeze, thou bit - ter sky, That dost not

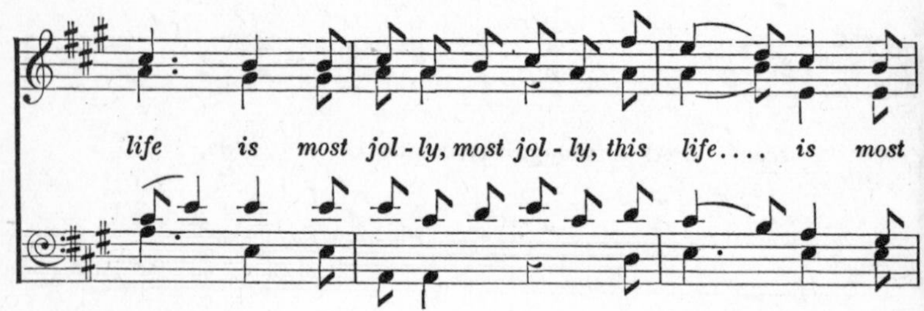

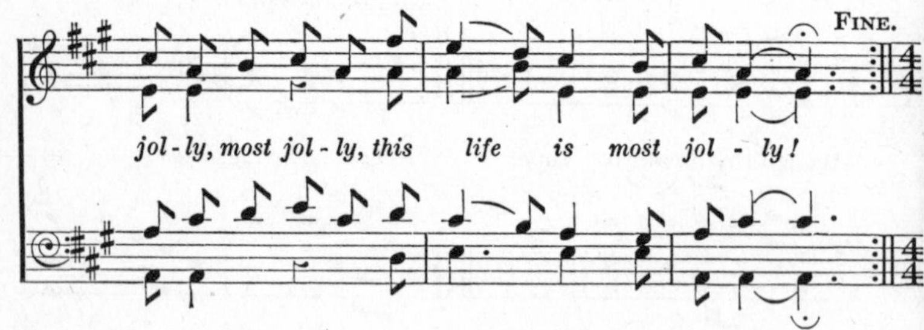

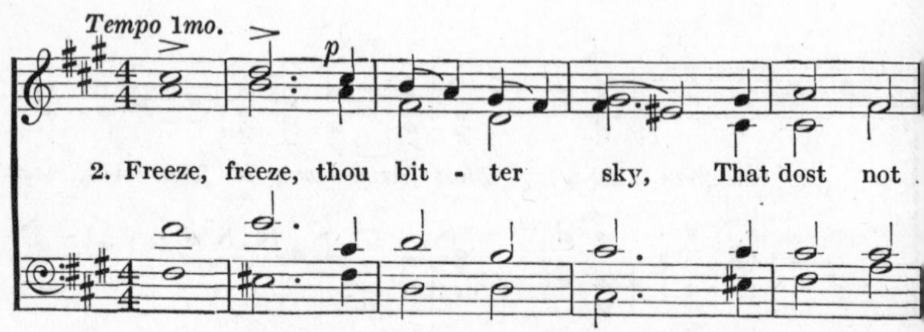

From *As You Like It*, Act II. Dr. Arne (1710–78) does not include the chorus, as Stevens (1757–1837) does.

172 MAKE WE MERRY

(CHRISTMAS, SECULAR)

Allegro con spirito. ♩. = about 100.
MARTIN SHAW.
f
Make we mer-ry, both more and less, For
now is the time of Chris-te-mas, of Chris-te-mas, of Chris-te-mas.
mf
2 Let no man come in-
mf

-to this hall, Nor groom, nor page, nor yet mar-shall,
But that some sport he bring withal.
3 If that he say he cannot sing, Some o-ther sport then let him bring, That

it may please at this feast-ing.
4 If he say he naught can do, Then, for my love, ask him no mo'
But to the stocks.... then let him go.

f
5. Make we mer-ry, both more and less, For now is the time of
f
Chris - te - mas, of Christ - mas, of Christ - mas, of
Christ - - - - - - - - - - - - - mas.

Martin Shaw. c. 1500.

MAKE we merry, both more and less,
For now is the time of Christmas.

2 Let no man come into this hall,
Nor groom, nor page, nor yet marshall,
But that some sport he bring withal.

3 If that he say he cannot sing,
Some other sport then let him bring,
That it may please at this feasting.

4 If he say he naught can do,
Then, for my love, ask him no mo'
But to the stocks then let him go.

5. Make we merry, both more and less,
For now is the time of Christmas.

1. more and less] in the old sense, 'great and small'. 4. mo'] more. stocks] The Lord of Misrule at Christmas often had stocks, pillory, and gibbet.

From the *Commonplace Book* of Richard Hill (cf. No. 36).

173 THE GOLDEN CAROL

(CHRISTMAS: EPIPHANY)

Allegro vivace. R. VAUGHAN WILLIAMS.

1 Now is Chris - te - mas y-come, Fa-ther and Son to-
Marcato.
-gether in one, Ho - ly Ghost, as ye be one, In fere - a, God
send......... us good new year - - a.

[*Copyright*, 1928, *by R. Vaughan Williams.*]

2 I will you sing with all my might, Of a child so

fair in sight, A maid - en bare on Christ - mas night, So

still - a, As.......... it was his will - a.

3 Three king - es came fro Gal - i - lee To Beth - le - hem, that

fair ci - ty, For to of - fer and to see, By
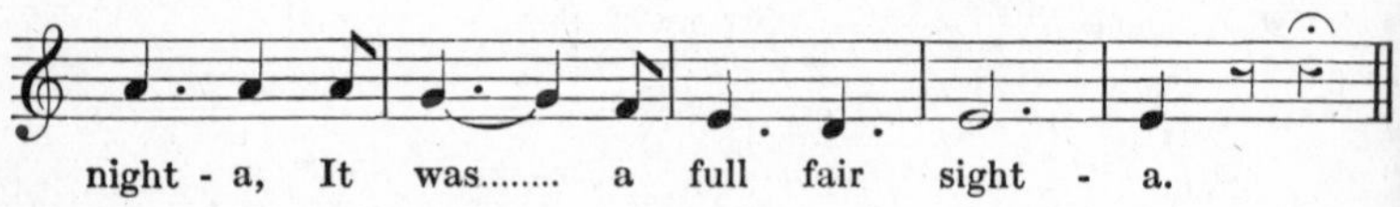
night - a, It was........ a full fair sight - a.

4 As they came forth with their offer - ing, They met with Her-od, that
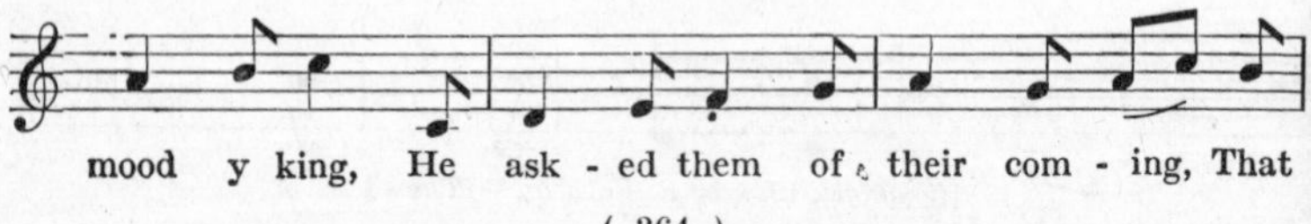
mood y king, He ask - ed them of their com - ing, That

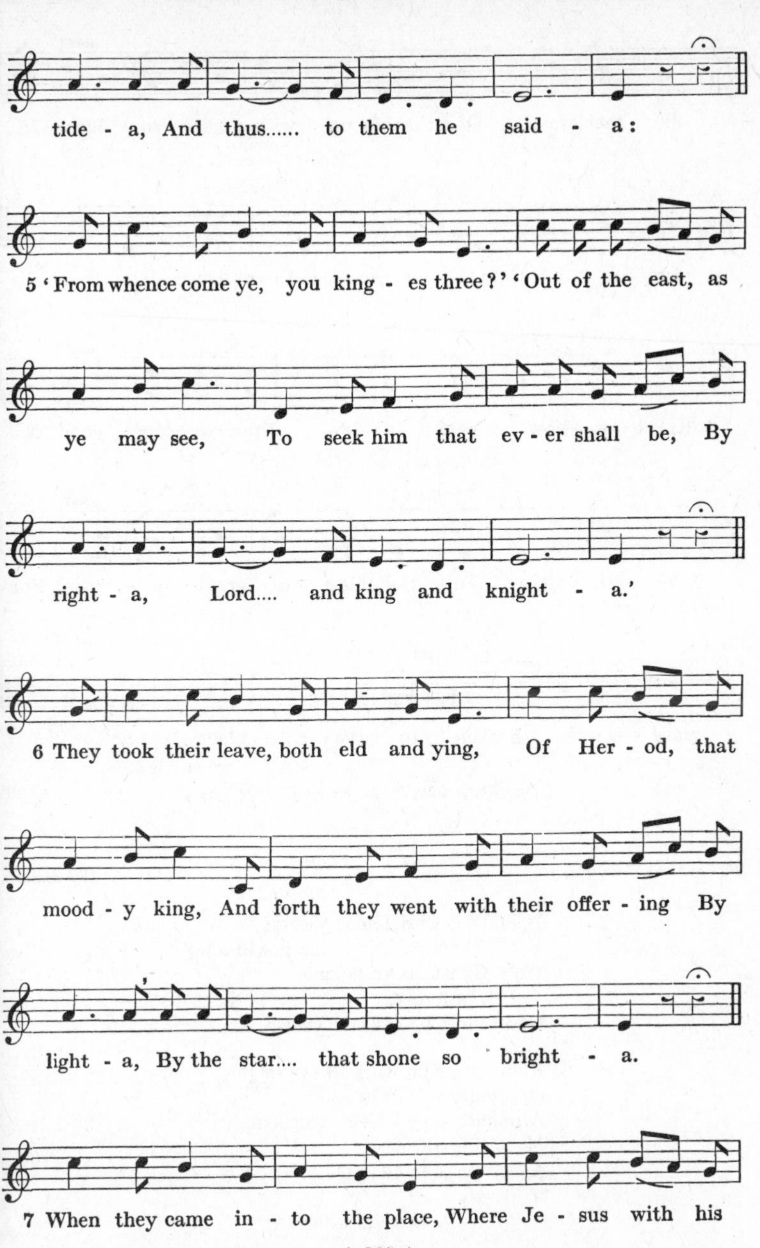
tide - a, And thus...... to them he said - a:
5 'From whence come ye, you king - es three?' 'Out of the east, as
ye may see, To seek him that ev - er shall be, By
right - a, Lord.... and king and knight - a.'
6 They took their leave, both eld and ying, Of Her - od, that
mood - y king, And forth they went with their offer - ing By
light - a, By the star.... that shone so bright - a.
7 When they came in - to the place, Where Je - sus with his

mo - ther was, Of-fer'd they up with great so - lace, In

fere - a, Gold,.... in - cense, and myrrh - a.

8. Kneel we now here a - down; Pray we in good de -

- vo - ti - oun, To that king of great re - nown, For

grace - a, In heaven to have a place - a.

R. Vaughan Williams. *15th century.*

NOW is Christèmas y-come,
Father and Son together in one,
Holy Ghost, as ye be one,
In fere-a,
God send us good new year-a.

2 I will you sing with all my might,
Of a child so fair in sight,
A maiden bare on Christmas night,
So still-a,
As it was his will-a.

1. In fere] together.

3 Three kingès came fro Galilee
To Bethlehem, that fair city,
For to offer and to see,
By night-a ;
It was a full fair sight-a.

4 As they came forth with their offering,
They met with Herod, that moody king,
He asked them of their coming,
That tide-a,
And thus to them he said-a :

5 'From whence come ye, you kingès three?
'Out of the east, as ye may see,
To seek him that ever shall be,
By right-a,
Lord and king and knight-a.'

6 They took their leave, both eld and ying,
Of Herod, that moody king,
And forth they went with their offering
By light-a,
By the star that shone so bright-a.

7 When they came into the place,
Where Jesus with his mother was,
Offered they up with great solace,
In fere-a,
Gold, incense, and myrrh-a.

8. Kneel we now here a-down ;
Pray we in good devotioun,
To that king of great renown,
For grace-a,
In heaven to have a place-a.

6. eld and ying] old and young. 7. Where] orig. MS., 'There' with this meaning.

This, which has most right to the name, 'Golden Carol', was printed by T. Wright from the Bodleian MS. Eng. Poet. e. 1 (*c.* 1460–90) in his *Songs and Carols* (Percy Society), 1847; also by Sandys in his *Christmas Tide*, 1852; A. H. Bullen (*Carols and Poems*, 1885) prints another version from *Notes and Queries*. Miss E. Rickert (*Ancient English Christmas Carols*, 1910) gives two versions, one in sixteen verses and without the tag. We have used that by Mr. F. Sidgwick in *Ancient Carols*, 1908. No tune has survived. Cf. Nos. 146 and 165.

174 WELCOME YULE

(CHRISTMAS, ST. STEPHEN, ETC.: CANDLEMAS)

SOLO VOICE. SYDNEY H. NICHOLSON.

Welcome Yule, thou merry man, In wor-ship of this ho-ly day!
With vigour.
rit.
tempo.
f
Wel-come Yule, Wel - - come Yule. 1 Wel-come be thou,
hea - ven-king, Wel - come born in one morn - ing,
Wel - come for whom we shall sing Wel - come Yule,
Verses 1–4.
rit.
Last verse.
rit.
Wel - - - - come Yule. Wel - - - come Yule.

S. H. Nicholson. *15th century.*

WELCOME Yule, thou merry man,
In worship of this holy day!
Welcome be thou, heaven-king,
Welcome born in one morning,
Welcome for whom we shall sing
Welcome Yule.

2 Welcome be ye, Stephen and John,
Welcome Innocents every one,
Welcome Thomas, Martyr one:

3 Welcome be ye, good New Year,
Welcome Twelfth Day, both in fere,
Welcome Saintès lief and dear:

4 Welcome be ye, Candlemas,
Welcome be ye, queen of bliss,
Welcome both to more and less:

5. Welcome be ye that are here,
Welcome all, and make good cheer,
Welcome all another year!

3. in fere] together. lief] beloved.

Sloane MS. 2593 (cf. No. 36), of the beginning of the fifteenth century or *temp.* Henry VI. Another version in the Bodleian Douce MS. 302, the collection of John Awdlay, the blind chaplain, *c.* 1430, printed in Sandys' *Christmastide*, 1852. See Preface, p. x.

175 THE VIRGIN'S CRADLE HYMN

(NATIVITY.)

som - - num vi - det, Dor - - - - - mi, Je - - - - su!
som - - num vi - det, Dor - - - - - mi, Je - - - - su!
som - - num vi - det, Dor - - - - - mi, Je - - - - su!
som - - num vi - det, Dor - - - - - mi, Je - - - - su!
rall. , mf (a tempo).
blan - - du - - - le! Si non
rall. , mf (a tempo).
blan - - du - - - le! Si................. non
rall. , mf (a tempo).
blan - - - - - - - - - - - du - le! Si................. non
rall. , mf (a tempo).
blan - - du - - - le! Si non
rall.
mf (a tempo).

dor - mis, ma - - - - - - ter plo - - - - - rat
dor - - - - - mis, ma - - - - - ter plo - - - - - rat
dor - - - - - mis, ma - - - - - ter plo - - - - - rat
dor - - - - - mis, ma - - - ter plo - - - - - rat
In - ter fi - la can - tans o - rat, Blan - - - de,
In - ter fi - la can - tans o - rat, Blan - - - de,
In - ter fi - la can - tans o - rat, Blan - - - de,
In - ter fi - la can - tans o - rat, Blan - - - de,

E. Rubbra. *Pr. S. T. Coleridge*, 1772–1834.

DORMI, Jesu! Mater ridet
  Quae tam dulcem somnum videt,
    Dormi, Jesu! blandule!
Si non dormis, mater plorat
Inter fila cantans orat,
    Blande, veni, somnule.

2. Sleep, sweet babe! my cares beguiling:
Mother sits beside thee smiling;
    Sleep, my darling, tenderly!
If thou sleep not, mother mourneth,
Singing as her wheel she turneth:
    Come, soft slumber, balmily!

Coleridge copied the Latin words from a print in a German village, and paraphrased them as above, under the title 'The Virgin's Cradle Hymn'. These verses are therefore akin to such Cradle Hymns as the Chester Nuns' Song (No. 67), 'Lullay, my liking' (No. 182), and the Lute Book Lullaby (No. 30).

176 HERRICK'S ODE

(NATIVITY)

ARMSTRONG GIBBS.

Armstrong Gibbs. *Robert Herrick*, 1591–1674.

IN numbers, and but these few,
I sing thy birth, O Jesu,
Thou pretty baby, born here,
With superabundant scorn here,
Who for thy princely port here,
Hadst for thy place
Of birth, a base
Out-stable for thy court here.

2 Instead of neat enclosures
Of interwoven osiers;
Instead of fragrant posies
Of daffodils and roses,
Thy cradle, kingly stranger,
As gospel tells,
Was nothing else
But here a homely manger.

3 But we with silks, not crewels,
With sundry precious jewels,
And lily-work will dress thee;
And, as we dispossess thee
Of clouts, we'll make a chamber,
Sweet babe, for thee,
Of ivory,
And plastered round with amber.

4. The Jews, they did disdain thee,
But we will entertain thee
With glories to await here
Upon thy princely state here,
And, more for love than pity,
From year to year
We'll make thee here
A free-born of our city.

177 OUT OF YOUR SLEEP

(NATIVITY)

Rather slowly. [*Copyright, 1928, by Martin Shaw.*] MARTIN SHAW.

(Tied in vv. 4, 5, 6.)
(v. 4.) (vv. 4, 6.)
the bell.
(v. 4.) (v. 5.)
FA-BURDEN TO VERSES 3 & 5.
3 Now man is bright-er than the sun; Now
5 Now man he may to hea-ven wend; Now
3 Now man is bright-er than the sun;
5 Now man he may to hea-ven wend;
3 Now man is, &c.
5 Now man he, &c.
3 Bless-ed be God,
5 This is no nay,

Martin Shaw.

15*th century.*

OUT of your sleep arise and wake,
For God mankind now hath y-take
All of a maid without any make ;
Of all women she beareth the bell.

2 And through a maidè fair and wise
Now man is made of full great price ;
Now angels knelen to man's service,
And at this time all this befell.

3 Now man is brighter than the sun ;
Now man in heaven on high shall won ;
Blessèd be God this game is begun
And his mother empress of hell.

4 That ever was thrall, now is he free ;
That ever was small, now great is she ;
Now shall God deem both thee and me
Unto his bliss, if we do well.

5 Now man he may to heaven wend ;
Now heaven and earth to him they bend ;
He that was foe now is our friend.
This is no nay that I you tell.

6. Now blessèd Brother, grant us grace,
At doomès day to see thy face,
And in thy court to have a place,
That we may there sing thee nowell.

3. won] win. 4. deem] judge. 5. no nay] not to be denied.

This fine carol is from the Selden MS. at Oxford, *c.* 1450. The tune is founded on a Danish chime.

178 IN EXCELSIS GLORIA FIRST TUNE.

(NATIVITY)

A. H. Brown.
mf
f
1 When Christ was born of Ma - ry free, In Beth - lem in that fair ci - ty,
Angels sung e'er with mirth and glee, In ex-cel - sis glo - ri - a,
p
Chorus.
ff
In ex-cel - sis glo - ri - a, In ex-cel - sis glo - ri - a,

D.S.
In ex - cel - sis glo - ri - a, In ex - cel - sis glo - ri - a.
Verse 2.
Herd - men be - held, &c.
Verse 4.
Then, dear Lord, &c.

Arthur H. Brown.

1456.

Christo paremus cantica,
In excelsis gloria.

WHEN Christ was born of Mary free,
In Bethlem in that fair city,
Angels sung e'er with mirth and glee,
In excelsis gloria.

2 Herdmen beheld these angels bright—
To them appearèd with great light,
And said, 'God's son is born this night':

3 This king is come to save his kind,
In the scripture as we find;
Therefore this song have we in mind:

4. Then, dear Lord, for thy great grace,
Grant us the bliss to see thy face,
Where we may sing to thy solace:

Harleian MS. 5396 (1456). Printed Wright, &c., and Chambers and Sidgwick. Original tune lost; A. H. Brown's tune appeared in Bramley & Stainer, 1871. Beyond the modernizing of the spelling, the following lines of the original only are altered: 'This king is comen to save kinde', 'Then Lord, for thy gret grace'.

178 IN EXCELSIS GLORIA

SECOND TUNE.

(NATIVITY)

SOLO VOICE.
MARTIN SHAW.
Christ-o pa-re-mus can-ti-ca, In ex-cel-sis glo-ri-a.
(Omit in v. 4.)

(Verse 2.)

'In ex-cel-sis glo - - - ri - a.' ....
'In ex-cel-sis glo - - ri - a.'

Martin Shaw. 1456.

Christo paremus cantica,
In excelsis gloria.

WHEN Christ was born of Mary free,
In Bethlem in that fair city,
Angels sung e'er with mirth and glee,
In excelsis gloria.

2 Herdmen beheld these angels bright—
To them appearèd with great light,
And said, 'God's son is born this night':

3 This king is come to save his kind,
In the scripture as we find;
Therefore this song have we in mind:

4. Then, dear Lord, for thy great grace,
Grant us the bliss to see thy face,
Where we may sing to thy solace:

Harleian MS. 5396 (1456). Printed Wright, &c., and Chambers and Sidgwick. Original tune lost; A. H. Brown's tune appeared in Bramley & Stainer, 1871. Beyond the modernizing of the spelling, the following lines of the original only are altered: 'This king is comen to save kinde', 'Then Lord, for thy gret grace'.

179 THE QUEST

(THE PASSION)

SOPRANO. *Con moto.* J. BRAHMS.

1 Saint Ma-ry goes a-seek-ing Through Jew-ry up and
2 O look, for she has found him; By Herod's house stood

ALTO.

1 Saint Ma-ry goes a-seek-ing Through Jew-ry up and
2 O look, for she has found him; By Herod's house stood

TENOR.

1 Saint Ma-ry goes a-seek-ing Through Jew-ry up and
2 O look, for she has found him; By He-rod's house stood

BASS.

1 Saint Ma-ry goes a-seek-ing Through Jew-ry up and
2 O look, for she has found him; By Herod's house stood

down, Through Jew-ry up and down, Un-til God the Lord she
he, By Herod's house stood he, What sor-row for her to

down, Through Jew-ry up and down, Un-til God the Lord she
he, By Her-od's house stood he, What sor-row for her to

down, Through Jew-ry up and down, Un-til God the Lord she
he, By Her-od's house stood he, What sor-row for her to

down, Through Jew-ry up and down, Un-til God the Lord she
he, By Her-od's house stood he, What sor-row for her to

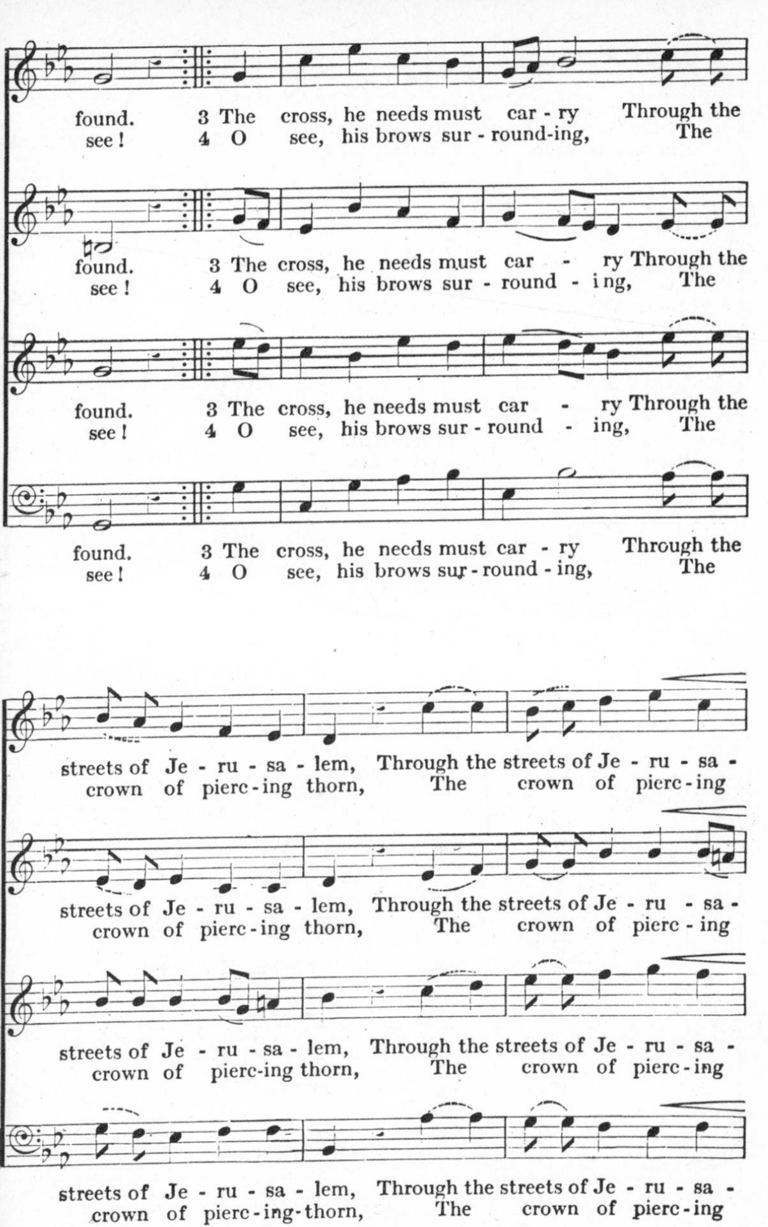

found. 3 The cross, he needs must car - ry Through the
see! 4 O see, his brows sur - round-ing, The
found. 3 The cross, he needs must car - ry Through the
see! 4 O see, his brows sur - round - ing, The
found. 3 The cross, he needs must car - ry Through the
see! 4 O see, his brows sur - round - ing, The
found. 3 The cross, he needs must car - ry Through the
see! 4 O see, his brows sur - round - ing, The
streets of Je - ru - sa - lem, Through the streets of Je - ru - sa -
crown of pierc - ing thorn, The crown of pierc - ing
streets of Je - ru - sa - lem, Through the streets of Je - ru - sa -
crown of pierc - ing thorn, The crown of pierc - ing
streets of Je - ru - sa - lem, Through the streets of Je - ru - sa -
crown of pierc-ing thorn, The crown of pierc - ing
streets of Je - ru - sa - lem, Through the streets of Je - ru - sa -
crown of pierc - ing - thorn, The crown of pierc - ing

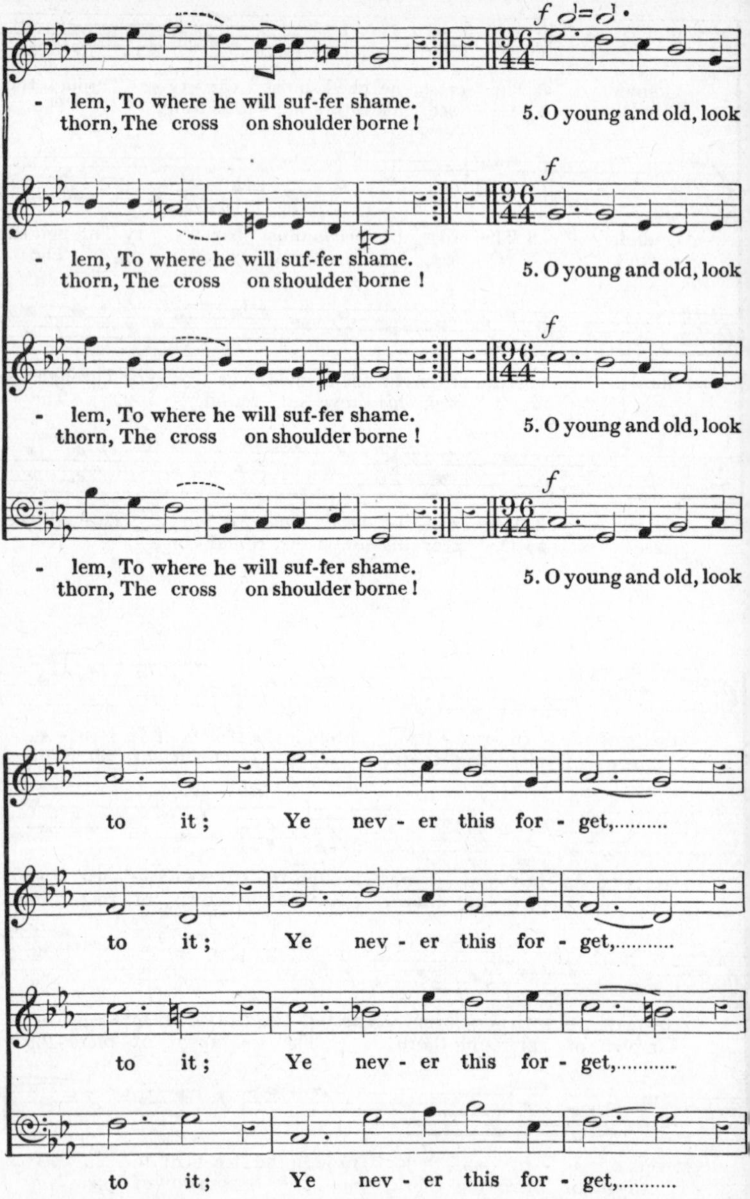

f 96/44

- lem, To where he will suf-fer shame.
thorn, The cross on shoulder borne!

5. O young and old, look

f 96/44

- lem, To where he will suf-fer shame.
thorn, The cross on shoulder borne!

5. O young and old, look

f 96/44

- lem, To where he will suf-fer shame.
thorn, The cross on shoulder borne!

5. O young and old, look

f 96/44

- lem, To where he will suf-fer shame.
thorn, The cross on shoulder borne!

5. O young and old, look

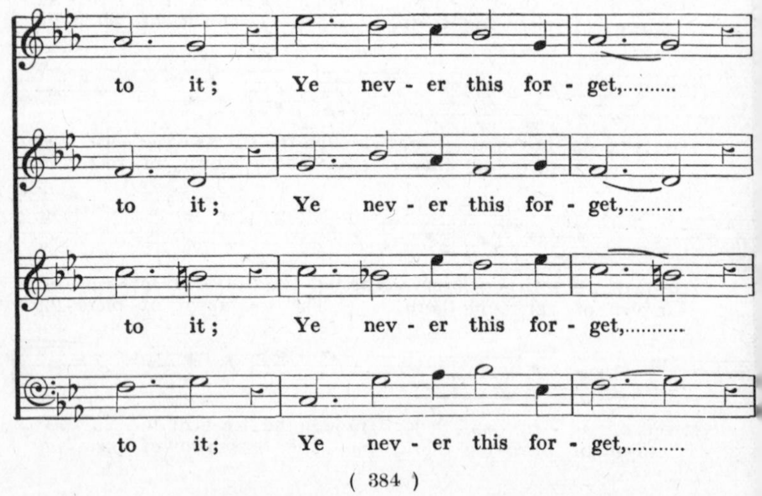
to it; Ye nev - er this for - get,..........
to it; Ye nev - er this for - get,..........
to it; Ye nev - er this for - get,..........
to it; Ye nev - er this for - get,..........

f
That his wounds set wide high Hea-ven's gate!
That his wounds set wide high Hea-ven's gate!
That his wounds set wide high Hea-ven's gate!
That his wounds set wide high Hea-ven's gate!

J. Brahms, 1833–97. *Traditional. Tr. H. T. Wade-Gery.*

SAINT Mary goes a-seeking
  Through Jewry up and down,
Until God the Lord she found.

2 O look, for she has found him;
  By Herod's house stood he,
What sorrow for her to see!

3 The cross, he needs must carry
  Through the streets of Jerusalem,
To where he will suffer shame.

4 O see, his brows surrounding,
  The crown of piercing thorn,
The cross on shoulder borne!

5. O young and old, look to it;
  Ye never this forget,
That his wounds set wide high Heaven's gate.

'Maria's Wallfahrt' ('Maria ging aus wandern') is given here as it was set by Brahms in his *Marienlieder*, with a new translation of the words. The second line in each verse is repeated. Cf. No. 93.

180 ADAM LAY YBOUNDEN

(GENERAL, MEDIEVAL)

Allegretto.
PETER WARLOCK.
1 A-dam lay y-
mf
-boun-den, Boun-den in a bond; Four thou-sand win-ter
Thought he not too long. 2 And all was for an ap-ple, An ap-ple that he

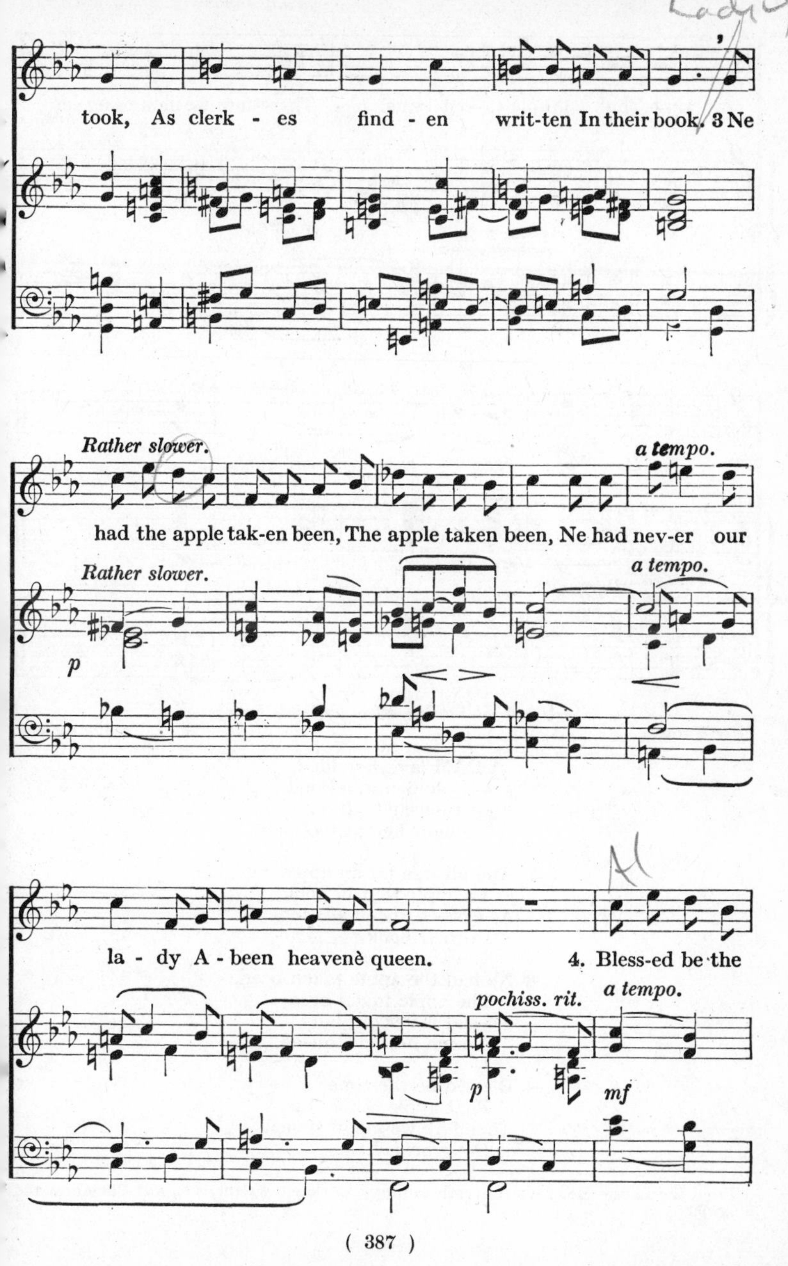
took, As clerk - es find - en writ-ten In their book. 3 Ne
Rather slower.
a tempo.
had the apple tak-en been, The apple taken been, Ne had nev-er our
p
la - dy A - been heavenè queen. 4. Bless-ed be the
pochiss. rit.
mf

time That ap-ple ta-ken was. There-fore we moun sing - en
f cres.
De - o gra - ci - - as!
ff allargando.

Peter Warlock. *c. 15th century.*

ADAM lay ybounden,
   Bounden in a bond;
Four thousand winter
   Thought he not too long.

2 And all was for an apple,
   An apple that he took,
As clerkès finden written
   In their book.

3 Ne had the apple taken been,
   The apple taken been,
Ne had never our lady
   A-been heavenè queen.

4. Blessèd be the time
   That apple taken was.
Therefore we moun singen
   Deo gracias!

From the Sloane MS. 2593 (fifteenth century). Printed Wright, &c., and Chambers and Sidgwick.

181 BALULALOW

(GENERAL)

SOPRANO SOLO.
Slow and very quiet throughout.
PETER WARLOCK.
1 O
muted strings.
p legato e tranquillo.
poco rit.
pp
con Ped.
my dear heart, young Je - sus sweet, Pre - pare thy
a tempo.
cra - dle in my spreit, And I sall rock thee

in my heart, And ne - ver mair from thee de -

poco rit.

part.

S
A

(closed lips) Mm. . . . .

T
B

Chorus alone.

mf a tempo.
2. But I sall praise thee ev - er -
(still closed) Mm
(open) Ah
(open) Ah
sempre legato.
(open) Ah
(Very slight aspiration every 3rd beat of the bar.)
ma cantabile.
muted strings.
pp
Chorus.

more, With sang - is sweet un - to thy
Mm
Ah
Ah
Ah

quasi 4/4
gloir; The knees of my heart sall I
Mm.......................................
Ah.......................................
Ah.......................................
espressivo.
Ah.......................................

poco rit. al fine.
bow, And sing that richt Ba - lu - la -
Mm...... (open) Ah..........
Ah..........
Ah..........
Ah..........

Peter Warlock. *Wedderburn*, 1567.

O MY dear heart, young Jesus sweet,
Prepare thy cradle in my spreit,
And I sall rock thee in my heart,
And never mair from thee depart.

2. But I sall praise thee evermore,
With sangis sweet unto thy gloir;
The knees of my heart sall I bow,
And sing that richt *Balulalow*.

1. spreït] spirit. sall] shall. 2. sangis] songs. gloir] glory.

From 'Ane Sang of the birth of Christ' ('I come from heaven to tell'), a piece of fifteen stanzas, from *Ane Compendious Buik of Godly and Spirituall Sangis*, 1567, by the brothers James, John, and Robert Wedderburn. The whole poem is a translation of the Christmas Eve Carol which Luther wrote for his son Hans, 'Vom Himmel hoch', first published in *Geistliche Lieder*, 1535. Luther's tune is in *Songs of Praise*, No. 365.

182 LULLAY MY LIKING

(GENERAL, MEDIEVAL)

REFRAIN. Allegretto
GUSTAV HOLST.
p
Lul - lay my lik - ing, my dear son, my sweet - ing;
p
pp
Lul - lay my dear heart, mine own dear dar - ling!
SOLO. 1st verse.
p
1 I saw a fair maid - en Sit - ten and sing: She
lul - led a lit - tle child, A swee - te lord - ing:
REFRAIN.
p
Lul - lay my lik - ing, my dear son, my sweet - ing;
p
pp
Lul - lay my dear heart, mine own dear dar - ling!

SOLO. 2nd verse.
mf
2 That e - ter - nal lord is he That made al - le thing ; Of
al - le lord - es he is Lord, Of al - le king - es king :
REFRAIN.
p
Lul - lay my lik - ing, my dear son, my sweet - ing ;
p
pp
Lul - lay my dear heart, mine own dear dar - ling !
SOLO. 3rd verse.
3 There was mic - kle mel - o - dy At that child - es birth : Al - though
they were in heaven's bliss They ma-de mic - kle mirth :
REFRAIN.
p
Lul - lay my lik - ing, my dear son, my sweet - ing ;

p
pp
Lul - lay my dear heart, mine own dear dar - ling!
Chorus. 4th verse.
mf
f
4 Angels bright they sang that night And saiden to that child 'Blessed be
thou, and so be she That is both meek and mild':
Refrain.
p
Lul - lay my lik - ing, my dear son, my sweet - ing;
p
pp
Lul - lay my dear heart, mine own dear dar - ling!

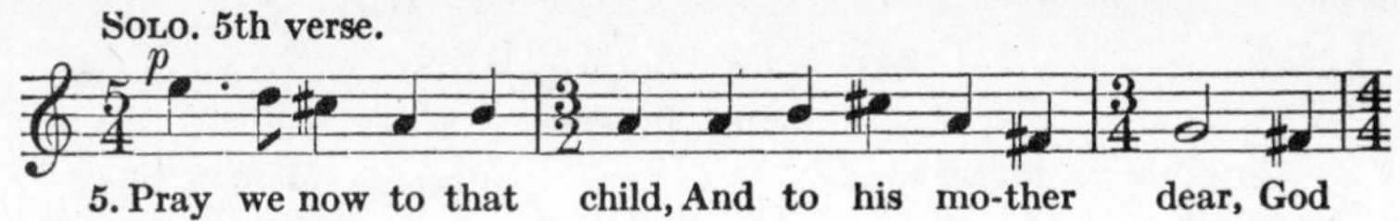
SOLO. 5th verse.
p
5. Pray we now to that child, And to his mo-ther dear, God

grant them all his bless - ing That now mak - en cheer :

REFRAIN.
p
Lul - lay my lik - ing, my dear son, my sweet - ing;

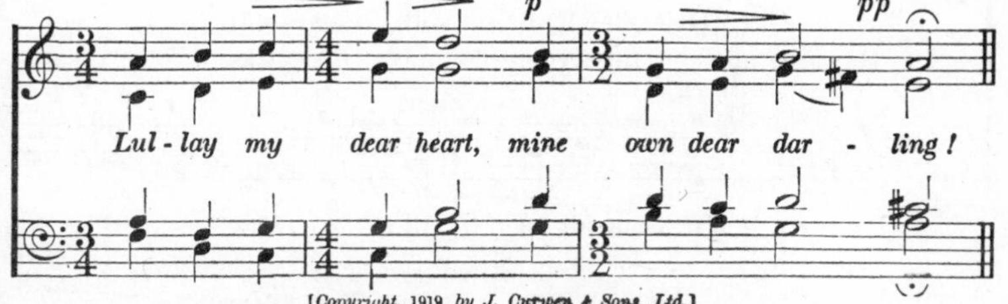
p
pp
Lul - lay my dear heart, mine own dear dar - ling!

G. Holst. *15th century.*

LULLAY my liking, my
dear son, my sweeting;
Lullay my dear heart, mine
own dear darling!

I saw a fair maiden
Sitten and sing:
She lullèd a little child,
A sweetè lording:

Lullay my liking, my dear
son, my sweeting;
Lullay my dear heart, mine
own dear darling!

2 That eternal lord is he
That made allè thing;
Of allè lordès he is Lord,
Of allè kingès king:

3 There was mickle melody
At that childès birth:
Although they were in heaven's bliss
They madè mickle mirth:

4 Angels bright they sang that night
And saiden to that child
'Blessed be thou, and so be she
That is both meek and mild':

5. Pray we now to that child,
And to his mother dear,
God grant them all his blessing
That now maken cheer:

2. eternal] *orig.* 'eche', with the same meaning. 3. mickle] much.
Words from the Sloane MS. (see Nos. 116, 174, 180, 183).

183 I SING OF A MAIDEN

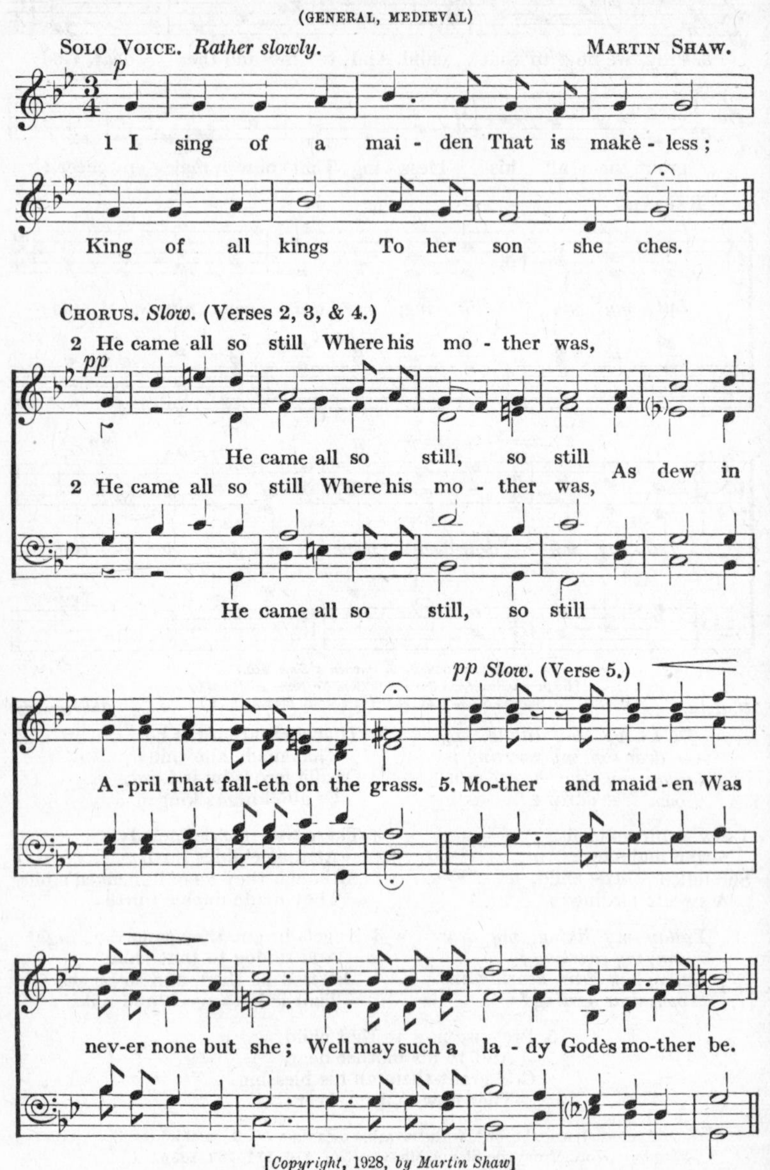
(GENERAL, MEDIEVAL)
SOLO VOICE. Rather slowly.
MARTIN SHAW.
p
1 I sing of a mai - den That is makè - less;
King of all kings To her son she ches.
CHORUS. Slow. (Verses 2, 3, & 4.)
pp
2 He came all so still Where his mo - ther was,
He came all so still, so still
As dew in
2 He came all so still Where his mo - ther was,
He came all so still, so still
A - pril That fall-eth on the grass.
pp Slow. (Verse 5.)
5. Mo-ther and maid - en Was
nev-er none but she; Well may such a la - dy Godès mo-ther be.

[*Copyright*, 1928, *by Martin Shaw*]

Martin Shaw. *15th century.*

I SING of a maiden
That is makèless;
King of all kings
To her son she ches.

2 He came all so still
Where his mother was,
As dew in April
That falleth on the grass.

3 He came all so still
To his mother's bowr,
As dew in April
That falleth on the flower.

4 He came all so still
Where his mother lay,
As dew in April
That falleth on the spray.

5. Mother and maiden
Was never none but she;
Well may such a lady
Godès mother be.

1. makèless] mateless, i. e. matchless. ches (pronounce to rhyme with 'less')] chose. 2, 4. Where] *orig.* MS. 'There,' with this meaning. all so] *orig.* 'also', as.

This famous little classic is also in the Sloane MS. Of its 'ineffable grace' Prof. Saintsbury says: 'In no previous verse had this Aeolian music—this "harp of Ariel"—that distinguishes English at its very best in this direction . . . been given to the world' (*Short History of English Literature*, 1913, p. 202). If ever there was a tune, it has been lost.

184 ALL BELLS IN PARADISE

(GENERAL)

TREBLE SOLO.
MARTIN SHAW.
1 O-ver yon-der's a park, which is new-ly be-gun:
CHORUS.
p
All bells in Pa-ra-dise I heard them a-ring,
SOLO.
Which is sil-ver on the out-side and gold with-in:
mf CHORUS.
And I love sweet Je-sus a-bove.... all thing.

Martin Shaw. *Traditional.*

OVER yonder's a park, which is newly begun:
All bells in Paradise I heard them a-ring,
Which is silver on the outside and gold within:
And I love sweet Jesus above all thing.

2 And in that park there stands a hall:
Which is covered all over with purple and pall:

3 And in that hall there stands a bed:
Which is hung all round with silk curtains so red:

4 And in that bed there lies a knight:
Whose wounds they do bleed by day and by night:

5 At that bedside there lies a stone:
Which our blest Virgin Mary knelt upon:

6 At that bed's foot there lies a hound:
Which is licking the blood as it daily runs down:

7. At that bed's head there grows a thorn:
Which was never so blossomed since Christ was born:

If sung unaccompanied the alto, tenor, and bass sing ''m' with closed lips during the solo.

See No. 61 for the version with its traditional tune. This version was recovered in the middle of the nineteenth century in North Staffordshire and contributed to *Notes and Queries* in 1862, but without its tune. The theme is still eucharistic: v. 3 describes the altar with dorsal and riddels; v. 7 the Glastonbury thorn.

185 WITHER'S ROCKING HYMN

(GENERAL)

SOLO. *Lento con moto.* R. VAUGHAN WILLIAMS.

p
1 Sweet ba-by, sleep! What ails my dear? What ails my dar - ling
p
thus to cry? Be still, my child, and lend thine ear To
hear me sing thy lul - la - by.
pp
My pret-ty lamb, for-
pp Chorus unaccompanied.
sweet...............

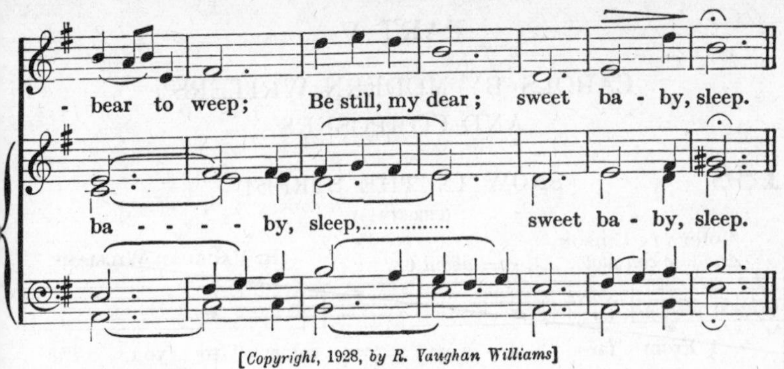
- bear to weep; Be still, my dear; sweet ba - by, sleep.
ba - - - - by, sleep,................ sweet ba - by, sleep.

[*Copyright*, 1928, *by R. Vaughan Williams*]

R. Vaughan Williams. *George Wither*, 1588–1667.

SWEET baby, sleep! What ails my dear?
What ails my darling thus to cry?
Be still, my child, and lend thine ear
To hear me sing thy lullaby.
My pretty lamb, forbear to weep;
Be still, my dear; sweet baby, sleep.

2 Whilst thus thy lullaby I sing,
For thee great blessings ripening be;
Thine Eldest Brother is a King,
And hath a kingdom bought for thee.
Sweet baby, then, forbear to weep;
Be still, my babe; sweet baby, sleep.

3 When God with us was dwelling here,
In little babes he took delight:
Such innocents as thou, my dear,
Are ever precious in his sight.
Sweet baby, then, forbear to weep;
Be still, my babe; sweet baby, sleep.

4 A little infant once was he,
And strength in weakness then was laid
Upon his virgin mother's knee,
That power to thee might be conveyed.
Sweet baby, then, forbear to weep;
Be still, my babe; sweet baby, sleep.

5 The King of kings, when he was born,
Had not so much for outward ease;
By him such dressings were not worn,
Nor suchlike swaddling-clothes as these.
Sweet baby, then, forbear to weep;
Be still, my babe; sweet baby, sleep.

6. The wants that he did then sustain
Have purchased wealth, my babe, for thee;
And by his torments and his pain
Thy rest and ease securèd be.
My baby, then, forbear to weep;
Be still, my babe; sweet baby, sleep.

George Wither's most famous lyrics were early written, 'Shall I wasting in despair' in 1615. He became a Puritan in 1623, and was raising a troop of horse in 1642. The 'Rocking Hymn' was in *Halelujah*, 1641.

PART V

CAROLS BY MODERN WRITERS AND COMPOSERS

186 SNOW IN THE STREET

(CHRISTMAS)

VOICES IN UNISON.
Andante con moto. 𝅗𝅥. = about 63.
R. VAUGHAN WILLIAMS.
1 From far a - way we come to you, The
ORGAN (OR VOICES IN HARMONY).
snow in the street and the wind on the door, To tell of great
ti - dings strange and true. Min-strels and maids stand

forth on the floor : From far a - way we come to you, To
tell of great ti - dings strange.......... and true.....

R. Vaughan Williams. *William Morris,* 1834–96.

FROM far away we come to you,
The snow in the street and the wind on the door,
To tell of great tidings strange and true. [*on the floor :*
Minstrels and maids stand forth
From far away we come to you, [*and true.*
To tell of great tidings strange

2 For as we wandered far and wide,
What hap do you deem there should us betide ?

3 Under a bent when the night was deep, [their sheep :
There lay three shepherds tending

4 'O ye shepherds, what have ye seen, [teen ?'
To slay your sorrow and heal your

5 'In an ox-stall this night we saw
A babe and a maid without a flaw :

PART II.

6 'There was an old man there beside ; [wide :
His hair was white, and his hood was

7 'And as we gazed this thing upon,
Those twain knelt down to the little one.

8 'And a marvellous song we straight did hear, [our care.'
That slew our sorrow and healed

9. News of a fair and a marvellous thing,
Nowell, nowell, nowell, we sing !

From William Morris's *The Earthly Paradise* (1868–70) in the poem, 'The Land East of the Sun and West of the Moon'. The carol begins 'Outlanders, whence came ye last', the first, second, and fourth verses being here omitted.

187

MID-WINTER

(CHRISTMAS)

In moderate time. GUSTAV HOLST.

The metre of this hymn is irregular. The music as printed is that of the first verse, and it can easily be adapted to the others.

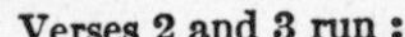
Verses 2 and 3 run :

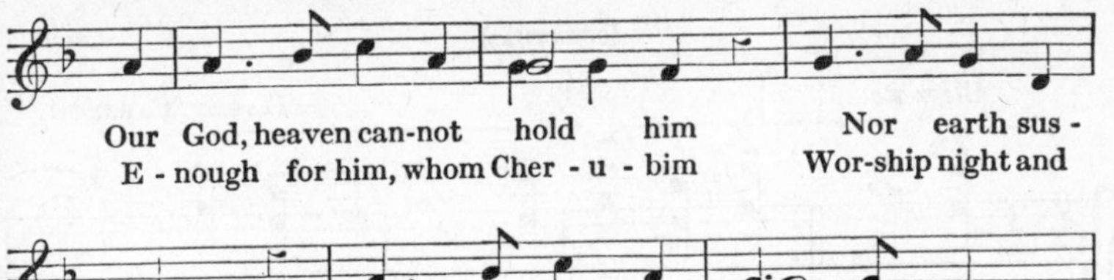
Our God, heaven can-not hold him Nor earth sus -
E - nough for him, whom Cher - u - bim Wor-ship night and

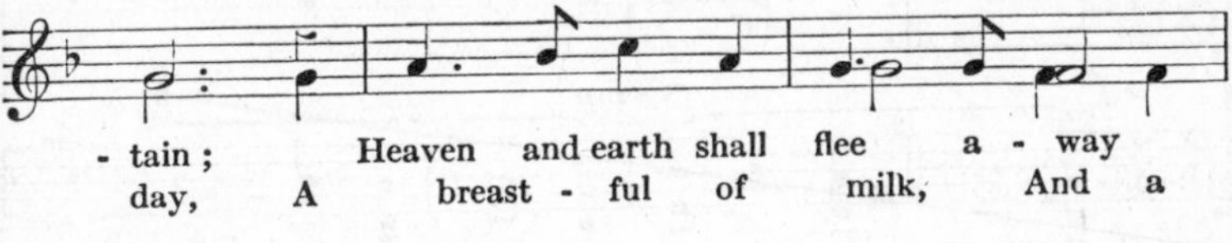
- tain ; Heaven and earth shall flee a - way
day, A breast - ful of milk, And a

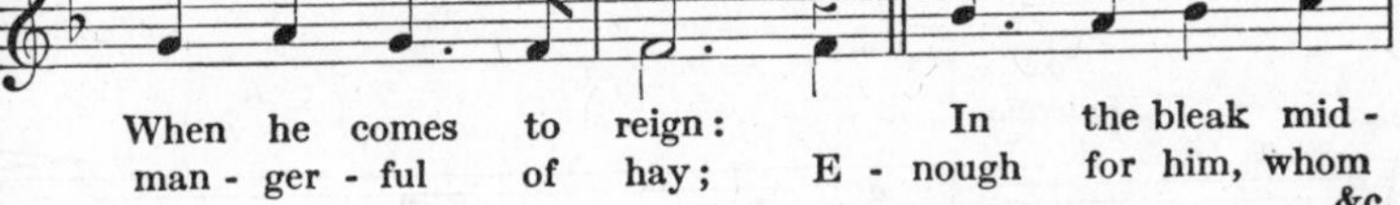
When he comes to reign : In the bleak mid -
man - ger - ful of hay ; E - nough for him, whom
&c.

G. Holst. *Christina Rossetti*, 1830–94.

IN the bleak mid-winter
  Frosty wind made moan,
Earth stood hard as iron,
  Water like a stone ;
Snow had fallen, snow on snow,
  Snow on snow,
In the bleak mid-winter,
  Long ago.

2 Our God, heaven cannot hold him
  Nor earth sustain ;
Heaven and earth shall flee away
  When he comes to reign :
In the bleak mid-winter
  A stable-place sufficed
The Lord God Almighty
  Jesus Christ.

3 Enough for him, whom Cherubim
  Worship night and day,
A breastful of milk,
  And a mangerful of hay ;
Enough for him, whom Angels
  Fall down before,
The ox and ass and camel
  Which adore.

4 Angels and Archangels
  May have gathered there,
Cherubim and Seraphim
  Thronged the air :
But only his mother
  In her maiden bliss
Worshipped the Belovèd
  With a kiss.

5 What can I give him,
  Poor as I am ?
If I were a shepherd
  I would bring a lamb ;
If I were a wise man
  I would do my part ;
Yet what I can I give him—
  Give my heart.

This poem, with its tune from the *English Hymnal* and *Songs of Praise*, is so much a carol that we feel bound to include it here also.

188 OUR BROTHER IS BORN

(CHRISTMAS)

Allegretto. HARRY FARJEON.

f
mp
p
con Ped.

Moderato.
p
1 Now ev - 'ry Child that dwells on earth, Stand
p

up, stand up and sing:........... The pass - ing night has
mf
mf

dim.
pp
giv - en birth Un - to the chil - dren's King......... Sing
pp
Ped. * Ped. *
sweet as the flute, Sing clear as the horn, Sing
joy of the Chil - dren, Come Christ - mas the morn:
cres.

cres.
rit.
f Allegretto.
Lit - tle Christ Je - sus Our bro - ther is born............
f
p
5. Now
mp
p
p
Moderato.
all the An - gels of the Lord, Rise up on Christ - mas

mf
*Even:........ The pass-ing night will hear the Word That
mf
f
Poco meno mosso.
is the voice of *Heaven. Sing sweet as the flute, Sing
f
clear as the horn, Sing joy of the An-gels, Come

* Pronounce nearly as one syllable.

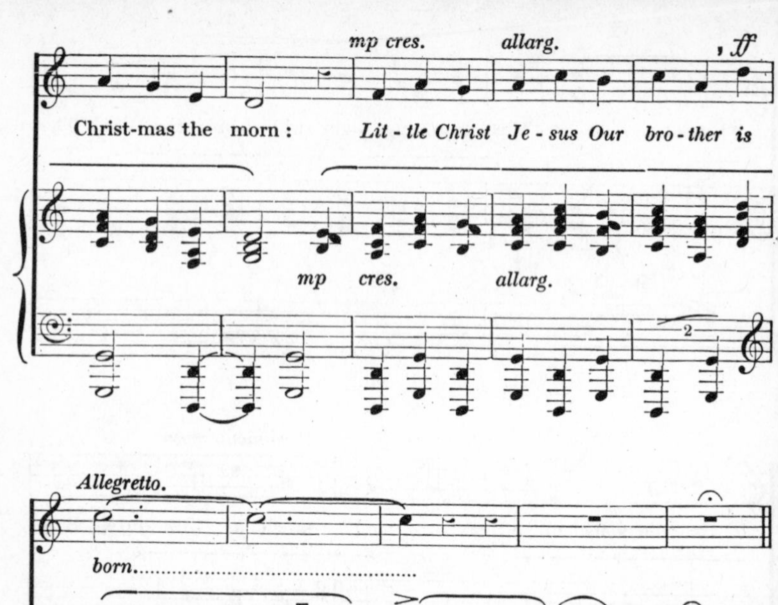

For high voices this carol may be transposed to key E.

Harry Farjeon. *Eleanor Farjeon.*

NOW every Child that dwells on earth,
  Stand up, stand up and sing :
The passing night has given birth
Unto the children's King.
Sing sweet as the flute,
Sing clear as the horn,
Sing joy of the Children,
Come Christmas the morn :
  Little Christ Jesus
  Our brother is born.

2 Now every star that dwells in sky,
Look down with shining eyes :
The night has dropped in passing by
A Star from Paradise.
Sing sweet as the flute,
Sing clear as the horn,
Sing joy of the Stars,
Come Christmas the morn :

3 Now every Beast that crops in field,
Breathe sweetly and adore :
The night has brought the richest yield
That ever the harvest bore.
Sing sweet as the flute,
Sing clear as the horn,
Sing joy of the Creatures
Come Christmas the morn :

4 Now every Bird that flies in air,
Sing, raven, lark and dove :
The night has brooded on her lair
And fledged the Bird of love.
Sing sweet as the flute,
Sing clear as the horn,
Sing joy of the Birds,
Come Christmas the morn :

5. *Now all the Angels of the Lord,
Rise up on Christmas Even :
The passing night will hear the Word
That is the voice of Heaven.
Sing sweet as the flute,
Sing clear as the horn,
Sing joy of the Angels,
Come Christmas the morn :

189 MERRY CHRISTMAS

(CHRISTMAS: SECULAR)

VOICES IN UNISON.
With animation. 𝅗𝅥 = about 84.
MARTIN SHAW.
mp
*
On Christ-mas Eve the bells were rung, On
Christ-mas Eve the mass was sung;......
The dam-sel donn'd her kir-tle sheen, The
hall was dress'd with hol-ly green;......
mf
Forth to the wood did

* May be sung as a solo, the Chorus joining in 'Then drink,' &c.

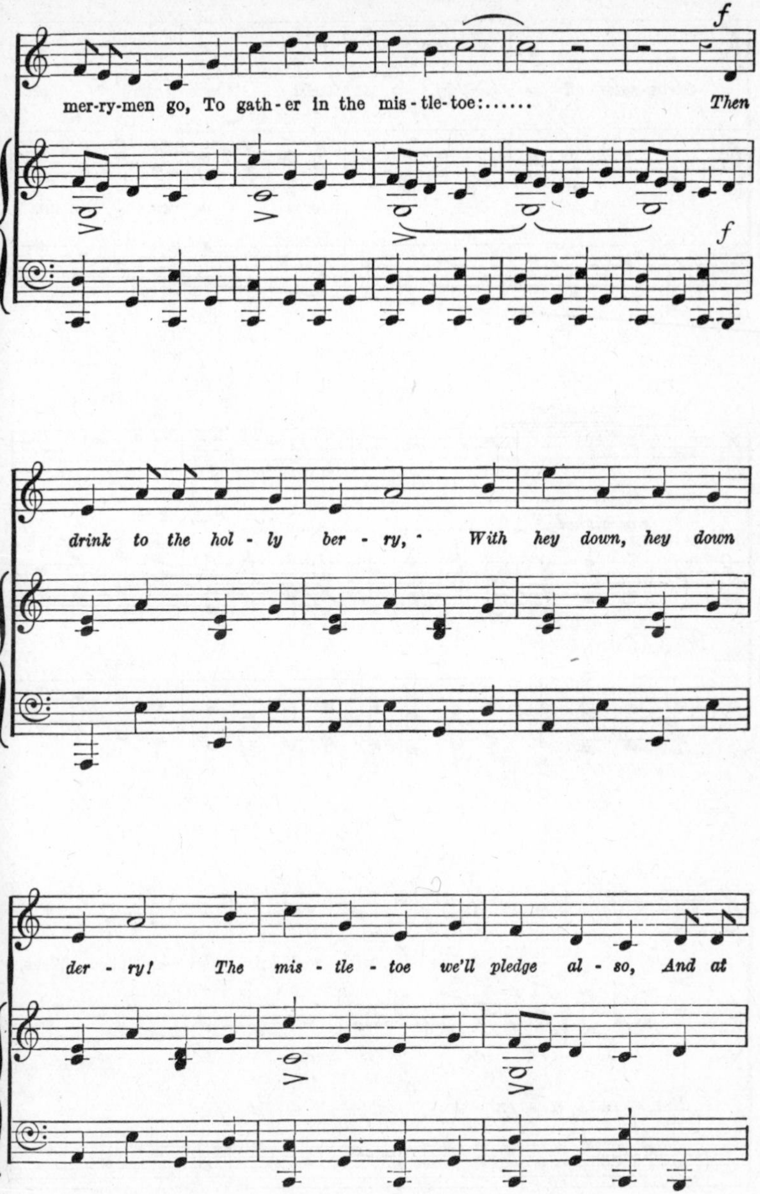

f

mer-ry-men go, To gath-er in the mis-tle-toe:...... *Then*

f

drink to the hol-ly ber-ry, With hey down, hey down

der-ry! The mis-tle-toe we'll pledge al-so, And at

Christ-mas all be mer-ry, At Christ - mas all be
cres - - - cen - - do.

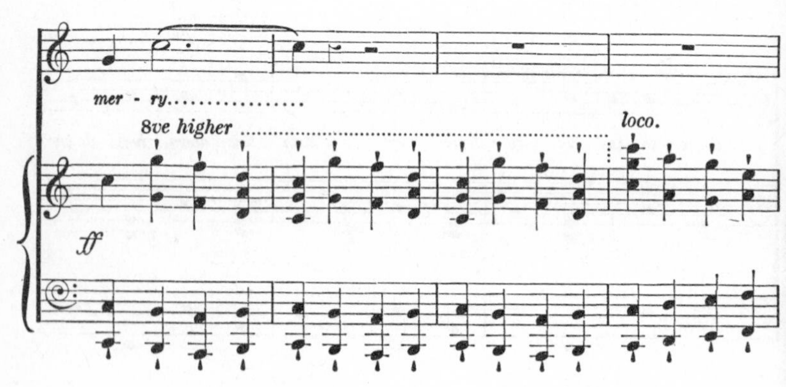
mer - ry.................
8ve higher
loco.
ff

f
2. The fire, with well-dried logs sup-plied, Went
dim - in - u - en - do.
f

roar - ing up the chim - ney wide;......
Then came the mer - ry

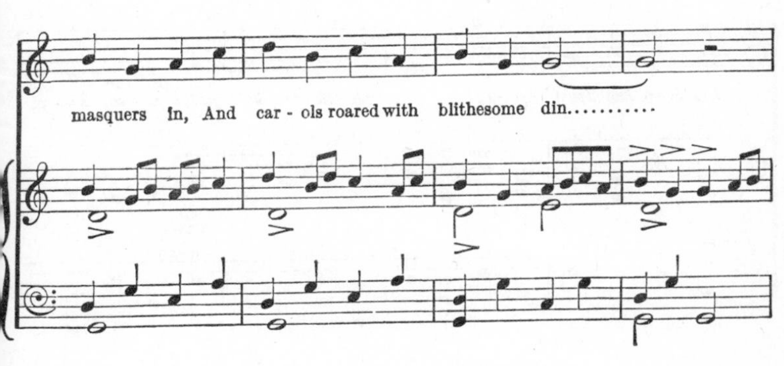
masquers in, And car - ols roared with blithesome din...........

Eng - land is mer - ry Eng - land, when Old Christ - mas brings his

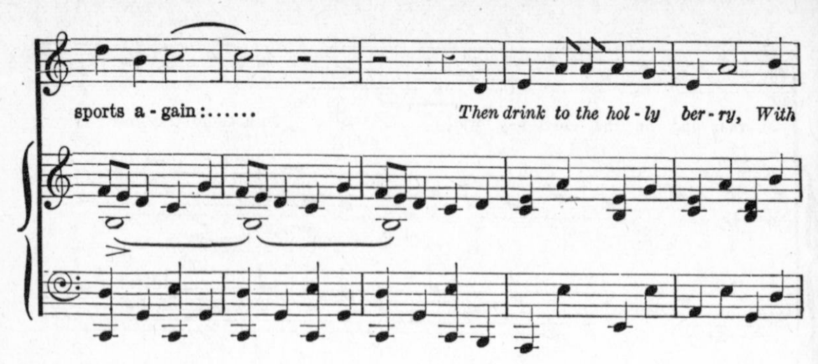
sports a-gain:......
Then drink to the hol-ly ber-ry, With

hey down, hey down der-ry! The mis-tle-toe we'll pledge al-so, And at

cres - - - cen - - do.
Christ-mas all be mer-ry, At Christ mas all be
cres - - - cen - - do.

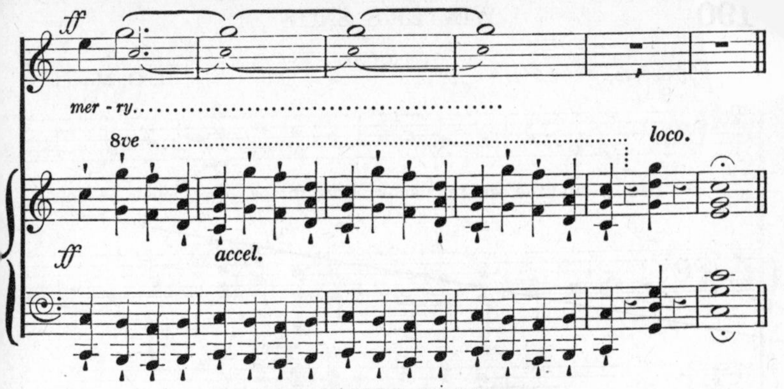

Martin Shaw. *Adapted from Sir Walter Scott*, 1771–1832.

ON Christmas Eve the bells were rung,
On Christmas Eve the mass was sung;
The damsel donned her kirtle sheen,
The hall was dressed with holly green;
Forth to the wood did merry-men go,
To gather in the mistletoe:

Then drink to the holly berry,
With hey down, hey down derry!
The mistletoe we'll pledge also,
And at Christmas all be merry,
At Christmas all be merry.

2. The fire, with well-dried logs supplied,
Went roaring up the chimney wide;
Then came the merry masquers in,
And carols roared with blithesome din.
England is merry England, when
Old Christmas brings his sports again:

The above lines are taken from *Marmion*, introduction to Canto VI; with a traditional refrain added.

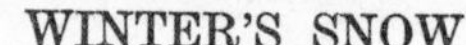

(CHRISTMAS)

Moderato.
SOLO.

R. O. MORRIS.

p 1 See a-mid the win-ter's snow, Born for us on earth be-low;

See the ten-der Lamb ap-pears, Pro-mised from e - ter-nal years.

CHORUS.

f *Hail, thou ev - er - bless - ed morn; Hail, re-demp-tion's hap-py dawn;*

The tune by John Goss to which this Carol is usually sung cannot be printed here owing to copyright difficulties.

Sing thro' all Je - ru - sa - lem, Christ is born in Beth-le - hem.

R. O. Morris. *E. Caswall,* 1814–78.

SEE amid the winter's snow,
Born for us on earth below;
See the tender Lamb appears,
Promised from eternal years:

Hail, thou ever-blessèd morn;
Hail, redemption's happy dawn;
Sing through all Jerusalem,
Christ is born in Bethlehem.

2 Lo, within a manger lies
He who built the starry skies;
He who throned in height sublime
Sits amid the cherubim:

3 Say, ye holy shepherds, say
What your joyful news to-day;
Wherefore have ye left your sheep
On the lonely mountain steep?

4 'As we watched at dead of night,
Lo, we saw a wondrous light;
Angels singing "Peace on earth"
Told us of the Saviour's birth:'

5. Sacred infant, all divine,
What a tender love was thine,
Thus to come from highest bliss
Down to such a world as this:

THE CHRISTMAS TREE

glad,...... all chil - - dren to - night!
sf
cres - - - - cen - - - - do.
mf
f
2 The
mo - ther sings of our Lord's good grace Where-by the Child who
mf

saved our race Was born..... and a - dored in a
con espressione
sf
low - - - - - ly place. 3 Once more the shep-herds,
p
as she sings, Bend low, and an - gels touch their strings: With
mf
mf

'Glo - ry' they hail the King...... of kings. 4 The
chil - dren lis - ten - ing round the tree Can hear the heaven - ly
p
mf
min - strel - sy, The man - - - ger's mar - - - vel
mf
p cres.

they........ can see.
5. Let ev - er - y house be
mf
rea-dy to-night—The chil - dren gather'd, the can-dles a - light—That
mu - - sic to hear,.... to see....... that sight.
con espressione.
sf
mf

P. Cornelius, 1824–74. *Do., Tr. H. N. Bate.*

THE holly 's up, the house is all bright,
The tree is ready, the candles alight:
Rejoice and be glad, all children to-night!

2 The mother sings of our Lord's good grace
Whereby the Child who saved our race
Was born and adored in a lowly place.

3 Once more the shepherds, as she sings,
Bend low, and angels touch their strings:
With 'Glory' they hail the King of kings.

4 The children listening round the tree
Can hear the heavenly minstrelsy,
The manger's marvel they can see.

5. Let every house be ready to-night—
The children gathered, the candles alight—
That music to hear, to see that sight.

Carl August Peter Cornelius, nephew of the painter, Peter Cornelius, was both composer and poet; he was born at Mainz, and worked much with Liszt. Among his most famous works are the *Weihnachtslieder*, from which this carol, 'Christbaum', is taken, Cf. No. 193.

THE SNOW LIES THICK

(CHRISTMAS)

GEOFFREY SHAW.

TENOR SOLO (Verses 1 & 4).

mf
1 The snow lies thick up - on the earth To-
4 But see, but see! the child's a-wake! His
Andante con moto.
mf
Senza Ped.

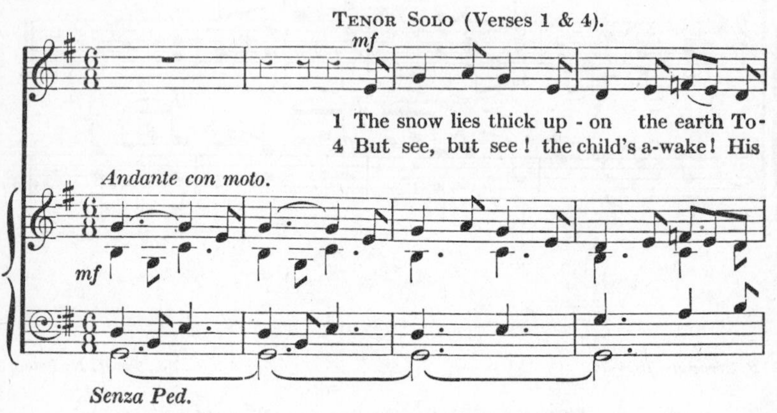

CHORUS.

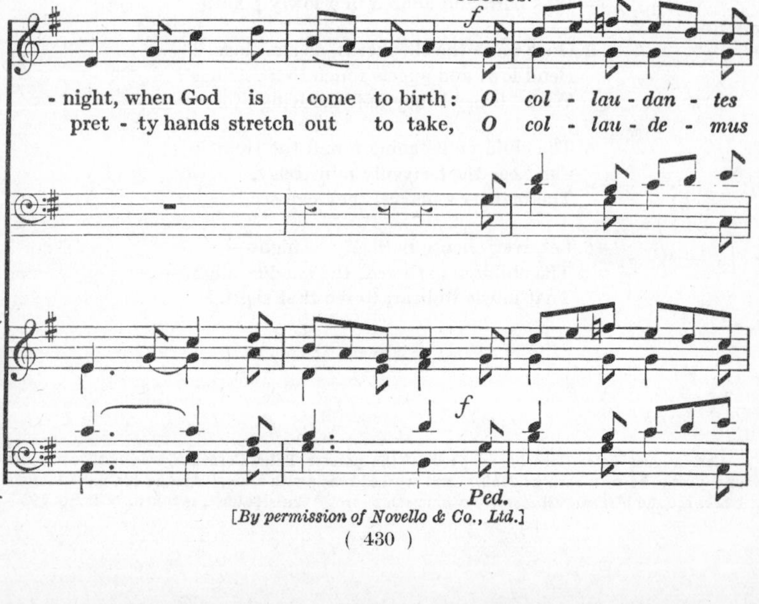

f
- night, when God is come to birth: O col - lau - dan - tes
pret - ty hands stretch out to take, O col - lau - de - mus
f
Ped.

[By permission of Novello & Co., Ltd.]

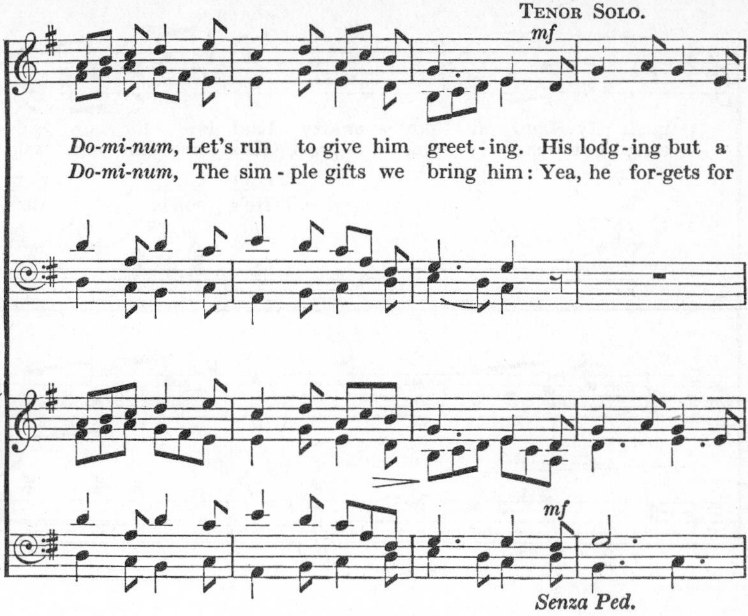

TENOR SOLO.
mf
Do-mi-num, Let's run to give him greet - ing. His lodg - ing but a
Do-mi-num, The sim - ple gifts we bring him: Yea, he for-gets for
mf
Senza Ped.

sta - ble, see! Where ox and ass his cour - tiers be, The
ve - ry love The glo - ry of his home a - bove, Nor

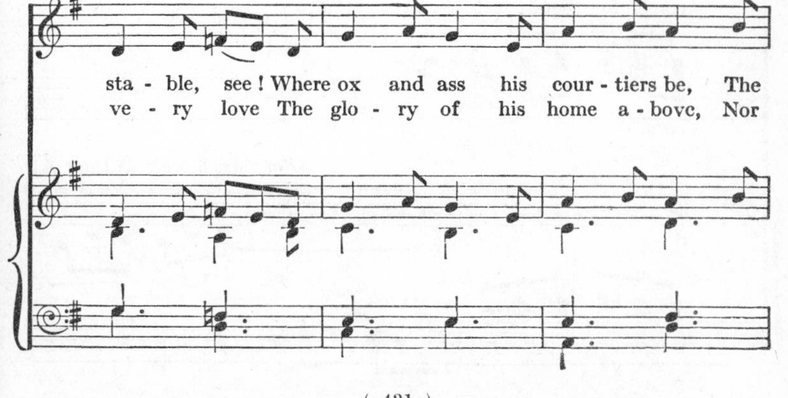

CHORUS.

f

migh - ty Lord in pov - er - ty Laid low for our sal -
cares but on - ly this to prove, He's come for our sal -

Laid low,.............. Laid
He's come,........... He's

f

Ped.

(For verse 5 begin at letter **A.***)*

- va - tion !
- va - tion.

low for our sal - va - tion.
come for our sal - va - tion.

(For verse 5 begin at letter **A.***)*

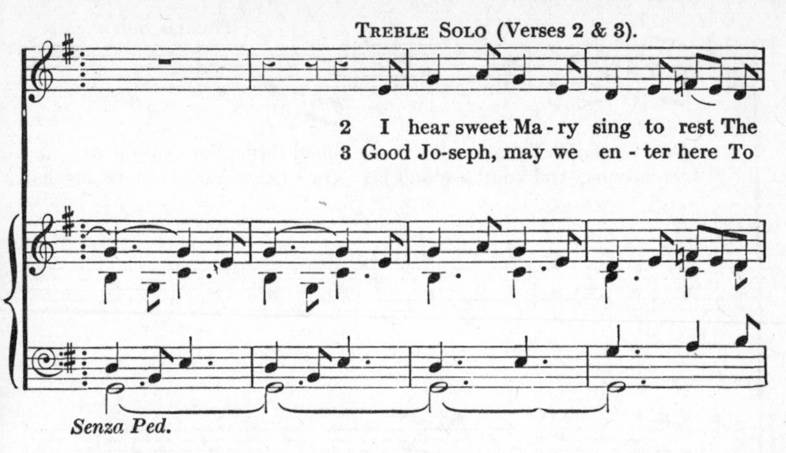
TREBLE SOLO (Verses 2 & 3).
2 I hear sweet Ma - ry sing to rest The
3 Good Jo-seph, may we en - ter here To
Senza Ped.

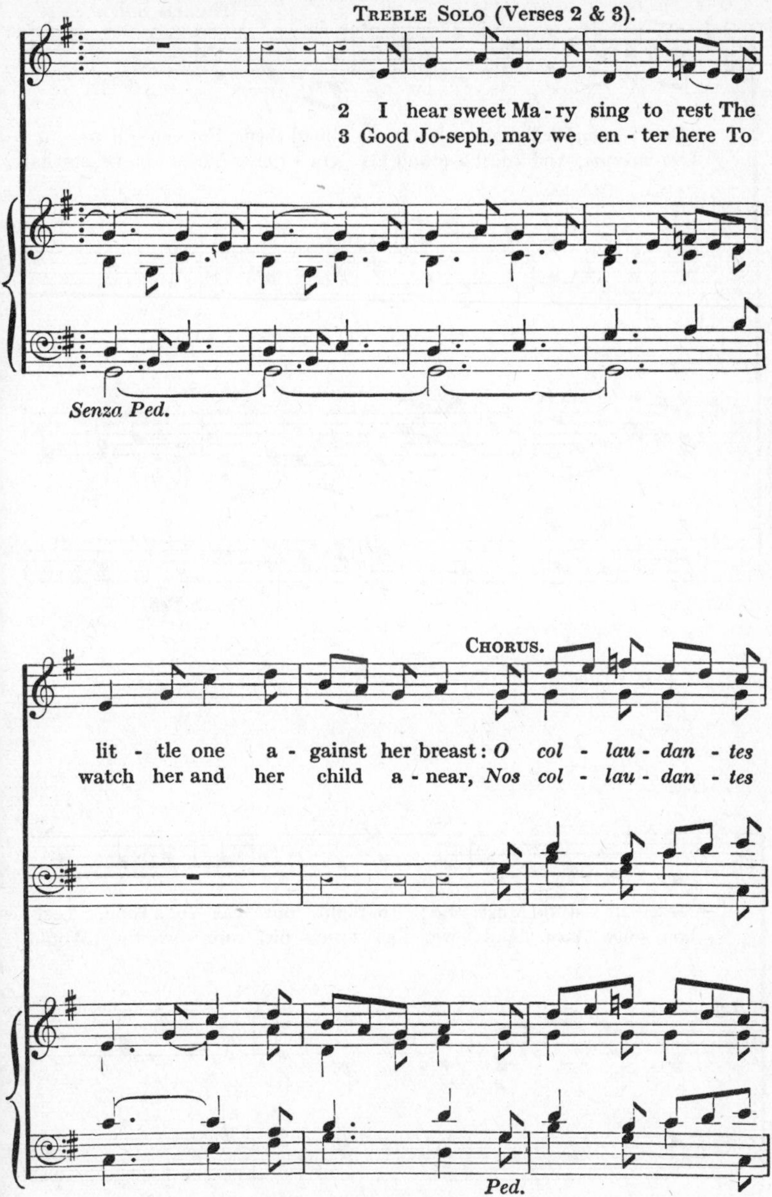

CHORUS.

lit - tle one a - gainst her breast : *O col - lau - dan - tes*
watch her and her child a - near, *Nos col - lau - dan - tes*

Ped.

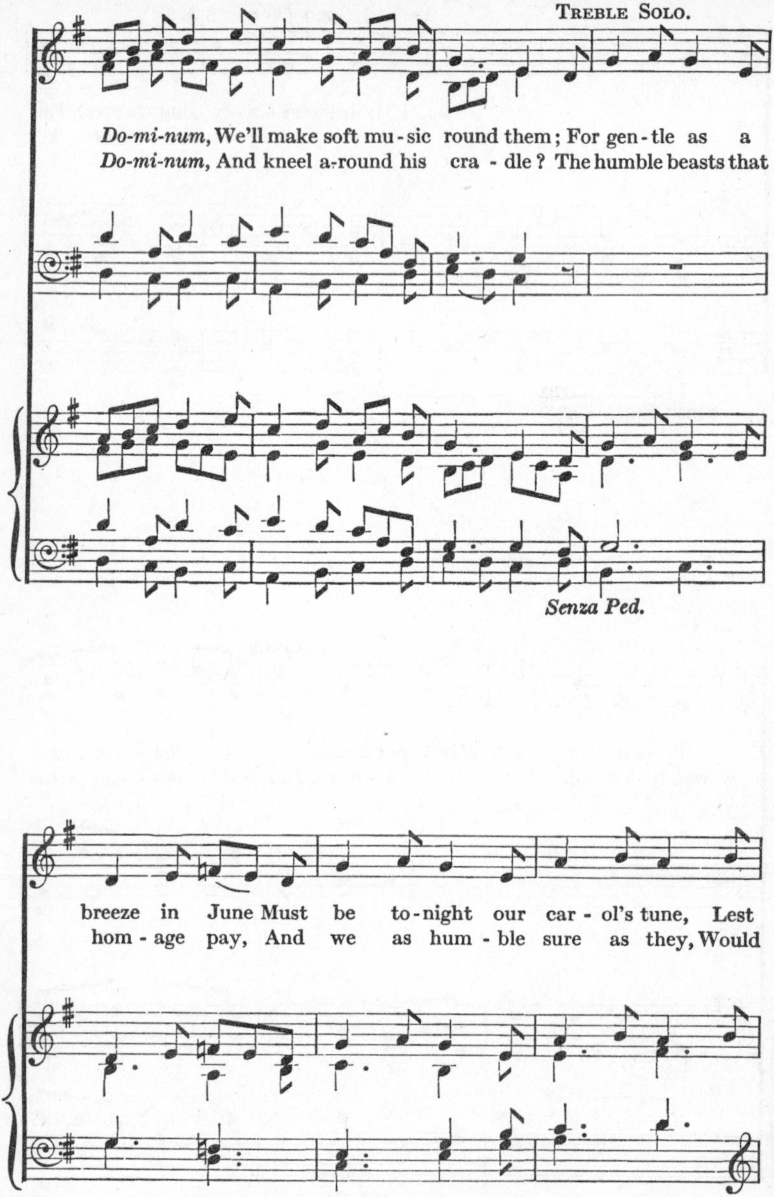

TREBLE SOLO.

Do-mi-num, We'll make soft mu - sic round them; For gen - tle as a
Do-mi-num, And kneel a-round his cra - dle? The humble beasts that

Senza Ped.

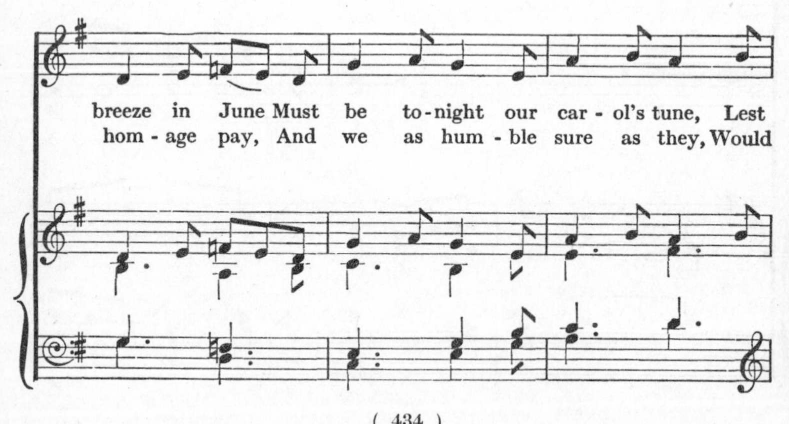
breeze in June Must be to-night our car - ol's tune, Lest
hom - age pay, And we as hum - ble sure as they, Would

Chorus.
That's born
O'er him
we a-wake the babe too soon
keep still watch to break of day
That's
O'er
That's born for our sal-
O'er him that brings sal-
p
p
Ped.
(For verse 4 go back to the beginning.)
born for our sal-va-tion.
him that brings sal-va-tion.
-va- -tion.
-va- -tion.
(For verse 4 go back to the beginning.)

CHORUS (Verse 5).

A

f

5. Then let us great, and let us small, And

A

f

Ped.

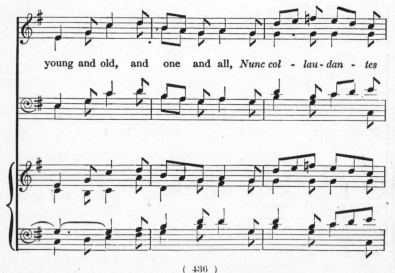

young and old, and one and all, *Nunc col - lau - dan - tes*

Do-mi-num, With dance and song draw hith-er! Bring boughs of hol - ly
green and red To deck a - bout his lit - tle bed, This

ff

ve - ry God, who lays his head So low for our sal -

So low,.............. So

ff

rall.

- va - - tion...

low for our sal - va - tion.............

rall.

Geoffrey Shaw. *Selwyn Image.*

THE snow lies thick upon the earth
To-night, when God is come to birth:
O collaudantes Dominum,
Let 's run to give him greeting.
His lodging but a stable, see!
Where ox and ass his courtiers be,
The mighty Lord in poverty
Laid low for our salvation!

2 I hear sweet Mary sing to rest
The little one against her breast:
O collaudantes Dominum,
We'll make soft music round them;
For gentle as a breeze in June
Must be to-night our carol's tune,
Lest we awake the babe too soon
That 's born for our salvation.

3 Good Joseph, may we enter here
To watch her and her child a-near,
Nos collaudantes Dominum,
And kneel around his cradle?
The humble beasts that homage pay,
And we as humble sure as they,
Would keep still watch to break of day
O'er him that brings salvation.

4 But see, but see! the child 's awake!
His pretty hands stretch out to take,
O collaudemus Dominum,
The simple gifts we bring him:
Yea, he forgets for very love
The glory of his home above,
Nor cares but only this to prove,
He 's come for our salvation.

5. Then let us great, and let us small,
And young and old, and one and all,
Nunc collaudantes Dominum,
With dance and song draw hither!
Bring boughs of holly green and red
To deck about his little bed,
This very God, who lays his head
So low for our salvation.

193 THE KINGS

(EPIPHANY)

Rather slowly, the accompanying Chorale with breadth.
P. CORNELIUS.
1. Three Kings from Per - sian lands a - far To Jor-dan fol-low the
p
point-ing star: And this the quest of the trav-el-lers three, Where the
p
new born King of the Jews may be. Full roy - al gifts they bear for the
p

King; Gold, in-cense, myrrh are their of - fer - ing.
2. The star shines
out with a stead - fast ray;
The Kings to Beth - le - hem
make their way,
And there in wor-ship they bend the knee, As Ma-ry's
p
p

child in her lap they see; Their roy - al gifts they show to the
p

King, Gold, in - cense, myrrh are their of - fer - ing.

3. Thou child of man— lo, to Beth - le - hem

The Kings are trav - 'lling— tra - vel with them !
The star of mer-cy, the star of grace, Shall lead thy heart to its rest-ing-
p un poco più mosso.
- place. Gold, incense, myrrh thou canst not bring ; Of-fer thy heart to the
rit.
a tempo.
f

in - fant King,
Of - fer thy heart!
p

P. Cornelius, 1824–74. *Do., Tr. H. N. Bate.*

THREE Kings from Persian lands afar
To Jordan follow the pointing star:
And this the quest of the travellers three,
Where the new born King of the Jews may be.
Full royal gifts they bear for the King;
Gold, incense, myrrh are their offering.

2 The star shines out with a steadfast ray;
The Kings to Bethlehem make their way,
And there in worship they bend the knee,
As Mary's child in her lap they see;
Their royal gifts they show to the King,
Gold, incense, myrrh are their offering.

3. Thou child of man—lo, to Bethlehem
The Kings are travelling—travel with them!
The star of mercy, the star of grace,
Shall lead thy heart to its resting-place.
Gold, incense, myrrh thou canst not bring;
Offer thy heart to the infant King,
Offer thy heart!

'Die Könige'. also from the *Weihnachtslieder*. The old Christmas tune 'Wie schön leuchtet' (No. 104) forms the accompaniment.

194

KINGS IN GLORY

(CHRISTMAS: EPIPHANY)

MARTIN SHAW.
Allegro. TREBLE SOLO (Verses 1, 3, and 5).
CHORUS.
p
1. Three Kings in great glo - ry of hor - ses and men, Of
3. Come mon-archs, and en - ter, your Mon - arch is here, Your
5. Then sim - ple and gen - tle, and fool - ish and wise, And
Allegro.
p
Senza Ped.
Ped.
SOLO.
hor - ses and men, In haste come a - rid - ing o'er
Mon - arch is here, Doff crowns, on the bare sod fall
fool - ish and wise, Come a - dore the great Lord of the
Senza Ped.

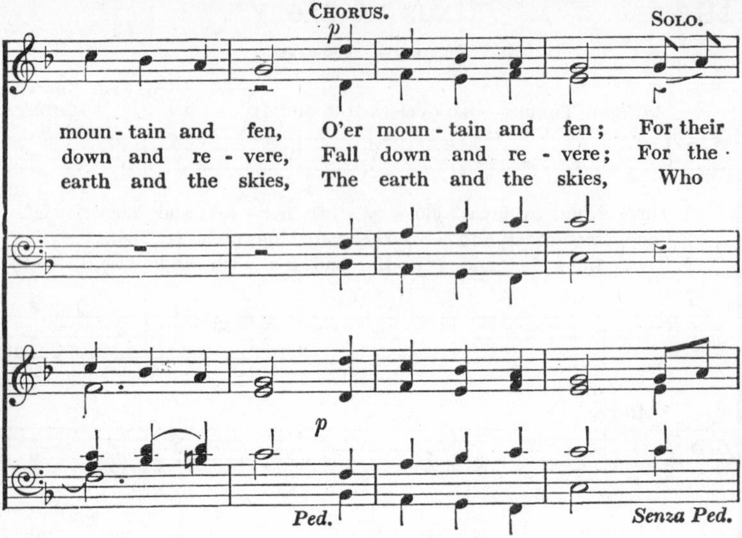

CHORUS. SOLO.

p

moun - tain and fen, O'er moun - tain and fen; For their
down and re - vere, Fall down and re - vere; For the
earth and the skies, The earth and the skies, Who

p

Ped. *Senza Ped.*

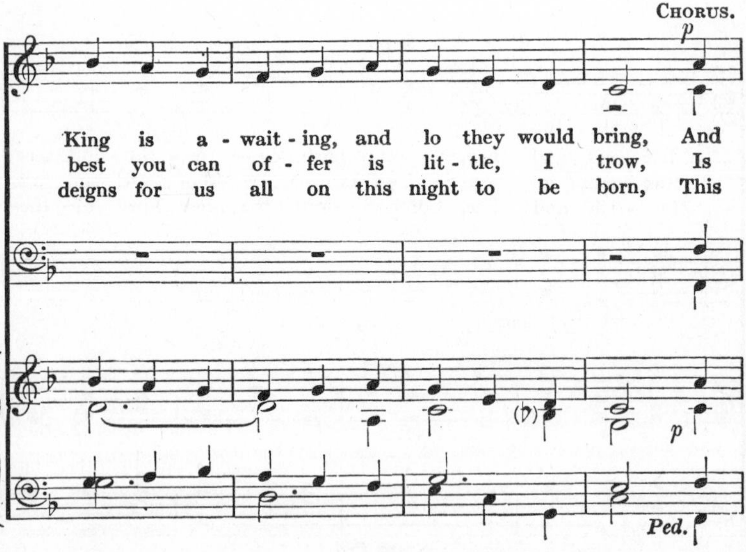

CHORUS.

p

King is a - wait - ing, and lo they would bring, And
best you can of - fer is lit - tle, I trow, Is
deigns for us all on this night to be born, This

(♭)

p

Ped.

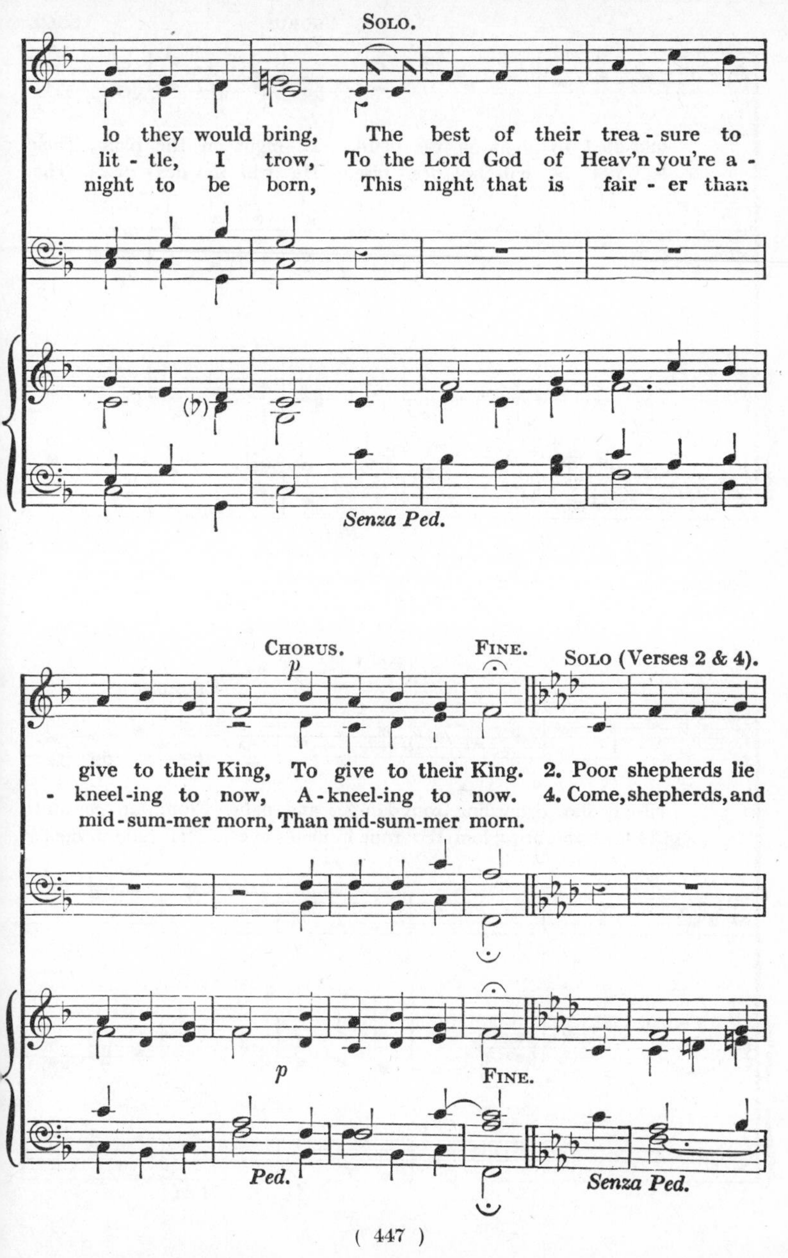
Solo.
lo they would bring, The best of their trea - sure to
lit - tle, I trow, To the Lord God of Heav'n you're a -
night to be born, This night that is fair - er than
(♭)
Senza Ped.
Chorus.
p
Fine.
Solo (Verses 2 & 4).
give to their King, To give to their King. 2. Poor shepherds lie
- kneel-ing to now, A-kneel-ing to now. 4. Come, shepherds, and
mid-sum-mer morn, Than mid-sum-mer morn.
p
Fine.
Ped.
Senza Ped.

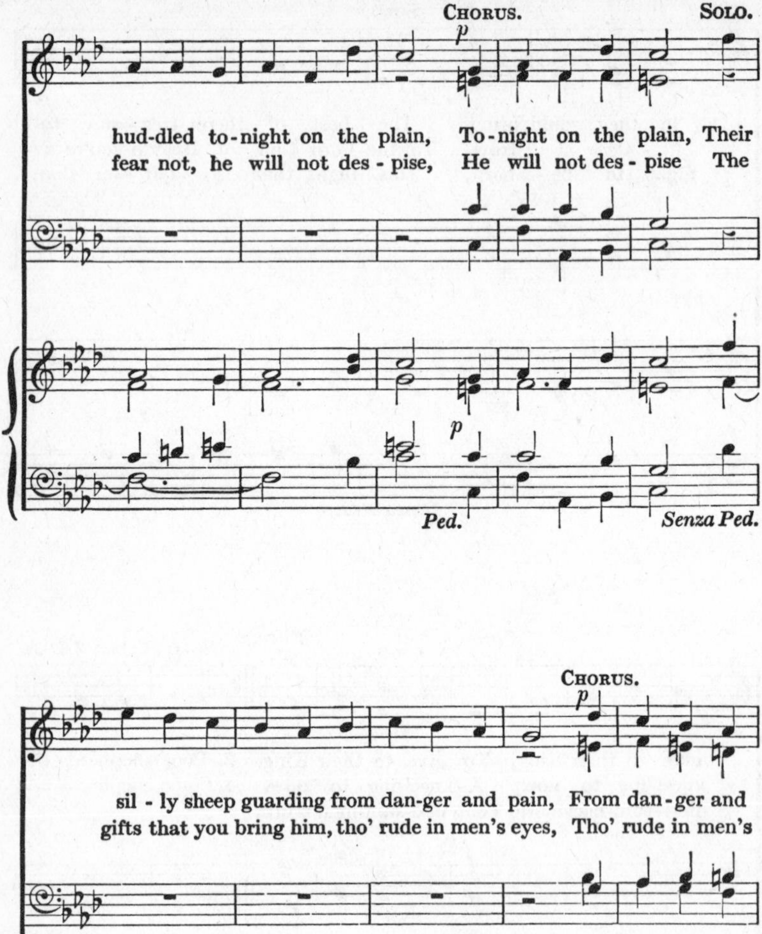

CHORUS. *p* SOLO.

hud-dled to-night on the plain, To-night on the plain, Their
fear not, he will not des-pise, He will not des-pise The

p

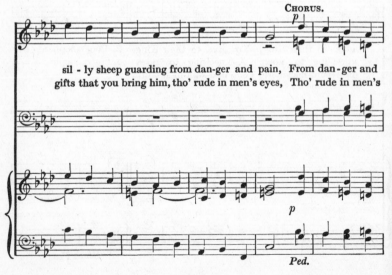

Ped. *Senza Ped.*

CHORUS. *p*

sil - ly sheep guarding from dan-ger and pain, From dan-ger and
gifts that you bring him, tho' rude in men's eyes, Tho' rude in men's

p

Ped.

Solo. Chorus.

p

pain; For the wolves howl a-round them, and bit-ter the air, And
eyes. See, he's not ar-rayed here in pur-ple and gold, In

p

Senza Ped. *Ped.*

Solo.

bit-ter the air, That blows o'er the snow-field all fro - -
pur-ple and gold, God's Lamb lies as help-less as lamb ....

Senza Ped.

Chorus.
All fro - - - - zen and bare.
As lamb......... of your fold.
- - - - zen and bare, All fro - - zen and bare.
.... of your fold, As lamb.... of your fold.
p
p
Ped.

Martin Shaw. *Selwyn Image.*

THREE Kings in great glory of horses and men,
Of horses and men,
In haste come a-riding o'er mountain and fen,
O'er mountain and fen;
For their King is a-waiting, and lo they would bring,
And lo they would bring,
The best of their treasure to give to their King,
To give to their King.

2 Poor shepherds lie huddled to-night on the plain,
To-night on the plain,
Their silly sheep guarding from danger and pain,
From danger and pain;
For the wolves howl around them, and bitter the air,
And bitter the air,
That blows o'er the snow-field all frozen and bare,
All frozen and bare.

3 Come monarchs, and enter, your Monarch is here,
Your Monarch is here,
Doff crowns, on the bare sod fall down and revere,
Fall down and revere;
For the best you can offer is little, I trow,
Is little, I trow,
To the Lord God of Heaven you're a-kneeling to now,
A-kneeling to now.

4 Come, shepherds, and fear not, he will not despise,
He will not despise
The gifts that you bring him, though rude in men's eyes,
Though rude in men's eyes.
See, he's not arrayed here in purple and gold,
In purple and gold,
God's Lamb lies as helpless as lamb of your fold,
As lamb of your fold.

5. Then simple and gentle, and foolish and wise,
And foolish and wise,
Come adore the great Lord of the earth and the skies,
The earth and the skies,
Who deigns for us all on this night to be born,
This night to be born,
This night that is fairer than midsummer morn,
Than midsummer morn.

195 KINGS OF ORIENT

(EPIPHANY)
J. H. HOPKINS, JUN.
J. H. HOPKINS, JUN. (arr. M.S.).
GASPAR.
1 We three kings of O - ri - ent are; Bear - ing
5. Glo - rious now, be - hold him a - rise, King, and
MELCHIOR.
1 We three kings of O - ri - ent are; Bear - ing
5. Glo - rious now, be - hold him a - rise, King, and
BALTHAZAR.
gifts we tra-verse a - far Field and foun - tain,
God, and sac - ri - fice! Heaven sings al - le -
gifts we tra-verse a - far Field and foun - tain,
God, and sac - ri - fice! Heaven sings al - le -

moor and moun - tain, Fol - low - ing yon - der star:
- lu - ya, Al - le - lu - ya the earth re - plies:
moor and moun - tain, Fol - low - ing yon - der star:
- lu - ya, Al - le - lu - ya the earth re - plies:
REFRAIN (after each verse).
O star of won - der, star of night,
Star with roy - al beau - ty bright, West - ward lead - ing,

still pro - ceed - ing, Guide us to thy per - fect light.
INTERLUDE.
(Fl. or Ob.)
(Clar.)
MELCHIOR.
2 Born a king on Beth - le - hem plain, Gold I bring, to crown him a - gain— King for ev - er, ceas - ing nev - er, Ov - er us all to reign:
GASPAR.
3 Frank - in - cense to of - fer have I; In - cense owns a De - i - ty nigh: Prayer and prais - ing, all men rais - ing, Wor-ship him, God most high:
BALTHAZAR.
4 Myrrh is mine; its bit - ter per - fume Breathes a life of gath - er - ing gloom; Sorrow - ing, sigh - ing, bleed - ing, dy - ing, Sealed in the stone - cold tomb:

For verse 5 go back to the beginning.

Verses 2, 3, and 4 should be sung as solos for men's voices, the accompaniment and refrain remaining unchanged.

John Henry Hopkins, 1820–91. **Do.**

The Kings.

WE three kings of Orient are ;
Bearing gifts we traverse afar
Field and fountain, moor and mountain,
Following yonder star :

O star of wonder, star of night,
Star with royal beauty bright,
Westward leading, still proceeding,
Guide us to thy perfect light.

Melchior.

2 Born a king on Bethlehem plain,
Gold I bring, to crown him again—
King for ever, ceasing never,
Over us all to reign :

Gaspar.

3 Frankincense to offer have I ;
Incense owns a Deity nigh :
Prayer and praising, all men raising,
Worship him, God most high :

Balthazar.

4 Myrrh is mine ; its bitter perfume
Breathes a life of gathering gloom ;
Sorrowing, sighing, bleeding, dying,
Sealed in the stone-cold tomb :

All.

5. Glorious now, behold him arise,
King, and God, and sacrifice !
Heaven sings alleluya,
Alleluya the earth replies :

The verses may be sung dramatically, in a hall or in church, the three kings entering in procession as they sing the first verse. Standing together (and each holding a casket), each may turn to the people to sing his verse, all forming round an imaginary crib for the choruses and v. 5. This last verse may then be sung full, the three kings returning to their places during the last two lines of the chorus.

This carol is one of the most successful modern examples. It was both written and composed (*c.* 1857) by Dr. J. H. Hopkins, Rector of Christ's Church, Williamsport, Pennsylvania, who died at Troy, New York, in 1891. See his *Carols, Hymns, and Songs*, New York, 1882.

196 BLAKE'S CRADLE SONG

(GENERAL)

2 Sweet sleep, with soft down
3 Sleep, sleep, hap - py child,
4 Sweet babe, in thy face
Weave thy brows an in - fant crown. Sweet sleep,
All cre - a - tion slept and smiled; Sleep, sleep,
Ho - ly im - age I can trace. Sweet babe,
An - gel mild, Hov - er o'er my hap - - py
hap - py sleep, While o'er thee thy mo - - ther
once like thee, Thy Ma - ker lay, and wept for
3
3

R. Vaughan Williams. [*Copyright*, 1928, *by R. Vaughan Williams*] *William Blake*, 1757–1827.

SWEET dreams, form a shade
O'er my lovely infant's head:
Sweet dreams of pleasant streams
By happy, silent, moony beams.

2 Sweet sleep, with soft down
Weave thy brows an infant crown.
Sweet sleep, Angel mild,
Hover o'er my happy child.

3 Sleep, sleep, happy child,
All creation slept and smiled;
Sleep, sleep, happy sleep,
While o'er thee thy mother weep.

4 Sweet babe, in thy face
Holy image I can trace.
Sweet babe, once like thee,
Thy Maker lay, and wept for me,

5 Wept for me, for thee, for all,
When he was an infant small.
Thou his image ever see,
Heavenly face that smiles on thee,

6. Smiles on thee, on me, on all;
Who became an infant small.
Infant smiles are his own smiles;
Heaven and earth to peace beguiles.

From the *Songs of Innocence*, etched in 1789.

197 THE CROWN OF ROSES

(Tschaikovsky's 'Legend')

(GENERAL)

p
pp
troop of chil - dren by, And see - ing ro - ses on the
tree, With shouts they plucked them mer - ri - ly.
f
3 'Do you bind ro - ses in your hair?' They cried, in
'Do you bind ro - ses in your hair?' They cried, in
3 'Do you bind ro - ses in your hair?' They cried, in
pp
scorn, to Je - sus there. The boy said hum - bly: 'Take, I

p cres.
pray, All but the nak - ed thorns a - way.' 4. Then of the
ff
thorns they made a crown, And with rough fin - gers pressed it
p cres - - - cen - - - do. ff
down, Till on his fore - head fair and young Red drops of
p
blood......... like ro - ses sprung........
p
like ro - ses sprung, like ro - ses sprung........

P. I. Tschaikovsky, 1840–93. *Plechtchéev, Tr. G. D.*

WHEN Jesus Christ was yet a child
He had a garden small and wild,
Wherein he cherished roses fair,
And wove them into garlands there.

2 Now once, as summer-time drew nigh,
There came a troop of children by,
And seeing roses on the tree,
With shouts they plucked them merrily.

3 'Do you bind roses in your hair?'
They cried, in scorn, to Jesus there.
The boy said humbly: 'Take, I pray,
All but the naked thorns away.'

4. Then of the thorns they made a crown,
And with rough fingers pressed it down,
Till on his forehead fair and young
Red drops of blood like roses sprung.

The Russian composer, Peter Ilich Tschaikovsky, was born in 1840 and died at St. Petersburg in 1893. From his *Chansons pour la Jeunesse*, Moscow, 1883: Plechtchéev wrote the words, which were translated into German by Hans Schmidt.

APPENDIX

ADDITIONAL FOLK TUNES WHICH ARE PROPER TO CERTAIN CAROLS IN PART I OF THIS BOOK

1

A VIRGIN MOST PURE

(PART 1, No. 4)

Tune noted by Cecil Sharp in Shropshire, 1911, and printed in the *Journal of the Folk-Song Society*, vol. v, p. 24.

2 ON CHRISTMAS NIGHT (Sussex Carol)

(PART 1, No. 24)

Tune noted by the late Dr. Culwick in 1904, from his mother, who had heard it many years previously in the streets of Dublin. The tune is printed in the *Journal of the Folk-Song Society*, vol. ii, p. 126.

3 (1) THE MOON SHINES BRIGHT (Bellman's Song)

(Part 1, No. 46)

Voices in Unison. [R. V. W.]

Organ.

Tune noted by Miss Lucy Broadwood, in Surrey, in 1894. Printed in the *Journal of the Folk-Song Society*, vol. i, p. 176.

---

3 (2) THE MOON SHINES BRIGHT (Bellman's Song)

(Part 1, No. 46)

[R. V. W.]

Tune noted at Kingsclere, Hants, by the late Godfrey Arkwright, in 1897, and printed in the *Journal of the Folk-Song Society*, vol. i, p. 178. Harmonies from the *English Hymnal*, where the tune is called 'Newbury' and set to hymn 16.

4 THE HOLY WELL

(Part 1, No. 56)

[R. V. W.]

Tune noted by Cecil Sharp, at Camborne, 1913. Printed in the *Journal of the Folk-Song Society*, vol. v, p. 4.

5 DIVES AND LAZARUS

(PART 1, No. 57)

[R. V. W.]

Tune noted for Mrs. Leather at Eardisley, Herefordshire, by Miss Andrews and Dr. Darling, in 1905. Harmonies from the *English Hymnal*, where the tune is called 'Eardisley', and is set to hymn 601.

6 (I) COME ALL YE WORTHY CHRISTIAN MEN (Job)

(PART 1, No. 60)

[*By permission of Novello & Co., Ltd.*]

Tune noted by W. Percy Merrick and printed in the *Journal of the Folk-Song Society*, vol. i, p. 74. Also published as a solo song in *Folk Songs from Sussex* (Novello).

6 (2) COME ALL YE WORTHY CHRISTIAN MEN (Job)

(PART 1, No. 60)

Tune noted by R. Vaughan Williams, near Horsham, in 1904, and printed in the *Journal of the Folk-Song Society*, vol. ii, p. 118.

7 THE CHERRY TREE CAROL

(Part 1, No. 66)

[M. S.]

Tune from Dr. E. F. Rimbault's *Old English Carols*, 1865.

THE CAROLS ARRANGED

FOR USE THROUGHOUT THE YEAR.

Titles are printed in italic, and when the beginning of the first line is used as a title, this part is printed in italic.

The carols classed under the heading *Nativity* are suitable for Christmas, but can also be sung in church at any time outside Lent throughout the year. On more informal occasions the Christmas carols themselves can sometimes be sung outside the Christmas season. The danger can thus be lessened of many beautiful Christmas carols being never sung, and the spirit of Christmas can be more widely diffused.

ADVENT.

NO. (*For the Fourth Sunday, see also Christmas Eve.*)

5 *Praise of Christmas.* All hail to the days. (*Also Christmas*)
134 *If ye would hear* the angels sing.
115 *Joseph and Mary.* O Joseph being an old man. (*Also Christmas*)
133 *Carol of the Advent.* People, look East. (*Also November*)
114 *No room in the Inn.* When Caesar Augustus
41 *Righteous Joseph.* When righteous Joseph. (*Also General*)

CHRISTMAS EVE.

(*Also for Christmas.*)

123 *Chanticleer.* All this night shrill chanticleer
51 *The Sinners' Redemption.* All you that are to mirth
66 *Cherry Tree Carol.* (*Part* 2.) As Joseph was a-walking
168 *Ben Jonson's Carol.* I sing the birth was born to-night
134 *If ye would hear* the angels sing. (*Also Advent*)
138 *O little town* of Bethlehem
189 *Merry Christmas.* On Christmas Eve the bells
24 *Sussex Carol.* On Christmas night all Christians sing
1 *Christmas Eve.* The Lord at first did Adam make

CHRISTMAS.

From the week before Christmas to February 2nd.
(*See also under* Nativity.)

116 *A babe is born* all of a may. (*Also Epiphany*)
73 *Dutch Carol.* A child is born in Bethlehem
2 *A child this day* is born
118 *Susanni.* A little child there is yborn. (*Also Epiphany*)
74 *Flemish Carol.* A little child on the earth. (*Also New Year*)
4 *A virgin most pure*, as the prophets do tell
169 *Tyrley, Tyrlow.* About the field they piped full right
5 *Praise of Christmas.* All hail to the days. (*Also Advent*)
119 *Angels from the realms* of glory. (*Also Epiphany*)
3 *Sunny Bank.* As I sat on a sunny bank (I saw three ships)
170 *New Prince, new pomp.* Behold a simple tender babe
6 *Irish Carol.* Christmas Day is come
7 *Hereford Carol.* Come all you faithful Christians
8 *Somerset Carol.* Come all you worthy gentlemen
10 *Come, love we God.* (*Also Epiphany*)
135 *Earthly friends* will change and falter
76 *Es ist ein' Ros' entsprungen*
186 *Snow in the Street.* From far away we come to you

THE CAROLS ARRANGED.

CHRISTMAS, Etc., SECULAR.

ST. STEPHEN (December 26th).

NO.

ST. JOHN (December 27th).

174 *Welcome Yule.* Welcome be thou. (*Also Christmas, etc., Candlemas*)

INNOCENTS' DAY (December 28th).

120 *In Bethlehem, that fair city.* (*Also Christmas*)
55 *The Miraculous Harvest.* Rise up, rise up. (*Legendary*)
80 *Three Kings* are here. (*Also Epiphany*)
92 *Puer Nobis.* Unto us a boy is born. (*Also Christmas*)
174 *Welcome Yule.* Welcome be thou. (*Also Christmas, etc., Candlemas*)
140 *The Band of Children.* What songs are these. (*Also Epiphany to Lent*)

NEW YEAR.

(*cf.* Christmas.)

44 *The Lamb of God.* Awake, Awake, ye drowsy souls. (*Also Passion*)
12 *God rest you merry (London).* (*Also Christmas*)
15 *Wassail Song.* Here we come a-wassailing. (*Also Christmas*)
50 *Nos Galan.* Now the joyful bells a-ringing
28 *Greensleeves.* The old year now away is fled
174 *Welcome Yule.* (*Also Christmas, etc.*)
83 *Congaudeat.* With merry heart let all. (*Also Christmas, etc.*)

JANUARY AND FEBRUARY.

(*cf. Epiphany, Candlemas, etc.*)

141 *January Carol.* Earth to-day rejoices

EPIPHANY.

January 6th to Septuagesima.

116 *A babe is born* all of a may. (*Also Christmas*)
118 *Susanni.* A little child there is yborn. (*Also Christmas*)
119 *Angels, from the realms* of glory. (*Also Christmas*)
10 *Come love we God.* (*Also Christmas*)
9 *Dark the night* lay. (*Also General*)
13 *God's dear Son* without beginning. (*Also Christmas*)
117 *Immortal Babe,* who this dear day. (*Also Christmas*)
23 *Make we joy* now in this feast. (*Also Christmas*)
173 *Golden Carol.* Now is Christèmas ycome. (*Also Christmas*)
121 *Falan-tiding.* Out of the orient crystal skies. (*Also Christmas*)
78 *Personent hodie* voces puerulae. (*Also Christmas*)
79 *Quem pastores* laudavere. (*Also Christmas*)
25 *Gallery Carol.* Rejoice and be merry. (*Also Christmas*)
27 *The first Nowell* the angel did say. (*Also Christmas*)
54 *King Herod and the Cock.* There was a star. (*Legendary*)
165 *Golden Mornings.* They saw the light. (*Also General*)
29 *This new Christmas Carol.* (*Also Christmas*)
193 *Three Kings from Persian lands*
194 *Three Kings in great glory*
80 *Three Kings.* Three Kings are here
195 *Kings of Orient.* We three kings of Orient
140 *The Band of Children.* *The stars shall light.* (*To Lent*)
83 *Congaudeat.* With merry heart. (*Also Christmas, etc.*)

THE CAROLS ARRANGED.

SUNDAYS AFTER EPIPHANY.

NO. *See* Epiphany. *Also* General, *especially :—*

65 *The Decree.* Let Christians all
69 *The Saviour's work.* The babe in Bethlem's manger
70 *Joys Seven.* (*verses* 1–5.) The first good joy
139 *Infinite Light.* The greatness of God. (*Also Lent, etc.*)
72 *Wondrous Works.* When Jesus Christ was twelve years old
167 *Carol of the Kingdom.* When Jesus was a baby

Also Nativity, especially :—

141 *January Carol.* Earth to-day rejoices

NATIVITY.

(*Suitable both for Christmas and for General use.*)

85 *Puer Natus.* A boy was born in Bethlehem
34 *Poverty.* All poor men and humble
123 *Chanticleer.* All this night shrill chanticleer
175 *The Virgin's Cradle Hymn.* Dormi, Jesu (Sleep, sweet babe)
141 *Earth to-day rejoices.* (*Jan. and Feb.*)
124 *Summer in Winter.* Gloomy night embraced the place
84 *The Cradle.* He smiles within his cradle
142 *Children's Song.* How far is it to Bethlehem
86 *In Dulci Jubilo*
176 *Herrick's Ode.* In numbers, and but these few
87 *Rocking.* Little Jesus, sweetly sleep
88 *Waking-Time.* Neighbour, what was the sound
35 *Sans Day Carol.* Now the holly. (*Also Passion, Easter*)
36 *Salutation Carol.* Nowell . . . This is the salutation. (*Also Annunciation*)
89 *Sion's Daughter.* O Sion's daughter, where art thou
177 *Out of your sleep* arise and wake
67 *Song of the Nuns of Chester.* Qui creavit coelum
125 *Rorate* coeli desuper
110 *Jesus of the Manger.* Sing, good company
30 *Lute-book Lullaby.* Sweet was the song
91 *In the Town.* Take heart, the journey 's ended
37 *The Angel Gabriel* from God. (*Also Annunciation*)
69 *The Saviour's Work.* The babe in Bethlem's manger. (*Also General*)
143 *The World's Desire.* The Christ-child lay
38 *The Holly and the Ivy.* (*Also Lent, Autumn*)
90 *Song of the Ship.* There comes a ship a-sailing
92 *Puer Nobis.* Unto us a boy is born
113 *Spanish Carol.* Up now, laggardly lasses
39 *This Endris Night*
40 *Wonder Tidings.* What tidings bringest thou
178 *In Excelsis Gloria.* When Christ was born

CANDLEMAS, *Feb.* 2.

126 *Candlemas Eve.* Down with the rosemary and bays. (*And till Refreshment Sunday*)
17 *All in the Morning.* (*Part* 1.) It was on Christmas Day
174 *Welcome Yule.* (*Also Christmas, etc.*)

THE CAROLS ARRANGED.

NO. **ANNUNCIATION,** *March* **25.**

100 *The Message.* A message came. (*Also General*)
52 *Angelus ad Virginem.* (*Also General*)
102 *Gabriel's message* does away. (*Also General*)
36 *Salutation Carol.* Nowell . . . This is the salutation. (*Also Nativity*)
37 *The Angel Gabriel* from God. (*Nativity*)
41 *Righteous Joseph.* When righteous Joseph. (*Also Advent, General*)

LENT.

First four weeks.

100 *The Message.* A message came. (*Also Annunciation*)
71 *My Dancing Day.* (*Part* 2.) Into the desert
144 *White Lent.* Now quit your care
45 *Sussex Mummers' Carol.* O mortal man. (*Also Passion*)
42 *Remember,* O thou man (*verses* 1, 2, 3, 6)
38 *The Holly and the Ivy.* (*Also Nativity, Autumn*)
66 *Cherry Tree Carol.* (*Part* 3.) Then Mary took. (*Also Passion*)

Also General Carols, especially :—

51 *The Sinners' Redemption.* All you that are
161 *The Shepherd.* Down in the valley
61 *Down in yon forest*
102 *Gabriel's message* does away
65 *The Decree.* Let Christians all
105 *The Garden.* Lord Jesus hath a garden
184 *All Bells in Paradise.* Over yonder 's a park
139 *Infinite Light.* The greatness of God
46 *The Bellman's Song.* The moon shines bright
166 *Carol of Service.* Up, my neighbour
72 *Wondrous Works.* When Jesus Christ was twelve years old
197 *The Crown of Roses.* When Jesus Christ was yet a child
167 *Carol of the Kingdom.* When Jesus was a baby

REFRESHMENT SUNDAY.

(*4th Sunday, Mid-Lent.*)

145 *Mothering.* It is the day of all the year.

PASSIONTIDE.

Last fortnight in Lent.

43 *The Seven Virgins.* All under the leaves
146 *The Merchants' Carol.* As we rode down. (*Also Palm Sunday*)
44 *The Lamb of God,* Awake, Awake. (*Also Easter*)
17 *All in the Morning.* (*Part* 2.) It was on Holy Wednesday. (*Also Easter*)
35 *Sans Day Carol.* Now the holly. (*Also Nativity*)
45 *Sussex Mummers' Carol.* O mortal man. (*Also Lent*)
93 *Mary's Wandering.* Once Mary would go
179 *The Quest.* Saint Mary goes
46 *Bellman's Song.* The moon shines bright. (*Also Lent, General*)
66 *Cherry Tree Carol.* (*Part* 3.) Then Mary took. (*Also Lent*)
197 *The Crown of Roses.* When Jesus Christ was yet a child. (*General*)
72 *Wondrous Works.* (*Part* 2) When they bereaved his life

PALM SUNDAY.

(*cf.* Passiontide.)

NO.

146 *The Merchants' Carol.* As we rode down

HOLY WEEK AND GOOD FRIDAY.

See Passiontide.

EASTERTIDE.

Easter Day till Ascension Day.

(*cf. Spring.*)

44 *The Lamb of God.* (*Part* 2.) It was early. (*Also Passion*)
71 *My Dancing Day.* (*Part* 3.) Before Pilate. (*Also Ascension*)
147 *Easter Carol.* Cheer up, friends and neighbours
148 *Christ the Lord is risen*
94 *Easter Eggs*
102 *Gabriel's Message.* (*General*)
104 *How brightly beams* the morning star. (*Also General*)
152 *Festival Carol.* How great the harvest is. (*Till Trinity*)
17 *All in the Morning.* (*Part* 2.) It was on Holy Wednesday
95 *Now glad of heart* be every one. (*Till Trinity*)
149 *Love is come again.* Now the green blade riseth
35 *Sans Day Carol.* Now the holly
96 *Hilariter.* The whole bright world. (*Also Spring, etc.*)
150 *The world itself* keeps Easter Day
97 *The Secret Flower.* This child was born. (*Also Whitsuntide*)
151 *Athens.* 'Twas about the dead of night
72 *Wondrous Works.* (*Part* 2.) When they bereaved. (*Passion, till Ascension*)

ASCENSIONTIDE.

71 *My Dancing Day.* (*Part* 3.) Before Pilate. (*Also Easter*)
127 *God is ascended* up on high
152 *Festival Carol.* How great the harvest is. (*Easter to Trinity*)
95 *Now glad of heart* be every one. (*Also Easter, Trinity*)
70 *Joys Seven* (*verses* 1, 6, 7.) The first good joy
72 *Wondrous Works.* (*Part* 2.) When they bereaved. (*Also Passion, Easter*)

WHITSUNTIDE

And the Holy Spirit.

59 *Welsh Carol.* Awake were they only. (*Also General*)
152 *Festival Carol.* How great the harvest is. (*Easter to Trinity*)
97 *The Secret Flower.* This child was born. (*Also Saints, etc.*)
153 *Song of the Spirit.* When Christ blessed his disciples
154 *The Spirit.* Winds of God unfailing. (*Also General*)

TRINITY SUNDAY.

(*cf.* General, Praise.)

152 *Festival Carol.* How great the harvest is. (*Also Easter, etc.*)
95 *Now glad of heart* be every one. (*Also Easter, etc.*)
96 *Hilariter.* The whole bright world. (*Also Easter, etc.*)

OTHER FESTIVAL OCCASIONS.

(*cf.* General : Praise.)

NO.

Saints' Days.

100 *The Message.* A message came. (*General*)
156 *Summer Time.* Lift your hidden faces
105 *The Garden.* Lord Jesus hath a garden. (*General*)
132 *Psalm of Sion.* O mother dear, Jerusalem. (*General*)
97 *The Secret Flower.* This child was born. (*Also Easter, etc.*)
99 *Flower Carol (verses* 3, 4, 5.) Through each wonder
166 *Carol of Service.* Up, my neighbour

Dedication, etc.

162 *Bell Carol.* In every town and village
44 *The Lamb of God.* (*Part* 2.) It was early. (*Missionary, etc.*)
88 *Waking-Time.* Neighbour, what was the sound. (*Missionary, etc.*)
111 *The Builders.* Sing, all good people
139 *Infinite Light.* The greatness of God. (*Missionary, etc.*)
166 *Carol of Service.* Up, my neighbour. (*Missionary, etc.*)

SPRING.

126 *Candlemas Eve.* Down with the rosemary
155 *April.* Now April has come
98 *Spring has come.* Now the spring has come again
129 *Pleasure it is.* (*Also Summer, Harvest*)
99 *Flower Carol.* Spring has now unwrapped the flowers
96 *Hilariter.* The whole bright world. (*Also Easter, etc.*)

MAY.

47 *May Carol.* Awake, awake, good people all
48 *May-Day Garland.* I've brought you here a bunch of may
49 *Furry Day Carol.* Remember us poor Mayers all

SUMMER.

101 *Gems of Day.* All the gay gems of day. (*General, Evening*)
156 *Summer Time.* Lift your hidden faces
99 *Flower Carol.* Spring has now unwrapped the flowers
157 *Summer Carol.* The dawn-wind now is waking
128 *Now welcome, Summer,* with thy sunnè soft
129 *Pleasure it is.* (*Also Spring, Harvest*)
96 *Hilariter.* The whole bright world. (*Also Spring, etc.*)

HARVEST.

158 *Fields of corn,* give up your ears
129 *Pleasure it is.* (*Also Spring, Summer*)
159 *Golden Sheaves.* Sing to the Lord of harvest

AUTUMN.

158 *Fields of corn,* give up your ears
63 *Green grow'th the Holly.* (*General*)
38 *The Holly and the Ivy.* (*And till after Christmas*)

THE CAROLS ARRANGED.

NO. **WINTER.**

63 *Green grow'th the Holly.* (*General*)
50 *Nos Galan.* Now the joyful bells a-ringing
133 *Carol of the Advent.* People, look East

GENERAL.

(*Carols classed under* Nativity *are also suitable for general use.*)

100 *The Message.* A message came
34 *Poverty.* All poor men and humble
101 *Gems of Day.* All the gay gems of day. (*Evening*)
51 *The Sinners' Redemption.* All you that are
57 *Dives and Lazarus.* As it fell out
58 *Jacob's Ladder.* As Jacob with travel
59 *Welsh Carol.* Awake were they only. (*Also Whitsuntide*)
60 *Job.* Come all you worthy Christian men
9 *Dark the night* lay. (*Also Epiphany*)
161 *The Shepherd.* Down in the valley
61 *Down in yon forest*
103 *The Birds.* From out of a wood
102 *Gabriel's Message* does away. (*Also Annunciation, Easter*)
63 *Green grow'th the Holly.* (*Seasons*)
104 *How brightly beams* the morning star
145 I know a lovely angel-game
162 *Bell Carol.* In every town and village
163 *The Three Traitors.* It was about the deep
17 *All in the Morning.* It was on Christmas Day (*omitting starred verses*)
65 *The Decree.* Let Christians all
165 *Paean.* (*Part* 2.) Lift up your heads
105 *The Garden.* Lord Jesus hath a garden
131 *Coverdale's Carol.* Now blessed be thou
106 *So, Brother.* Now brothers lift your voices
108 *The Kingdom.* O, I have seen a King's new Baby
109 *O Little One sweet*
132 *Psalm of Sion.* O mother dear, Jerusalem
181 *Ane Sang.* O my dear heart
184 *All Bells in Paradise.* Over yonder 's a park
26 *Saint Stephen* was a holy man. (*Also Dec.* 26)
111 *The Builders.* Sing all good people
110 *Jesus of the Manger.* Sing, good company, frank and free
69 *The Saviour's Work.* The babe in Bethlem's manger. (*Also Nativity*)
70 *Joys Seven.* The first good joy
139 *Infinite Light.* The greatness of God
46 *Bellman's Song.* The moon shines bright. (*Also Passion*)
165 *Golden Mornings.* They saw the light
68 *The Truth from Above.* This is the truth
112 *Eia.* To us in Bethlem city
71 *My Dancing Day.* To-morrow shall be
166 *Carol of Service.* Up, my neighbour
64 *A New Dial.* (*In those twelve days.*) What are they
72 *Wondrous Works.* When Jesus Christ was twelve years old
197 *The Crown of Roses.* When Jesus Christ was yet a child
167 *Carol of the Kingdom.* When Jesus was a baby
41 *Righteous Joseph.* When righteous Joseph. (*Also Advent, etc.*)
154 *The Spirit.* Winds of God unfailing. (*Also Whitsun*)

THE CAROLS ARRANGED.

GENERAL: CRADLE SONGS.

NO. *cf.* Nativity *for Cradle Songs of the Nativity.*

130 *Watts's Cradle Song.* Hush! my dear
185 *Wither's Rocking Hymn.* Sweet baby, sleep
196 *Blake's Cradle Song.* Sweet dreams

GENERAL: LEGENDARY.

53 *The Carnal and the Crane.* As I passed by a river-side
56 *The Holy Well.* As it fell out one May morning
163 *The Three Traitors.* It was about the deep
66 *Cherry Tree Carol.* Joseph was an old man
55 *The Miraculous Harvest.* Rise up, rise up, you merry men all
54 *King Herod and the Cock.* There was a star in David's land
197 *The Crown of Roses.* When Jesus Christ was yet a child

GENERAL: MEDIEVAL.

180 *Adam lay ybounden*
52 *Angelus ad Virginem*
62 *All and Some.* Exortum est in love
182 *Lullay my Liking.* I saw a fair maiden
183 *I sing of a Maiden*
177 *Out of your sleep* arise and wake. (*Nativity*)
67 *Song of the Nuns of Chester.* Qui creavit coelum

GENERAL: PRAISE.

160 *Angels holy,* high and lowly
152 *Festival Carol.* How great the harvest is. (*Also Easter, etc.*)
165 *Golden Mornings.* (3, 4.) O ever thought be of his grace
107 *Praise to God* in the highest
164 *Carol of Beauty.* Praise we the Lord
99 *Flower Carol (verses* 3, 4, 5.) Through each wonder. (*Also Spring*)

SUITABLE FOR USE IN PROCESSION.

2 *A child this day* is born. (*Christmas*)
4 *A Virgin most pure.* (*Christmas*)
119 *Angels, from the Realms.* (*Christmas*)
160 *Angels holy,* high and lowly. (*General*)
152 *Festival Carol.* How great the harvest is. (*Easter to Trinity*)
17 *All in the Morning.* It was. (*Christmas to Easter*)
105 *The Garden of Jesus.* Lord Jesus hath a garden. (*General, and Saints*)
137 *Masters in this Hall.* (*Christmas*)
173 *The Golden Carol.* Now is Christèmas ycome. (*Christmas*)
111 *The Builders.* Sing all good people. (*General, and Dedication*)
27 *The First Nowell.* (*Christmas*)
192 *The snow lies thick* upon the earth. (*Christmas*)
194 *Kings in Glory.* Three Kings. (*Epiphany*)

For Conclusions of Services or Concerts, see " Praise " ; *also the following verses:* 16 *Good-bye* ; 44 (Pt. 3), *Good Wishes* ; 45 (4–6), *Sussex Mummers* ; 49 (6), *Furry Day* ; 99 (5), *Flower Carol* ; 104 (3), *How brightly* ; 129, *Pleasure it is* ; 152 (4, 5), *Festival Carol* ; 165 (Pt. 2), *Paean* ; etc.

NOTES ON THE USE OF CAROLS

The following notes are the result of consultation and experiment.

Waits customarily sing during the week before Christmas. Properly organized from good choirs, they might supplant the casual choir-boys and sturdy but unmusical beggars who are a nuisance at so many front doors. Waits may be accompanied by wind-instruments, but harmoniums are as fatal to carols as to hymns. It is often worth while to announce the day and the district beforehand, together with a charity to which the money will be given after expenses have been deducted.

Carol Parties. Sometimes a dozen or two men and women from a choral society visit people by arrangement in their own houses, the host inviting a party to listen to carols for an hour, and making a small contribution to a charity. A whole round of half-hour parties can be managed by car on Christmas Eve.

Private Houses and Schools. There is often amateur carol singing in private houses and at school breaking-up parties. But sometimes on such occasions nearly all the carols sung are poor imitations: amateur singers and school teachers need the warning that strong commercial interests are engaged in pushing inferior songs of all descriptions; and the true carol is still obscured by the false, because the nature of carols has not been fully understood. The simplest remedy is to choose from the traditional tunes.

Concert Rooms and Parish Halls. No concerts are so popular as those which consist of carols. Since crowded audiences are assured, it is worth while to obtain the best musical help and to pay professional musicians, and local orchestras and bands. Such concerts can be made even more delightful by interspersing two or three carols sung dramatically (*e.g.* Nos. 20, 26, 48, 49, 64, 77, 88, 90, 173, 195). Costume can also be used; and in any case it is perhaps best to avoid evening clothes. Some may come on as a party of waits to sing carols like Nos. 15, 30, 31. Carol concerts need not be only in the period between Advent Sunday and Septuagesima: Lent, Easter, and Spring carol concerts should, for instance, be very popular.

In Church. Groups of carols, both during and after a service, are a good way of marking Easter and other festivals, as well as Christmas. In some churches carols are sung on Easter Day and other festivals instead of an evening sermon. On ordinary Sundays appropriate carols would form a sound and very popular substitute for anthems in many churches.

Children's Services. It has been found a good plan to sing a carol to the children on any Sundays throughout the year when a good singer can be got.

Carol Services. We have suggested in the Preface a new type of informal popular service, to be announced as a "Carol Service," and to be held on every Sunday throughout the year, in the afternoon, or in the evening. The name will at once attract; and, if the music chosen is really carol music, the whole service will have a delightful character. We suggest that this Carol

Service should last from one hour to an hour and a quarter, but not longer; and that it should take something like the following form :—

1, Short Prayer ; 2, Hymn or Carol ; 3, First Reading ; 4, Carol A ; 5, Poetry ; 6, Carol B ; 7, Notices ; 8, Carol C ; 9, Second Reading ; 10, Carol D ; 11, Short Lecture or Address ; 12, Hymn or Carol ; 13, Lord's Prayer and Grace.

In this scheme, perhaps the carols marked A and B might be in the main for a choir or quartet, and those numbered C and D of a more congregational character. If carols are sung for Nos. 2 and 12, the people's share would be further increased. Should still more carols be wanted, a solo carol might be substituted sometimes for No. 5, or for some other number. The First Reading in this example is from the Bible, the Second is from some other source, as a rule. All the readings and other parts are meant to be short—about the length of the Gospels in the Prayer Book. It has been found that improvised versicles and responses have a remarkable effect upon the general tone of these gatherings ; they may be taken from the carol itself, announced when it is given out, and then repeated by the person in charge and the people before the carol is sung. Sometimes the refrain can be thus used, sometimes the opening lines, sometimes another couplet from the carol. The congregation can also be brought in by some verses being allotted to them, as well as by their joining in the choruses.

INDEX OF COMPOSERS, SOURCES, ETC.

(There are sometimes two traditional tunes to one number.)

(The word "Traditional" may cover any date or era from the fifteenth to the eighteenth century.)

INDEX OF AUTHORS, SOURCES, ETC.

INDEX TO TITLES

INDEX TO TITLES

INDEX OF FIRST LINES

SET IN
GREAT BRITAIN
AT THE
UNIVERSITY PRESS
OXFORD
AND
PRINTED IN
THE NETHERLANDS
BY
KOCH AND KNUTTEL
GOUDA

~~Whence is that Goodly~~

~~In the Manger He Lies~~

~~Hope~~

1. Once in Royal

2. In Dulci Jubilo

3 Coventry Carol

4. Whence is that G F

5 In the Manger He Lies

6 – Crown of Roses

7. Infant King

8 A Virgin Most Pure

9 Dormi Jesu

10. Berlin